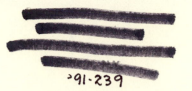

Culture and Christianity

Contributions to the Study of Anthropology

A Nilotic World: The Atuot-Speaking Peoples of the Southern Sudan
John W. Burton

Culture
and
Christianity

THE DIALECTICS OF TRANSFORMATION

Edited by George R. Saunders

Contributions to the Study of Anthropology, Number 2

GP

GREENWOOD PRESS
NEW YORK • WESTPORT, CONNECTICUT • LONDON

Library of Congress Cataloging-in-Publication Data

Culture and Christianity : the dialectics of transformation / edited
   by George R. Saunders.
      p.   cm. — (Contributions to the study of anthropology, ISSN
0890–9377 ; no. 2)
   Bibliography: p.
   Includes index.
   ISBN 0–313–26118–0 (lib. bdg. : alk. paper)
   1. Christianity and culture.   I. Saunders, George R., 1946–
II. Series.
BR115.C8C85   1988
261—dc19   88–5651

British Library Cataloguing in Publication Data is available.

Library of Congress Catalog Card Number: 88–5651
ISBN: 0–313–26118–0
ISSN: 0890–9377

First published in 1988

Greenwood Press, Inc.
88 Post Road West, Westport, Connecticut   06881

Printed in the United States of America

∞

The paper used in this book complies with the
Permanent Paper Standard issued by the National
Information Standards Organization (Z39.48–1984).

10   9   8   7   6   5   4   3   2   1

Copyright Acknowledgments

A version of Chapter 3, by Michael French Smith, was previously published as "From Heathen to Atheist: Changing Views of Catholicism in a New Guinea Village," in *Oceania* LI:40–52 (1980). It is reprinted here by permission.

A version of Chapter 4, by Peter Weston Black, was previously published as "The Teachings of Father Marino: Christianity on Tobi Atoll," in *Mission, Church, and Sect in Oceania* (A.S.A.O. Monograph No. 6). James A. Boutilier, Daniel T. Hughes, and Sharon W. Tiffany, eds. Pp. 307–354. Ann Arbor: University of Michigan Press. 1978. It is reprinted here by permission.

For Ted Schwartz
teacher, friend, and the real author of this book

Contents

Preface

This book has had a long, pleasant, and I hope fruitful germination. It began some years ago as a series of informal discussions among faculty and graduate students in the Department of Anthropology at the University of California in San Diego. Sharing an anthropological interest in religion and field experience in Christian societies, we were mystified by the paucity of serious anthropological studies of Christianity, and particularly the lack of systematically comparative work. For the 1976 meetings of the Southwestern Anthropological Association, Ted Schwartz organized a symposium entitled "Transformations of Christianity," where we made some initial attempts at analyzing how the religion, as a social and symbolic system, had been molded to quite diverse cultural contexts. Excited by particular ethnographic case studies and the similarities and differences of the historical processes illustrated, we continued the symposium for the next few years with a series of seminars at U.C.S.D. More recently, most of us have moved on to new positions in other places, but the discussions on Christianity and culture have continued at annual meetings and in correspondence. Here, finally, is at least the initial product of our meandering pilgrimage.

It is probably fortunate that this book represents a considerable condensation of the process that produced it. Some of our early discussions never got out of the vestibule and into the church. For example, we attempted in various ways to identify the content of some sort of "core reference system" of Christianity, an "essence" that remained intact through the many cultural transformations. This proved to be a much more difficult task than we at first imagined. As anthropologists, we almost immediately rejected the notion of finding the essence of Christianity in the official dogma of contemporary churches; we were interested instead in the religion as experienced by its ordinary practitioners, wherever they might be found. Given the difficulty that anthropologists have had even in defining "religion" (Spiro 1966), it is perhaps not surprising that our most probing discussions failed to elicit many features of Christianity that translated wholly and literally from one cultural context to another. All religions, or course, are cultural systems, and they are always embedded in patterns of human experience that are at least to some extent integrated—patterns in which political, economic, aesthetic, and other aspects of life are interlaced and perhaps even phenomenologically indistinguishable.

The best we were able to do, finally, was to identify a set of issues that seem to recur regularly in the transformation of Christianity. That is, Christianity seems to present particular problems in whatever cultural context it appears, though the solutions to the problems vary from place to place and time to time. Monotheism, for example, is a tendency rather than a reality in most of Christianity, and the conceptualization of the Trinity, the proliferation of saints, the deification of the Madonna, and the intrusion of other supernatural figures such as ancestors all become important aspects of the dialectical relationship of culture and Christianity. Similarly, Christianity is a particularly messianic religion, as is apparent even in its name, and yet its messianism is more an issue for polemics than a uniform body of belief and practice. Other recurrent issues include millenarianism and eschatological tendencies; the status of "charisma," personal revelation, prophecy, and mystical individualism; the forms of "power" attributed to the religion; and the tensions between direct or mediated salvation, between the immanence and transcendence of the supernatural, between congregational and hierarchial organizational structure, between justification and mystification of the political status quo, on the one hand, and revolutionary ideology on the other.

In short, our attempt to locate an essential Christianity—like many of our other discussions—resulted in happy frustration, perhaps akin to the enjoyment of an Escher print, which is always something other than it appears to be. I hope that the chapters that have resulted from our discussions are true to the complexity of Christianity itself, and that the resulting book has a unity and coherence that derives from something other than abstraction and simplification. That, at least, was our goal.

Many people contributed good counsel that has improved the book. Ted Schwartz, to whom it is dedicated, initiated the discussions and provided many of the most provocative ideas. Melford Spiro, Ed Hutchins, and F. G. Bailey also gave good criticism and advice, either in general ways or in specific comments. Michael Oppenheim, Martha Saunders, Leonard Thompson, and John Stanley offered useful critiques of the theoretical comments in the conclusion, though of course none of them should be blamed for its shortcomings. John Russell and Richard Swiderski wrote excellent ethnographic analyses of additional cases, which for various reasons did not find their way into the final book, but nevertheless contributed substantially to our thinking about the issues. An anonymous reviewer for Greenwood Press made especially valuable suggestions for the concluding chapter. Lawrence University provided funds and secretarial services for the production of the initial manuscript.

George R. Saunders' research and writing were also supported by a traineeship from the National Institute of Mental Health, a Fulbright Scholarship for Dissertation Research, and faculty research grants from Lawrence University. Stefano and Rita Borello, Carol, Josh, and Patrick Saunders all offered moral and practical support during the research period, and Melford Spiro and F. G. Bailey made useful suggestions for improving the manuscript.

Peter Weston Black's research in Tobi and Palau was financed by a grant (MH 12766) from the National Institute of Mental Health, and he gratefully acknowledges comments on his chapter by D. Korn, D. K. Jordan, R. Levy, R. McKnight, T. Schwartz, M. Spiro, S. Tiffany, and B. Webster.

Michael D. Murphy's chapter is based on ethnographic research conducted with the support of a National Institute of Mental Health Traineeship, and he notes the helpful comments of William Dressler, David Jordan, Milady Khoury, Richard Krause, Allen Maxwell, Claudia Murphy, Donald Tuzin, and Anne Woodrick. He is especially indebted to Marc Swartz, teacher and friend, for his amiable guidance during the period of fieldwork and afterward.

William Wedenoja's research was made possible by grants from the National Institute of Mental Health and the Organization of American States.

Geoffrey M. White acknowledges the support of a Foreign Area Fellowship from the Social Science Research Council and a grant (3201) from the Wenner-Gren Foundation for Anthropological Research. Peter Black gave comments which were particularly helpful in revising Chapter 2.

Finally, Chapter 10 bears my name as author, but is in fact a product of the collective discussions over a period of several years. All of the contributors to this book are in some sense co-authors of these general and theoretical observations. My thanks to all of them for their intelligent contributions, and also for their patience in seeing this book through to publication.

1

Introduction

GEORGE R. SAUNDERS

INTRODUCTION

Ever since the first Protestant Mission was established in San Francisco's Chinatown by Dr. William Speer in 1852, Christianity has been a recognized aspect of Chinese community life in the United States. Despite the fact that an estimated 20 percent of all Chinese living in the United States today are nominally Christian and 6.7 percent are active churchgoers (NACOCE 1980), the Christian church remains an anomalous institution with respect to both ethnic churches in general and Chinese immigrant associations in particular. On the one hand, it has not been considered a bastion of traditional culture in the sense of European ethnic churches. Historically, Christianity has played an important role in helping European immigrants to the United States adjust to their new environment, but that role has been, on the whole, conservative (Mohl and Betten 1981; M. Smith 1978). According to J. P. Dolan, the ethnic church, usually the Roman Catholic parish, preserved for the European immigrant his ethnic identity as well as his language, traditional values, customs, and beliefs.

The national parish aided the newcomers in becoming hyphenated Americans by providing them with a familiar experience in a strange environment. It was not necessary to sever their roots with the old country in order to pledge allegiance to a new flag. The ethnic parish assured them of this, and it helped to facilitate their accommodation to an adopted homeland (1975:162).

The ethnic churches of the European immigrants, therefore, have traditionally been forces of stability, providing continuity with the past for those concerned with adjusting to the present.

Unlike the Roman Catholic churches of the European immigrants, however, membership in a Chinese Christian church involves exposure to a completely been a dynamic system of symbols, ideals, and ideas in constant interaction with other systems in its environment. Its messages and meanings have been adapted regularly to the exigencies of new economic and social situations, new personnel, and to each ethnic, tribal, and national subculture and culture into which it has been introduced.

In this book, Christianity is of interest as a cultural system—that is, as a system of shared ideas, beliefs, and values expressed in public symbols and ritual. A fundamental assumption thus underlies all of the research presented here: Although the religion retains some constant features as it is transmitted from people to people or as it evolves within a single society, it is never a fixed, isolated or neatly bounded system. It is always open to modification and transformation, especially through its articulation of politics, economics, education and socialization, aesthetics, and non-Christian religions. Like other aspects of society and culture, Christianity can be expected to take on different forms and to have different functions and meanings in different settings. Though it might be possible to abstract the definitive elements of an "essential" Christianity, the primary goal of this book is precisely the opposite—to explore the complex processes of its transformation. There is of course some strand of unity stretching with Christianity across cultural and temporal frontiers, but our focus is rather the mutual adaptation of the religion and local culture—an interactive process. The authors of these chapters are all anthropologists, and, as might be expected, the research also deals mainly with the manifestations of the religion in the thoughts and actions of ordinary people, rather than with its codification and expression by the elite authorities of any church.

The book is not only concerned with the transformations of Christianity, but also with cases in which Christianity is the agent for change in other systems. Specifically, four types of transformation are considered here. The first is the adaptation of Christianity itself—of its ideology, symbolism, and institutional structure—to particular social conditions. The second is change in indigenous social organization effected through the influence of Christian doctrine, symbolism, the organization of the Christian church, or other aspects of contact with Christians. The third type, closely related but not identical to the second, is the transformation of indigenous culture as it makes a place for Christianity. The fourth type of transformation, and by no means the least important, is the modification of individual personality characteristics, cognitive style, or interpersonal behavior through contact with Christians and induction into one or another of the sects or denominations. Examples of these transformations are most readily found in instances of conquest, colonialism, and other contact between Christian and non-Christian societies, perhaps particularly in the missionary movement, which has been a major force in modern history (Beidelman 1982; Whiteman 1983; Salamone 1983). However, such transformations may also be internally generated, through individual visionary experiences or from changes in the relationships between religion and other sociocultural systems, especially political economy.

In anthropology, such transformations have typically been discussed along with "acculturation" (culture change via contact between cultures), and most often have been referred to as "syncretism." Since early in this century anthropologists have been concerned with the process by which a subordinate group adjusts to domination from another by adopting its ideas, beliefs, values, and institutional forms (or at least by modifying traditional social and cultural forms to make them more consonant with those of the dominant group). Religion has often been a central topic in these studies. However, our approach should be distinguished from "acculturation studies" in that we view the transformative process as continual, dynamic, and as both internally and externally stimulated—not simply and solely due to culture contact. Furthermore, our perspective regards these transformations as something other than syncretic composites of two or more religious systems. We are concerned with a Christianity that is *always* embedded in other systems and realized in concrete settings. Thus, in this book, Christianity is not coterminous with its official doctrine; it cannot be considered apart from the Christians who embody it. It is not a fully integrated and uniform system, composed of invariant elements, nor is it free of inconsistencies and paradoxes. Both Christianity and the local systems into which it has been introduced are flexible and dynamic, and they interact in a dialetical process that leads to transformations of both.

This book explores the transformative process and its results in a number of specific case studies. The chapters are organized roughly geographically, but there is also a kind of substantive logic to the order. The first chapters are ethnohistorical analyses of the introduction of Christianity into Melanesian and Micronesian societies, under the conditions of colonial and clientelist expansion by Western powers. These are followed by a case study from contemporary Korea, in which the missionaries are native Koreans. The sixth chapter is again ethnohistorical, but this time focuses on a colonial situation in the Western hemisphere, in Jamaica, and includes the complicating history of slavery and the politicization of Christianity during the emancipation struggle. The seventh chapter, on a Chinese Christian church in California, deals with the uses of religion among immigrants in the United States. The final two case studies deal with transformations in established (Catholic) churches in the United States and Italy. In general, then, the book moves from cases of cultural transformation through culture contact (and conflict) to cases of internally generated change. In the final chapter, we attempt to abstract some general propositions from the varied analyses that comprise the body of the book.

Chapter 2 on the missionization of the Solomon Islands demonstrates the significance of the colonial situation, but also presents the Solomon Islanders as active participants in the process of Christianization. Indeed, Geoffrey M. White describes conversion as "less a product of steady evangelization than an internally generated process in which people actively sought to learn the new religion." The active posture of indigenous groups in the missionization process is also emphasized by Michael French Smith and William Wedenoja, though it is clear from their work that conversion has a different meaning for the converts than for the missionaries. Earlier acculturation studies sometimes presented the subordinate group as the passive recipient of a new culture, but the studies in this book reflect recent attempts to recognize the dialectical process of culture contact (cf. Wolf 1982).

White's study of the Solomon Islands case introduces another theme reflected in several of the chapters of this book as well as in other recent anthropological studies of Christianity (Schneider and Lindenbaum 1987:2): Conversion to Christianity is often a pragmatic decision based on an assessment of the relative advantages of the religion in the immediate, this-worldly context. For Solomon Islanders, (Anglican) Christianity provided a rationale for rejecting ancestor worship and thus for ending the destructive cycle of headhunting for propitiation. The changes in religion, however, also entailed extensive changes in social organization, settlement patterns, and even in individual personality. The purging of ancestral shrines eliminated the connection between kinship and local territories, and thus permitted the relocation and amalgamation of diverse groups into larger villages. In this case, then, conversion to Christianity was accompanied by wholesale transformations of social and cultural life. Still, there remained some genuine similarities between traditional Solomon Islands religion and "the new way," in that the pragmatic and this-worldly approach to religion was in both cases a central characteristic.

Pragmatic considerations also motivated the conversion of the people of Kragur (on the island of Kairiru, Papua New Guinea) to Catholicism, and have likewise been a factor in the more recent skepticism about the religion. Smith's chapter deals generally with the problem of belief (and disbelief), and offers insight into the difficulties of integrating a pragmatic and instrumentalist indigenous approach to religion with a moralistic and salvationist Christianity. Smith cites the "inextricable interpenetration of moral and material issues" in Kragur as well as the immanence and immediacy of religion in the indigenous tradition. The people of Kragur thus paid little attention to ideas about heaven and hell, and instead anticipated that conversion to Catholicism would bring about a rapid material transformation of their way of life. In other words, conversion was expected to provide wealth and power. The results have been disappointing, and in recent years considerable disenchantment has become evident. This is perhaps not uncommon: in a discussion of Christianity in South Africa, Jean and John Comaroff recently remarked that "while the mission introduced a new world view, it could not deliver the world to go with it" (1986:1).

Smith's analysis also attends to the significant changes in attitudes of missionaries and church personnel since Vatican II (1963–65), and points out, interestingly, that villagers are not generally pleased with the liberalization, democratization, voluntarism, and desacramentalization of the past two decades. Rather, they see this as a kind of "inconstancy" on the part of the Mission, and in some cases even as evidence of conscious deception by earlier missionaries.

In the past few years, the Mission has begun encouraging indigenous ritual practices, but it is too late: in the wholesale conversions of the earlier part of the century important indigenous ritual knowledge was lost, and it can no longer be fully reconstructed. Some of the people of Kragur thus surmise that the Mission personnel intentionally attempted to deprive them of these important sources of power.

Finally, Smith's analysis raises one further important issue. The problem of belief is conditioned by both social and psychological parameters. Socially, for example, both the indigenous religious tradition and the mission Catholicism rely heavily on specialist practitioners, and thus some people are able to distance themselves by leaving the troubling inconsistencies of belief and ritual to be worked out by the experts. Psychologically, individuals seem to differ in their tolerance of ambiguity and inconsistency, and thus display greater or lesser ability to believe in the face of contradictions. These themes are echoed in some of the other chapters.

Peter Weston Black's chapter deals with the conversion to Roman Catholicism of the entire population of Tobi atoll (in the Western Carolines, Micronesia) in the 1930s by a Spanish Jesuit named Father Marino. Again, Black presents the conversion as involving the interaction of the missionary and of local actors, in a fascinating historical case. A century and a half of intermittent contact with Europeans and of local factionalism had brought the islanders to "an experiment in secularism" just prior to Father Marino's arrival. A dispute over the succession to the chieftainship combined with the influence of a resident Japanese impresario had led to the destruction of the chief's spirit house and of other ritual sites, resulting in the abandonment of much of traditional ritual. As in Kragur and the Solomon Islands, Tobian religion had been oriented primarily to practical goals such as the protection of the island and its inhabitants from disaster. Father Marino thus arrived at a time when the people felt particularly vulnerable and without a supernatural guardian. Catholicism was to fill this void.

Each of these first three cases of mass conversion, then, took place following considerable disruption of traditional social and cultural systems in the period of increasing contact with Europeans. Christianity was adopted in part because of its potential for supplementing or replacing traditional religious systems that were no longer functioning effectively under the changing circumstances. Disease, social disruption, and psychological stress all helped create a readiness for conversion, and the obvious power and wealth of the missionaries made Christianity an attractive alternative for indigenous people. The long-run commitments to Christianity may of course differ in the three cases: Black, for example, emphasizes the continuing religiosity of the Tobians, while Smith focuses on the development of religious skepticism and even atheism.

Black also investigates the "emic" Tobian interpretation of the newly introduced Catholic rituals, and notes the ways in which the new rituals have been related in meaning and function to traditional Tobian practices. The Tobian word for "baptism," for example, assimilates two traditional practices: fathers used to punish misbehaving sons by holding their heads under water, and shamans did the same to patients in order to treat them for insanity. Thus baptism is an appropriate ritual for curing "bad" or "crazy" behavior. Black similarly notes that some of the awe and respect that Tobians show for Father Marino derives from statements he made about resurrecting the dead. Indigenous Tobian culture had emphasized the interaction of ghosts and living humans, and ghosts are still greatly feared; a priest who claimed control of ghosts and who associated that power with Catholicism was thus an impressive man.

Christianity is not always so impressive when introduced to new contexts, however, and Griffin Dix's chapter describes the failure of the Christians in the Korean village of Ye-an to make many converts. Though attractive to a small number of marginalized villagers, particularly widows, Christianity was seen by the majority as clashing with important Confucian values. The village blend of Confucianism and shamanism emphasized harmonious social relationships, "propriety," and (again) specific rituals for particular and immediate ends, while Christianity was taken to overemphasize individual salvation, inner faith and commitment, and the afterlife. Dix's analysis points out the important social cleavages (such as gender and lineage status) reflected in the relative attractiveness of Christianity to some people but not to others. This chapter is also suggestive as an example of how "microhistorical" events—in this case a dispute over the way a young preacher handled an exorcism—can affect the long-term outcome of religious change. Such events, though apparently trivial, can be of enduring significance in relatively stable, small-scale communities.

Wedenoja's chapter, like most of the others in the book, is ethnohistorical, though (again like the others) written by an anthropologist with pertinent ethnographic field experience. He deals in depth with the rise of "Revival," a contemporary Creole religion in Jamaica. Revival blends elements of African religions and Christianity and had its origins in plantation slavery. Wedenoja presents Jamaican religion as central to the Creole culture that developed in the nineteenth century and stresses the continual innovation that has resulted in a rich, flexible, and dynamic symbolic system. Like the other versions of Christianity described in the book, Jamaican revivalism meets immediate personal and social needs, providing rituals for healing as well as a kind of psychological recreation through spirit possession.

Wedenoja's analysis makes quite clear the political implications of Jamaican religion at various historical junctures, but also notes that Christianity is exceptionally flexible in its political messages. The missionaries to Jamaica varied in their attitudes toward slavery, for example. The Anglicans—the first Christian ministers on the islands—ignored the slaves altogether; the Moravians in the 1750s argued to estate owners that Christianization would make for more diligent, reliable, and loyal slaves. The British Baptists and later the Methodists, however, actively supported abolition. Similarly, black Christians themselves took the Christian political message in different ways, frequently turning it to revolutionary causes. Indeed, Wedenoja argues that the revolutionary potential of religious movements is frequently underestimated, and he details the many rebellions led by Jamaican Christian leaders. Many of these were millenarian in character, as in the early twentieth century when J. L. TaBois predicted a world revolution that would bring the end of all mortgages and debts, the confiscation of property by the poor, and the establishment of a heavenly kingdom on earth. According to Wedenoja, social discontent and anti-establishment views are frequently expressed even today in Jamaican Pentecostalism. Though there is no doubt that religion may function as a psychological palliative, then, there is also no doubt that it may provide the inspiration for revolution.

Lawrence A. Palinkas' chapter concerns the development of the Chinese Christian community in San Diego, California, and focuses on two contemporary Mandarin-speaking churches. Immigrant churches have often helped new arrivals to adjust to life in the United States, but European ethnic churches have, on the whole, played a conservative role, helping immigrants to preserve their culture and providing continuity between the old and new. Though Chinese Christian churches have also had this function, Palinkas emphasizes rather their role in helping the immigrants change. Like Chinese Christian churches in other places, the San Diego churches provided English classes and housing for unmarried men and mediated between new immigrants and the English-speaking community. However, the San Diego Chinese Christian churches had some unique characteristics as well. In San Diego the Chinese community underwent an early dispersal throughout the city, rather than concentrating in a Chinatown. The churches functioned as a community center for a population that otherwise was integrated into ethnically diverse neighborhoods.

There are numerous ways in which Chinese culture and life in the United States present social and psychological dilemmas for individuals, and the contemporary churches provide a setting in which such conflicts can be ameliorated. Palinkas notes specifically the problems of submission to authority and reliance on kin groups, and he argues that the Christian churches maintain the values of submission while creating a nonkin reference group. The metaphor of a family is maintained through the church, which replaces the traditional kin support network. The churches also help individuals to resolve identity crises and to deal with old age in a cultural context where age no longer brings respect and power. All of this is accomplished through the apparently contradictory but in fact complementary processes of integration of the two cultural systems in some respects and distinction of the two in others, and the church becomes the arena in which such clarifications can take place.

Michael D. Murphy's analysis of the development of a Catholic Pentecostal prayer community in a conservative southern California parish takes us into a consideration of transformation in an established Christian religion. The Catholic "Charismatic Renewal" movement was generated in part by changes within the Catholic church itself following Vatican II, and in part through diffusion of Pentecostalism from Protestants to Catholics in the 1960s and 1970s. Murphy's analysis concerns the "politics" of transformation: the management of tensions between an emotionally inspired, "spontaneous," and potentially heretical religious experience and a conservative, somewhat authoritarian form ordinarily controlled by an established clergy and based on a formalized dogma. The central ritual elements of Charismatic Renewal, such as the gifts of prophecy and speaking in tongues, necessarily presented problems for Catholics who were deeply committed to staying in the good graces of the church.

The particular prayer community studied by Murphy was considered "clergy-led," in that it had the sanction of the parish priest and the leadership of the deacon, long a highly respected man in the parish. Murphy's chapter provides insight into the subtle methods by which the deacon managed both to encourage the fervent emotionalism generated in the prayer meetings and simultaneously to control the spontaneity and keep it within the bounds of acceptable Catholic religiosity. The process involved "the routinization of charisma" through careful preparation of the participants and tight management of the meetings themselves. For example, one of the "gifts of the Holy Spirit" used in the meetings was the power of "discernment," through which the leader and sometimes other members suggested that certain performances represented the work of Satan rather than of the Holy Spirit. An attack on the Virgin Mary, on one occasion, and on the infallibility of the Pope, on another, were quickly countered by such suggestions. As the prayer group developed and grew, such means allowed the group to walk the thin line between orthodoxy and heresy without running afoul of the Church, and in the process, an important transformation of standard American Catholicism was effected.

My own chapter deals with the politicization of religion at a different level, in the context of Italian national and local elections. Taking as "texts" a prayer and an "anti-prayer" composed prior to the 1980 elections, I analyze the ways in which the priest of a small alpine village and a group of local leftists play on the ambiguity of the relationship between religion and politics. Though Roman Catholicism might be presented as an apolitical religion, and though communism might be presented as an areligious political ideology, the opposition of the two in the electoral context creates transformations in both. The mutual relevance (or irrelevance) of politics and religion becomes a contested issue, and the symbolic content of Catholicism is changed accordingly. This final ethnographic study examines both social and psychological factors that bear on the politicization of religion, an extremely common (if not inevitable) process. I consider especially attitudes toward authority and dependency, the symbolic significance of the tension between social hierarchy and class solidarity, and the importance of the idea of "separate spheres" for men and women in Italian village life.

Though the relationship between culture and Christianity varies considerably in the ethnographic case studies presented in the book, there are also unquestionably some unifying and general features of the transformative process. In the final chapter, we attempt to draw out some theoretical implications and make some generalizations about the interaction of Christianity and culture.

The term "dialectics"—though used rather loosely and without formal definition—is taken seriously throughout the book, and especially in the overview provided in the concluding remarks. Though a "world religion," Christianity's world is a richly variegated one, and its introduction and evolution in any cultural context depend on the real and pragmatic actions of very different people working within distinct established structures. Its own symbols and institutional structure are manipulated along with local culture in a way that changes both. Still, Christianity does have some intrinsic content, and culture change does follow comprehensible patterns. Our goal in the chapters that follow is to contribute to the ongoing anthropological task of demystification of both.

2

Symbols of Solidarity in the Christianization of Santa Isabel, Solomon Islands

GEOFFREY M. WHITE

INTRODUCTION

The work of the Anglican Melanesian Mission in Santa Isabel represents one of the dramatic stories of socioreligious change in Melanesia. After some initial setbacks in the mid–nineteenth century, the Mission converted the entire population (about four thousand people comprising four major language groups) within two decades. Furthermore, this wholesale conversion was less a product of steady evangelization than an internally generated process in which people actively sought to acquire the new religion and participate in Christian ritual. The extensive societal transformation accompanying missionization was seen, from the indigenous point of view, as the result of a deliberate effort to revitalize self and society in the image of a "new life." This chapter explores the indigenous understandings and practices upon which the experience of Christianization has been constructed in Santa Isabel.

Early missionary work on the island was done in the context of escalating raids against Santa Isabel settlements by well-armed headhunters (White 1979). The raids depopulated large areas of the island and fomented several decades of social disruption in which many people were uprooted from their ancestral lands. Given this ongoing social and cultural upheaval, the socioreligious system introduced by missionaries was perceived as a means of redefining and revitalizing the institutions in crisis. The deliberate incorporation of new social forms during a period of personal stress and societal disintegration resembles the model of "revitalization movements" described by Anthony F. C. Wallace (1956) (cf. Guiart 1970). Just as revitalization movements seek to resolve social and psychological strain through *cultural transformation*, many Santa Isabel communities actively sought relief from the problems of raiding and killing by attempting to reforge an identity as "Christian people" living in a "new way" of life. Santa Isabel Christianity thus obtained much of its cultural meaning through con-

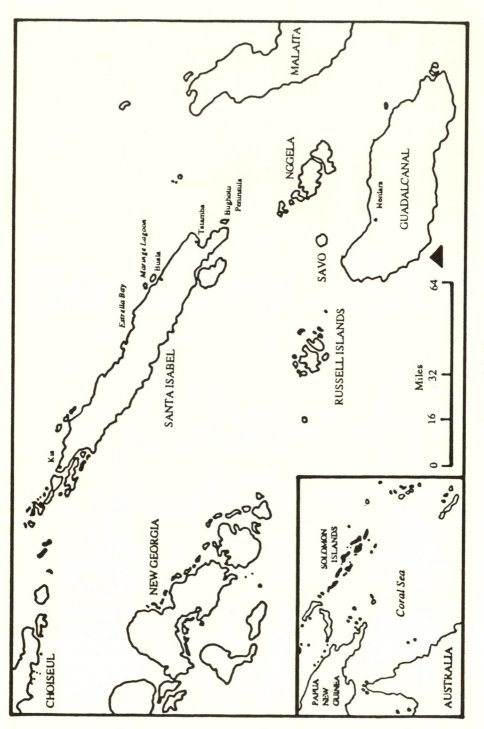

Solomon Islands

trastive images of the "new way" and the "way before"—images that continued to depend upon traditional frameworks of understanding for their significance and force.

The transition to the "new way" was marked by wholesale changes in social organization as well as in ritual life. For most of the population, conversion involved migration to relatively large coastal villages where Mission catechists conducted teaching and worship in village churches. The migration entailed a consolidation of traditional settlement patterns, as well as a shift in structures of power and authority as catechists and priests acquired many of the roles of traditional priests and chiefs. The social environment so created fostered the acquisition of Christian ideology, just as the new ideology rationalized and sustained the Mission social order. For example, a rationale for residential consolidation was offered in the ideals of peace, unity, and solidarity expressed in notions of Christian identity, in ritual activity conducted in village churches, and in feasts celebrating Christian occasions.

To understand Christianization as an internally generated process of change involving active attempts at redefining identity, it is necessary to explore the cultural significance of Christian identity and the practices that enact it. It is ironic that the "new life" could not even have been envisioned, much less actively pursued, were it not defined in large part on the basis of traditional goals and customs (that is, in the framework of a culturally constructed "behavioral environment") (Hallowell 1967). Christianization substituted an entire complex of Christian ritual and belief for traditional religious practices, fulfilling many of the same functions and acquiring many of the same meanings as in the indigenous symbolic system. After a brief account of social life in the pagan past, this chapter reviews the process of societal consolidation brought about by missionization and then examines cultural frameworks of understanding that give the process meaning for the people of Santa Isabel.

THE PAGAN PAST

This chapter is based on fieldwork done in the Maringe area of Santa Isabel (see map). The language of this region, spoken by more than half of the island's fourteen thousand inhabitants, is an Austronesian language referred to as Cheke Holo, "bush language," and specifically as A'ara in the villages where I worked (White et al. 1988). As indicated in the name of their language, residents of the Maringe area formerly inhabited the high mountains and valleys in the interior part of the island where they lived in small hamlets composed of only a few households. There were some canoe-building and fishing groups who lived along the coast, but more were inland dwellers who subsisted on swidden gardening. And still today, people derive their livelihood largely from subsistence horticulture.

Indigenous patterns of sociopolitical organization resemble those described for other islands in the Western Solomons (Oliver 1955; Scheffler 1965). Kinship relations and regional alignments provided the primary basis for social identity in the past. The idiom for tracing descent is matrilineal and exogamous clans are found in all parts of the island. Major forms of collective activity in the past included raiding (and defense from raiding), staging feasts for allies and rivals, and making propitiatory offerings at the shrines of deceased ancestors—all of which were occasions for dispersed peoples to cooperate and gather together. These activities were organized by local leaders or chiefs (*funei*) whose power was based on a combination of personal reputation and demonstrated accomplishments in feasting and warfare. The social influence and authority of traditional leaders was closely connected with their perceived access to powerful ancestral spirits (*na'itu*) and other supernatural forces that were presumed to provide them with personal power (or mana, *nolaghi*) in dealing with enemies or rivals as well as in gardening, fishing, or curing illness.

In many ways, the symbolic centers of the traditional universe were the ancestral shrines that dotted the landscape. The shrines, or *phadagi*, were constructed out of stones piled up to house the skulls and bones of important deceased ancestors. The descendants of the chiefs whose bones resided in a particular shrine would make periodic propitiatory offerings at the shrine in order to avoid ancestral retribution for not fulfilling ritual obligations and to seek their assistance in maintaining personal and community well-being. Ancestral spirits offended by their descendants could bring them harm in the form of illness or failure in important socioeconomic activities such as gardening. The shrines were an important symbol of the power of chiefs and priests who had inherited the knowledge and ritual paraphernalia to perform the proper rites. In addition, ancestral shrines were a Durkheimian emblem of the collective identity of those who shared common descent and of their relation to the land upon which the shrine was located.

The web of mutually supporting meanings and interdependencies among institutions of kinship, leadership, and land ownership began to unravel in the mid–nineteenth century after the first effects of contact with Europeans began to be felt in Santa Isabel. Beginning in the early part of the century, Europeans increasingly sailed into the Solomons archipelago for trading or labor recruiting. The chiefs who controlled this trade sought to obtain European goods, especially improved weapons in the form of steel axes and guns (White 1979; Jackson 1975; McKinnon 1975). These leaders and their followers were, in many instances, able to build up substantial arsenals of new weapons with which to dominate their neighbors (who often did not participate in the trade with Europeans) and further expand their economic resources. This cycle of trading and raiding reached its peak in the Western Solomons where a few notorious chiefs capitalized on their military dominance to go farther and farther afield in hunting and raiding expeditions. Although some chiefs in the Bughotu area in the southeastern portion of Santa Isabel were known to traders and profited from the new trade, much of the population, especially inland dwellers such as Cheke Holo speakers, did not. As a result, they became easy victims for raiding parties from the Western Solomons. In addition, internecine raiding appears to have escalated.

Documents left by European observers attest to the scale of headhunting raids during this period and to the devastating effects on Santa Isabel, where long stretches of coastline were left uninhabited (Woodford 1909). For Cheke Holo speakers, the response was either to move into regions at the highest elevations where people could take refuge in hilltop forts to defend against alien attackers (see Hocart 1922; Wilson 1935:13–14), or to flee to the southeastern tip of the island and enter into temporary alliance with powerful chiefs who had emerged in the Bughotu area. Given their inability to maintain adequate defenses (even the forts could be besieged until the defenders were forced to give up hostages) and, in many cases, their dislocation from ancestral lands, the prestige of chiefs and the ancestral spirits from whom they derived their power must have suffered greatly. It was in this context that representatives of the Melanesian Mission first arrived.

The Mission work was begun in the Bughotu area where the renowned chief, Bera, had built up a substantial store of weapons and a military following through trade with Europeans. Bera was none too eager to receive the "good news" and died in a resolutely pagan state, even though he had allowed Mission representatives to reside in his area and begin their teaching. The missionaries, such as Alfred Penny, tried to contribute in a practical way to dealing with the head-hunting problem by setting up an organized system of defense in which watch was kept and an early alarm given if a raiding party was sighted (Penny 1888:218). Later the missionary Henry Welchman took a more active role and considered traveling to the Western Solomons to present the notorious head-hunter Ingava with a peace offering (Welchman 1889–1908).

The Mission, however, contributed more than just improved defenses. It provided a rationale for peace and a ready-made cultural system with which to transform many of the beliefs and institutions connected with raiding. Mission teaching supplied a conception of supernatural power that could be assimilated to indigenous notions of mana, but was explicitly divorced from the practice of raiding. Whatever success the Mission stations had in defending against raids would have been interpreted as evidence of the strength of their religious teaching. Indigenous beliefs associated success in warfare with the efficacy of supernatural powers. The Mission offered a new source of supernatural power and gave some evidence of its effectiveness. In response to the necessity of maintaining both personal reputation and the prosperity of their followers, some leaders made the pragmatic decision to allow a new kind of ritual specialist in their midst, a Christian catechist teacher. The attitude of one particular chief toward the catechists reveals some of the cultural assumptions that lay behind acceptance of Christianity. Welchman visited Goregita at his fort and asked him about sending a catechist to teach him and his people the "new way":

Goregita told me, in answer to my question, that he was anxious to have a teacher to live with him. I asked him why, and he said he had been much troubled by the enemy, who harried him continually, and within a month, they had forced him to give them two of his people as captives: he had noticed that where there was a teacher, the people lived in peace, and they were seldom or never disturbed by raids. So he thought if I would send him a teacher, he also would be left alone. "Then you don't want your people to be taught?" I asked. "No, I only want one of your teachers to come and live here" (Melanesian Mission 1899:8).

The Bughotu chief Soga was the most successful and well documented of the leaders who first saw the potential benefits of Christianity as a source of power and prestige. He began courting the new teaching following the death of his predecessor, Bera. As early as 1884, Alfred Penny noted, "Soga and Voo came to see me. They are very amenable to have a teacher, we have arranged for Devi to go there and begin a school" (Penny, Diary: May 22, 1884). Five years later Soga was baptized Monilaws Soga (after the resident missionary at that time, R. M. Turnbull) along with his wife and about seventy followers (Armstrong 1900:273).

From that time until his death nine years later, Soga used the ideology of peace to form alliances extending into every region of Santa Isabel. His exploits were portrayed extensively in Mission publications as one of the dramatic examples of Christian transformation. Although it is difficult to judge the distortion in these records, Soga was a remarkable and perceptive individual who saw Mission teaching as a way of acquiring knowledge, prestige, and influence. Under the tutelage of Henry Welchman, he learned to read the Mission lingua franca, Mota, and eagerly read Mission texts. Soga possessed a voracious intellect and questioned Welchman closely on religious and historical points raised in his readings (Welchman, 1889–1908). He formed a close symbiotic relationship with Welchman, who provided advice and Mission backing for Soga's activities as peacemaker and alliance builder. Through the agency of Soga and other converted leaders, pacification and evangelization proceeded hand in hand. By the turn of the century, the entire Bughotu population had been converted and every part of the island contacted by Mission representatives.

Santa Isabel contrasts with other islands in the Solomons where recognized chiefs were not among the first converts, who tended to be recruited from the margins of society. In many cases, the spread of Christianity proceeded much more slowly elsewhere because of the lack of enthusiasm or outright resistance posed by powerful local leaders. In the Roviana area in the Western Solomons, once a notorious headhunting center, the Methodist Mission gained its first converts among "slaves" (probably taken from Santa Isabel or Choiseul) (Tippett 1967; Harwood 1978), and pacification seems to have demoralized much of the population, removing many of the traditional activities where chiefs had sought prestige and influence. As suggested by a man from the Western Solomons quoted by A. M. Hocart (1922:79): "No one is mighty now; they are all alike, they have no money; they cannot go headhunting; they all 'stop nothing.' " These contrasts in the social meanings of Christianity among early converts in the Western Sol-

omons had in Santa Isabel had consequences for the subsequent course of Christianization in the two areas. Whereas the Mission was seen as a revitalizing force
in Santa Isabel, revitalization in the Roviana area took the form of an indigenous
"breakaway" church, the Christian Fellowship Church, which split from the
Methodist Church after World War II (Harwood 1978).

The military strength of Soga and other Christian chiefs on Santa Isabel was
more important for pacification and defense than the organizational efforts by
missionaries and catechist teachers. Soga, like his predecessor Bera, had established regional dominance through success in the cycle of trading and raiding
described previously. Soga used his military resources, as well as the Christian
ideology of peace, to form alliances—as much through intimidation as evangelization (White 1979). These pacts, together with the suppression of local
raiding, strengthened the ability of Christian chiefs to withstand headhunting
attacks from the Western Solomons. For Soga, as a Christian, there had been
an initial setback in 1891 when about 150 New Georgians forced him and his
followers into their fort, where they were helpless to prevent the plundering of
their village and gardens. Ultimately, someone from their ranks had to be offered
in ransom (Armstrong 1900:292). Following this raid, however, Soga resisted
major headhunting forays on at least two occasions. The following year a group
of thirty headhunters attempted to purchase a victim from Soga, but he successfully refused. And in 1897, eight canoes of New Georgians were surrounded
by Soga with a large force and sent away in defeat, apparently without loss of
life (Melanesian Mission 1898:1–3, 7–8).

While Soga's efforts could not put an end to raiding parties originating in
the Western Solomons, the alliances he built through his evangelical efforts
must have helped improve defenses by reducing pressures from internecine warfare. Prior to the nonraiding pact, a community's safety and well-being depended
upon military alliances built up through feast exchanges and by participating in
raids against mutual enemies. The Christian ideology of peace, with its prohibition on killing as a way of dealing with rivals and enemies, provided a cultural
way out of the cycle of raiding and alliance building. In any case, the era of
headhunting was rapidly coming to an end as British authorities sought to punish
raiders (even using warships on one occasion to shell offending villages in the
Western Solomons) (Zelenietz 1979). Santa Isabel and New Georgia were
brought under the British Protectorate in 1901.

The Protectorate administration based in Nggela took on a distant, little-
noticed role in Isabel affairs. This was possible because of the thorough social
and cultural transformation forged by the Melanesian Mission. It was on Santa
Isabel that the Mission most deserved the appellation "true architect of the
British Solomon Island Protectorate" (Morrell 1960:349). In fact, after fifteen
years of colonial administration on the island, the acting resident commissioner
wrote the high commissioner for the Western Pacific that "The island of Ysabel
has received next to no Government supervision, the natives are quiet and
peacebal [sic], everyone being under the control of the Melanesian Mission"

(WPHC 4/11/8: 1915). What were the transformative processes that produced this Mission-based society, which seemed to find the colonial administration redundant?

SOCIAL CONSOLIDATION IN THE "NEW WAY"

Even before the British flag was raised on Santa Isabel, roughly one-fourth of the island population had been baptized (923 out of an estimated 4,000) (Melanesian Mission 1901:143). At that time there were forty-one catechists and fourteen Mission "schools" already established on the island. Once head-hunting raids dwindled at the turn of the century, the process of training catechists and setting up village schools accelerated rapidly. In 1903 Welchman established a Mission station on the small Bughotu island of Lilihigna, renaming it *Mara na Tabu* ("Sacred People," or "All Saints"). This station became a base for instructing catechists and coordinating their work around the island until Welchman's death from malaria in 1908. In 1903 a school had been established in Kia at the extreme northwestern end of the island, the number of catechists had grown to fifty-seven, and Welchman could report that "there is a great falling off in the number of adult baptisms in Bughotu. This is due to the fact that now all the people are Christians" (Melanesian Mission 1904:40).

A remarkable feature of Christianization in Santa Isabel is that the entire population was converted by a *single* mission, unlike most areas in Melanesia where competing missions introduced a number of denominations into the same area. In Santa Isabel, the ability of the Melanesian Mission to bring the whole population within its orbit is a product of the rapidity of conversion in the context of headhunting and pacification, as well as the deliberate policy of the British resident commissioner, Charles Woodford, to restrict competition among the various missions (Hilliard 1978:134). Subsequent to conversion of the whole island by the Melanesian Mission, Seventh Day Adventists succeeded in winning over two villages with a combined population of about 100.

The rapid spread of Mission influence on Santa Isabel should be seen in the context of the cultural meanings of conversion. Conversion entailed the adoption of a package of religious belief and ritual along with sociomoral ideals that rationalized major shifts in patterns of residence and leadership. These parallel transformations reinforced one another so that Mission ideology gave purpose and meaning to the new social order at the same time as societal changes facilitated the spread of Christianity as a (syncretic) cultural system. Among the important social changes contributing to the propagation of Christian teaching were the amalgamation of formerly dispersed peoples into relatively large coastal villages and the emergence of catechists and priests as powerful local leaders. The process of amalgamation, which had begun as a response to raiding headhunters, was further reinforced by the Mission policy of creating new settlements that would bring larger numbers of people into regular contact with the daily routines of Christian life. Firmly rooted in indigenous understandings

about persons and spirits (see White 1985a, 1985b), Mission ideology was a potent force in shaping and maintaining the new social order in these village amalgams. Christian moral precepts gained motivational force from the same reasoning about dangerous supernatural powers and the risks of moral transgression that had given the traditional religion its persuasive moral authority.

In local perceptions, the onset of peace was associated with the adoption of Christianity. The concurrent processes of pacification and migration to coastal villages imbued conversion in Santa Isabel with a sense of holistic change. The transformation was symbolized by the new identity adopted by individual persons and by whole communities: that of the "Christian person." Viewed against the backdrop of crisis caused by raiding headhunters, conversion promised to revitalize social life with renewed security and prosperity. During the first decade of this century, the desire for Mission teaching in the Maringe area reached millennial proportions. Welchman wrote in 1903 that "one great feature of this year's work is the demand for schools in the bush, and among bush people who have come out into the open" (Melanesian Mission 1904:37). This optimistic statement was made in part on the basis of evangelical work by a self-styled prophet who had received some minimal Mission instruction and set off on his own to convert people in the Maringe area. He succeeded in gathering an estimated 250 people into one village and helped to organize two other villages that later became centers of Mission teaching with regular catechists. The desire for catechists by groups yet uncontacted by missionaries was also observed on the neighboring island of Choiseul where headhunting had also taken a heavy toll (Goldie 1914:577, cited in Scheffler 1965:23).

Mission leaders organized and managed the new coastal villages. Bishop Cecil Wilson of the Melanesian Mission described the process as follows:

In our large islands . . . there are no villages until we make them . . . the people live in hamlets. . . . When we get Christians in any one spot, we gradually gather all the people together from that neighborhood so that we form a village in time. When the number is finished, and all the people have gathered together, there may be 150 of them (Melanesian Mission 1910:41–42, cited in Chapman and Pirie 1974:2.31).

This type of settlement differed sharply from pre-Western patterns of residence in which rights to land and identification with named regions were established through descent and expressed in the activities of chiefs. Important attachments to land and regional identity were constructed in the context of major feasts and enacted in rites of propitiation at ancestral shrines. Migration away from ancestral lands to villages in coastal regions could only have been accomplished with a concomitant transformation of social relations and identities. Just such a transforming process was provided by Christian conversion.

Nine villages were formed in the Maringe area between 1900 and 1910. These ranged in size from about 100 to 300 residents, indicating that most of the regional population came to reside in these village conglomerates. Once a Chris-

tian village was established and a building constructed to serve as chapel and school, pagans residing in the environs could more readily be evangelized and attracted into the village, perhaps to form an additional hamlet (*gruru*). Through such a process of accretion, villages typically included several discrete hamlets, each with one or more representative elders or chiefs. In this way, the distinctiveness of regional groups was maintained in a submerged form in the new village conglomerates. Many people maintained a village dwelling while residing for extended periods at garden sites several miles distant. Sunday prayer services and special ceremonial celebrations were well attended while the twice-daily prayers could be somewhat sparse.

Brief consideration of the formation of two Maringe Christian villages will illustrate the sociocultural processes associated with these residential changes. Both of the villages described, Sugarege and Buala, owed their origins to the flight from headhunters into the Bughotu area where the Mission was first established.

The people who lived near the shore of the Maringe lagoon were decimated by headhunting raids during the 1880s. For example, in 1881 an agent aboard a labor recruiting vessel observed the "remains of a cannibal feast, about 10 people had been killed and eaten there . . . the hair yet clung to the skulls" (Gaggin, September 1, 1881). By about 1890 some of the last surviving inhabitants of the Maringe lagoon migrated to Lagheba on the Bughotu peninsula for relief from continuing raids from the West. A group of about fifty men, women, and children was led by a chief named Getu who took his followers to live within the orbit of Soga's influence in Bughotu. Within a few years, Welchman wrote that Getu was "anxious for a school" (Diary: April 11, 1894). Welchman left Hugo Hebala, a Bughotu man trained at the Mission's Norfolk Island school, to build a school and instruct the Maringe people. In 1905 Hugo Hebala and Getu (baptized "John Selwyn Getu") led the colony of Lagheba Christians back to the Maringe lagoon to resettle the area and begin evangelizing others in the surrounding region.

When the move was made, Maringe landowners granted Hebala and the Mission two islands in the lagoon and a stretch of shoreline, as an expression of their desire to participate in the "new way." Work was begun immediately on building a church. Hebala and Getu asked Welchman to consecrate the structure even before it was finished. Their wish was soon granted as Welchman came to bless the church, with about 200 Christians inside the building and both Christians and pagans observing the ceremony from outside (Wilson 1935:80–81).

Hebala not only ministered to the group of transplanted Lagheba Christians, but was the dominant force in carrying Mission teaching throughout all of Maringe. He worked to attract pagans living near the lagoon to establish residence at Buala and attend the school there. He and other catechists trekked through the bush contacting pagan enclaves, drawing them into the new teaching. Within three years, Welchman reported,

Buala has been growing rapidly. A number of heathen have come down from the hills at the back, and have made a settlement for themselves almost adjoining the Church compound... they were attracted by the friendly nature of the Christians and by the peace of the place. Many have joined the baptismal class which now numbers 70.... Hugo, the deacon, had done much missionary work among the bush fold, and two or three places are ready for teachers (Melanesian Mission 1908:46–47).

Another example of one of the early Christian villages in Maringe is Sugarege. During the height of headhunting, people living in one of the Maringe regions fled south to the mountainous area bordering the Bughotu peninsula. There they divided and formed two settlements, Suasupa and Saile, managed by rival chiefs. One settlement was Christianized before the turn of the century while the other remained pagan. George Giladi, the sister's daughter's son of the chief of the pagan settlement, was taken to Norfolk Island for schooling. He later returned to work as a catechist under Welchman. After Welchman's death, he set out on his own to evangelize his own people and eventually led them back to their ancestral lands in Maringe. In the process, Giladi succeeded in bringing about a merger of the Suasupa and Saile settlements to form a new Christian village. And like Hebala, he sought fresh converts in the region where the new village was formed, expanding both his own influence and that of the Mission. The ground had hardly been cleared for the first settlement when Giladi engineered another move to include several additional groups in a larger village called Sugarege with a population of about 300. At its peak size, Sugarege was composed of seven named hamlets.

Sugarege (literally "branched house") got its name from the village church, constructed with three wings or "branches." It was consecrated in 1917 by Bishop Wood. The resident missionary Andrew Thomson described the church as "the finest church in the bush all inlaid work and raised on a wall of concrete and stone" (Thomson, Diary: April 26, 1917).

In the long run, maintenance of many of the Christian village amalgams proved unworkable. Five of the nine Maringe villages formed during the conversion period ultimately segmented into numerous splinter villages. Not long after the formation of Sugarege, a dispute over adultery caused an initial splintering of one group from the village. Giladi later departed with a sizable following to take up missionary work on the island of Makira, and Sugarege finally divided into several small fragments at the time of World War II. The process of aggregation and subsequent splintering of Sugarege is represented in Figure 1.1 with dates of movement for derivative villages. The final division of Sugarege was associated with the decision by a Mission priest, Fr. Stephen Talu, to lead his kin and followers to form a new settlement on their ancestral land, several miles further inland. This move followed from tensions between Talu and close relatives of Giladi, a rivalry that flared into numerous disputes and formal inquiries. Catechists and Mission priests, like the chiefs they often supplanted, could also become embroiled in competition for prestige and influence.

Figure 1.1
Merging and Subsequent Splitting of an Early Christian Village, with Approximate
Dates

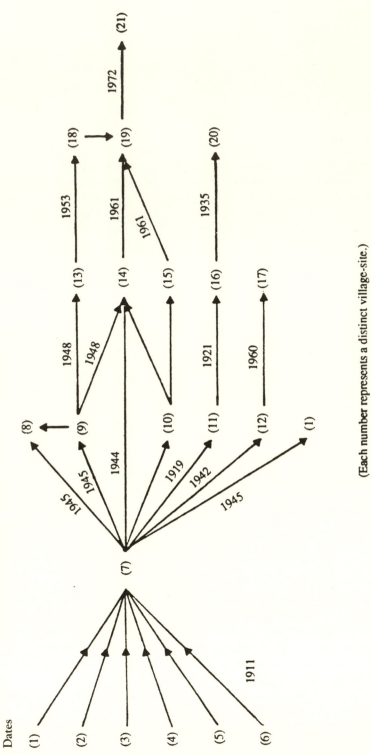

(Each number represents a distinct village-site.)

In addition to the competitive struggles of rivalrous leaders, sorcery fears and conflicts over adultery contributed to village splintering. Sorcery accusations would be expected in the new villages where large numbers of unrelated people, outside the sphere of trust defined by kinship ties, lived in close proximity to one another. Furthermore, large villages produced novel health problems and were easily devastated by epidemics of influenza, dysentery, and whooping cough—often interpreted as the product of sorcery.

The schismatic tendency of large hamlets and villages has been described elsewhere in the Solomons and Melanesia (Ross 1973:250; Schwartz 1963). It is rather the formation and persistence of relatively large Mission villages, a historical novelty in Santa Isabel, that requires explanation. By introducing a new complex of religious belief and ritual, Mission teaching both rationalized and motivated these changes in social organization. In particular, the Mission rhetoric of unity, brotherhood, and cooperation was embodied in the new, shared identity of the "Christian person" and regularly enacted in ceremonies carried out in village churches (White 1980). Ancestral shrines (*phadagi*) were replaced by churches as the major locus of supernatural power, and the previous pattern of competitive feasting was continued only in feasts marking Christian occasions such as Christmas, Easter, and village "church days."

Village churches and the ceremonies associated with them came to represent the collective identity of the new residential unit, the Mission village. The formation of villages in which ritual life was centered on village churches coincided with the declining importance of ancestral shrines. Indeed, the destruction and exorcism of ancestral shrines were major means by which missionaries and catechists demonstrated the ascendancy of the new teaching. So, for example, in one incident at Kia, Henry Welchman put a number of baptismal candidates to a test by having them destroy an ancestral shrine:

We proceeded to a small island at no great distance, and climbed the hill to a place where there were four well-built tombs, surrounded by skulls, each with the death blow in evidence. There was a momentary hesitation,—it is not a particularly cheerful business to defile your grandfather's grave, and to burn his bones, even for a brown man,—but it was only momentary, and the stones were rolled down the hill into the sea, and the bones in them made into a heap with the skulls of the victims who had been sacrificed to the dead man and a huge bonfire lighted over them. It is only a beginning; it will be a work of time to get rid of them all for the tombs are scattered all over the mainland (Melanesian Mission 1908:45–46).

Santa Isabel people were able to destroy or abandon their shrines only because they were acquiring a new set of beliefs and practices that could be used in many of the same ways, so as to protect themselves from the consequences of such desecrations.

People did not stop believing in ancestral spirits or "forest spirits." Rather, they began believing that the Christian God provided even more potent powers operating in many of the same contexts—for protection from malevolent forces, curing, and the acquisition of personal power, mana. In fact, this new source of power and protection was seized upon particularly as a way of dealing with many of the dilemmas and dangers associated with the pagan supernatural. Christian ritual procedures such as prayer, hymn singing, and priestly blessing were frequently invoked as a means of exorcising dangerous "forest spirits" from their known habitats, thus making the forest safer. Catechists and priests such as Hugo Hebala organized ceremonial processions into the forest to kneel and pray at the previous sacred sites to dispel spirits that had the power to cause sickness and injury.

As in the case of prayer services held at shrine sites, catechists and priests took the lead in using Christian ritual to confront suspected sorcerers. In Maringe, Hugo Hebala initiated a campaign to confront sorcerers and eradicate their destructive powers. During the 1920s he enlisted the assistance of the catechist Walter Gagai in a kind of "search and destroy" mission. Writing about this effort for the Mission publication *Southern Cross Log*, Hebala described the process as follows:

This last year I determined hotly within myself to make a thorough search amongst all the people for every old heathen thing that still remained hidden in their hearts, to get rid of them entirely. And one man was appointed, Walter Gagai by name, to go through all the villages, seeking out every person, and questioning them. And he succeeded completely. He sought for and found some things belonging to old times that they were still keeping hidden. And they all made full confession of everything, great or small, not one thing of any kind could they keep hidden in their breasts; and all of them in every village promised earnestly to renounce entirely those bad things of olden days, and to cleave with all their might to the teaching of Jesus Christ (Melanesian Mission, August 1925:123, cited in Whiteman 1983:351–52).

Some of the sorcerers so identified were then escorted to Buala where Hebala conducted a "spiritual cleansing." For each alleged sorcerer, Hebala conducted a ritual in the Buala church in which the person was asked to renounce sorcery and give up any ancestral relics or ritual paraphernalia connected with the practice. (Hebala's son, Nathaniel, recalls a substantial pile of sorcery objects accumulating in the church from this procedure.) Whether the person admitted to practicing sorcery or not, he or she was required to kiss the Bible as a sign of disavowal of any further involvement. It is generally believed that if anyone were to conceal sorcery in this situation, and still kiss the Bible, he or she would likely suffer death within a matter of weeks as retribution from God. Informants recall several such cases of denial and subsequent death.

Over forty years later, another priest, Eric Gnhokro, engaged in a similar campaign to deal with continuing fears of sorcery. Gnhokro, like Hebala, employed the ritual of Bible kissing with suspected sorcerers who, it is said, would die within six months if they attempted to conceal their deadly practice. Darrell L. Whiteman (1983a:581) was told of a case in which two brothers and a sister suspected of practicing sorcery died within three months of kissing the Bible at Gnhokro's request.

These somewhat dramatic uses of Christian ritual are preventive measures aimed at neutralizing or deflecting forces causing illness and death. The Mission introduced other, quieter measures as well. Christian crosses worn around the neck were adopted as a substitute for amulets traditionally worn for protection. This type of substitution was encouraged by missionaries, as indicated by Richard Fallowes (an English priest who worked in Isabel during the 1930s) in a letter home asking for things to be mailed to him, including "inexpensive small crosses for wearing round the neck. Charms were very much in demand in days gone by and the people feel happier wearing the Sacred Symbol round their necks" (Letter: November 17, 1932).

In addition to these methods of prevention, the Mission also introduced new remedies for illness. Since the most powerful healing practices traditionally drew upon spiritual assistance, especially from ancestor spirits, Christians turned to prayer, hymn singing, and blessings as replacements or supplements to earlier methods. Armstrong described the ritual remedies sought for a whooping cough epidemic in Bughotu:

the whooping cough continued raging, and a day was fixed for fasting and prayer, which was kept by all the Christians of Bugotu . . . at midday there was a special service for the removal of the sickness, at which a collection was made for the Mission. The churches were crowded at this service, the collection was equivalent to £10 of our money, a great sum, for Bugotu is very poor (1900:339).

The purging of ancestral spirits from religious ritual eliminated an important means of articulating ties of kinship and regional affiliation. At the same time that people began to move away from regions inhabited by their ancestors, an important ritual mechanism (ancestor propitiation) by which these affiliations had been expressed and socially affirmed was also being abandoned. Migration and conversion gave village churches much of the social significance formerly associated with ancestral shrines. Churches became both the ceremonial center of social life and the arena for acquiring mana and spiritual assistance.

In the Maringe area where newly formed Christian villages were built along the coast, the construction of a village church was usually the first major co-operative enterprise for village residents, as was the case for both Buala and Sugarege. But here again apparent changes belie underlying continuities. In many instances, stones from pagan ancestral shrines were used in the foundations for churches, still regarded as memorials to deceased ancestors. Certain days were (and still are) set aside to commemorate important ancestors with special church services. This rationale for church construction is reflected in the statement below attributed to George Giladi by one of his descendants who spent part of his boyhood in Sugarege. Giladi purportedly exhorted his followers to

Build a church! One big house for the Christian village and the church I'm working in as a memorial for Hofi and Baghovu [two discrete locales], as a memorial for our ancestors, for Soruhehe and Fatimana, Khegra and Hafe. This will be a memorial for my grandfathers and fathers.

The genealogical relations that connect the speaker to Giladi (catechist) and three of the four ancestors cited in the rationale for church construction (but given pseudonyms here) are depicted in Figure 1.2. (Note that the relations are consistent with the principle of uterine descent.)

The same informant who recalled Giladi's call to his followers to build the Sugarege church talked about the rationale for building the church in his own village—a large and costly building for a village of about fifty residents. He said that the church is a "memorial" for a number of ancestral shrines (*phadagi*) and listed the names of eight former shrines, going on to say:

These are ancestral shrines which, gathered together, make one shrine, Namono [village name]. Those are ancestral shrines and this one shrine of Christianity is put at Namono. . . . However many shrines there were before, this is the one shrine now. In order to gather together these various shrines, we call the chapel "all holy men."

This statement indicates that village churches, like ancestral shrines, serve an important function in symbolizing collective identity based on ties of descent (cf. Tippett 1967:271), while at the same time expressing the trend toward social consolidation represented in Christian villages. However, coparticipation in worship in churches is bounded less clearly by genealogical connections. The new God transcends particular ancestral spirits connected to specific individuals and descent groups. By invoking one deity for the same purposes that many spirits had been called upon previously, religious ritual became increasingly disconnected from small-scale, particularistic group definitions that could provide the lines for social divisiveness. The new Mission order redefined the social basis for co-participation in religious ceremonies, just as the new villages enlarged the scale of social settlements.

In addition to the expanded scale of ceremonies within a village, special communion services would typically draw attendance from a wide network of neighboring villages. Welchman noted the enthusiasm of people for receiving Holy Communion: "It was greedily accepted, the Communicants in many cases coming from a distance. Those who lived away in the bush stayed for days in order to make the most of the opportunity" (Melanesian Mission 1904:37). This enthusiasm, which is still evident today, derives from the understanding that Holy Communion is a source of Christian mana and a means of acquiring a mantle of spiritual protection, closely akin to the former rites of ancestor propitiation. The perceived similarity of Holy Communion and ancestor propitiation in Santa Isabel is evident in the words of a contemporary Isabel priest in a sermon given in a Maringe village. He used the words "propitiate" (*fafara*) and "ancestral shrine" (*phadagi*) in drawing the following analogy.

Figure 1.2
Genealogical Relations of Ancestors Cited in Rationale for Chapel Construction

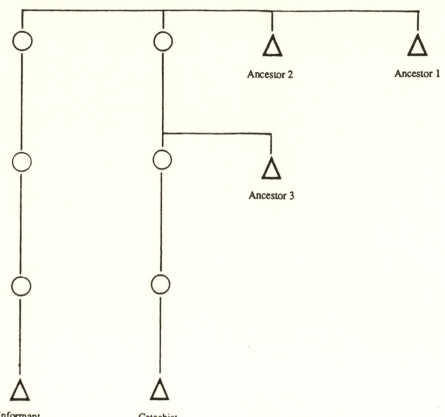

Whatever thing you or I want, come here [the church]. Ask for it in His name. . . . To get what? To get mana and strength. This is our shrine. Jesus Christ, his body and his blood, come to help you on this morning. This is our shrine. . . . It is just one name for us to receive mana.

The priest's words exemplify the manner in which the new variety of shrine, village churches, served to condense the focus of propitiatory rites to "just one name" from the plethora of individual spirits formerly propitiated in pagan ceremonies.

H. I. Hogbin's portrayal of Christianity on the neighboring island of Malaita (1958; 1970) reveals a number of parallels with Santa Isabel, despite substantial cultural differences between the two islands. His account of indigenous under-standings of worship in church services, based on the traditional model of ancestor propitiation, is a case in point:

Many of the Malaita converts still accept the concept of supernatural power but regard it as an attribute of God. He uses it, they say, to aid those who regularly go to church services, which they consider to be ceremonies in His honor and hence in a way similar to the sacrifices. Such attendances, nevertheless, are insufficient: the worshippers, to retain His favour, must in addition, obey the Commandments and certain other rules. The significance attached to the latter depends to a considerable extent on older ideas of right and wrong (1958:180).

In this passage, Hogbin points to links between conceptions of supernatural power and adherence to moral rules. The cultural reasoning that links moral transgression to personal harm infuses Christian ideology with much of its moral force.

As caretakers of the village church and proprietors of new ritual knowledge, catechists and Christian priests acquired many of the important social roles formerly associated with chiefs and pagan priests. Just as chiefs relied upon their links with potent spirits to act as guardians and representatives of their followers, Mission leaders increasingly became dominant sociopolitical figures because of their perceived role as sources of the new knowledge and the benefits to be gained from the "new way" of life. Redefining the sources of knowledge and power transformed the bases of political legitimacy, diminishing the prestige and influence of traditional leaders. Thus the rise of catechists (and later Mission priests) was paralleled by the decline of local chiefs. Guiart described a similar situation for Vanuatu:

Leaders now had to be experienced not in pig rearing, but in the work of God. Teachers and deacons were, naturally enough, the new men of authority in the world of Christianity that had been accepted, with its promise of a glowing future (1970:135).

Most of the early catechists working on Santa Isabel were trained at a school maintained by the Melanesian Mission on Norfolk Island, located 1,500 miles from the Solomons. After 1896 training was carried out at Siota on nearby Nggela. Catechists came away from Mission teaching with knowledge of Anglican religious belief and the Mission lingua franca, Mota. The absence of catechists from local life for extended periods of schooling allowed them a certain amount of detachment from ongoing rivalries and disputes. Upon returning, some catechists were able to transcend local divisions and act as mediators in unifying people under their leadership in Mission villages.

Not only did the cessation of raiding undercut one of the important roles of traditional chiefs, but Christianization also brought the end of major feasts (*diklo*) sponsored by chiefs as expressions of regional identity and accomplishment. Missionaries such as Welchman considered competitive feasting (which he referred to in his diaries as "great feasts") contrary to Mission ideals and prohibited catechists from participating in them. Instead, the "new way" of life transformed the patterns of feasting, so that large-scale feasts were held only to mark Christian occasions such as Christmas or the consecration of a new village church. Large feasts are almost always accompanied by religious ceremony and Holy Communion in the village church. The new pattern transformed, but by no means ended, the more personalistic mode of feasting sponsored by chiefs and their followers to demonstrate their accomplishments, build prestige, and promote alliances with other groups. Feasting is still very much a vehicle for promoting personal and community prestige, but its Christian rationale has muted the significance of public displays of food and wealth as expressions of group accomplishments and identity in relation to other groups. In the past, major feasts were the single most important occasion for the public recitation of regional identity and history in the form of speeches about genealogy, intermarriage, and migration movements among dispersed peoples.

Christmas, Easter, and "church days" are now the important obligatory occasions for village feasts. The "church day" is a celebration on the day of the patron saint of the village church. It is the one day annually on which a village will host a major feast and invite people from neighboring villages. "Church days" and other Christian feasts provide an opportunity for villagers to mobilize and express their shared identity as co-residents. This type of feasting also redraws the lines of rivalry according to village boundaries. So, for example, one informant speculated that when rain ruins the day of feasting and dancing for a "church day," it is probably caused by someone from another village performing weather magic to spoil the occasion. As village leaders and representatives of the "new way," catechists and priests have inherited important sociopolitical roles as organizers of Christian feasting. Catechists appear to have varied greatly in the degree to which they seized upon the role of sponsor for large feasts. However, the most renowned catechists (and, later, priests) such as Hebala and Giladi acquired their wide influence in large measure by pursuing some of the same channels of personal and political activity available to traditional leaders.

Similar to the ways chiefs had worked to build and maintain a following, catechists and priests such as Hebala and Giladi worked at forming and maintaining the unity of the Christian villages over which they presided. In some instances, resident catechists formed partnerships with traditional *funei* in order to manage and direct sociopolitical activity in the new residential centers, as in the case of Hugo Hebala and John Selwyn Getu at Buala. In other cases, catechists assumed the dominant role, as in the example of George Giladi at Sugarege. An old Maringe man who was a young boy at the time Sugarege was formed recalled that Giladi would call frequent village meetings and admonish the village residents that "You people must not go out [leave the village]. Stay here from generation to generation." And in order to validate the new amalgamation of social groups in Sugarege, he proclaimed that anyone who was born in the village automatically acquired rights to land in the region.

This kind of proclamation gives an indication of the sociocultural transformation entailed by conversion—away from the constructs of descent and ancestral lands to the more universalistic code of the Mission. Early catechists and priests were only able to succeed (to the extent that they did) in their attempt to meld together disparate groups when their actions derived moral force from the existing sociomoral universe. Conversion involved not only the adoption of a new religious creed, but the acquisition of a social identity (that of the "Christian person") rooted in indigenous understandings about persons, spirits, and social practice.

Catechists and Mission priests wielded weighty sanctions in attempting to win new converts and maintain the unity and moral order of large Christian villages. For example, by prohibiting a person from participating in prayer or communion services, a priest could remove an individual from the protective powers of the Christian God and make him or her vulnerable to the dangers of a behavioral environment populated with a wide variety of harmful forces, including possible retribution from pagan and Christian spirits alike. Hogbin (1958:198–99) noted this same point in his discussion of the emergence of missionaries and catechists as leaders with extensive social and political influence: "His authority to suspend members of his congregation is almost as powerful a weapon as that of the administration to pass sentences of imprisonment." These powers endowed Mission leaders with an aura of fear and respect in the eyes of their followers. European missionaries on Santa Isabel used these sanctions deliberately to perpetuate the unity of Christian villages. Richard Fallowes, a British priest who worked on the island in the 1930s, wrote in his diary that he had met with people in one of the coastal Maringe villages and "discussed at length the departure of certain people, 12 in number, from Nareabu. I made the rule that anyone who left a church village to live in a village where no church existed would remain excommunicate. The people concerned agreed to return to Nareabu" (Fallowes, Diary, November 7, 1931). Mission leaders were thus able to draw upon beliefs in the power and immediacy of the Christian supernatural to sustain some of the new forms of social organization that emerged during the era of conversion. However, the constant dialectic between the Mission ideals of solidarity and the numerous opportunities for transgression or conflict is evident in the high rate at which Santa Isabel people were placed outside the Church as punishment by the early missionaries. By 1908, one-tenth of all the converts on the island were excluded from church services for some period of time (Hilliard 1978:174).

CONCLUSION

This chapter has sketched social and cultural transformations accompanying Christianization in Santa Isabel within the framework of their locally interpreted significance. Because of the disruptive period of headhunting prior to conversion, social structural changes in Santa Isabel appear more thoroughgoing than elsewhere in the Solomons. Extensive societal reorganization, signaled by widespread shifts in patterns of residence and institutions of leadership, was possible because the changes were interpreted as a process of revitalization, symbolized by the adoption of a new identity (that of a "Christian person") and, indeed, way of life (the "new way").

I have argued that during the era of conversion concurrent societal and cultural transformations were mutually reinforcing. Just as notions of the "new way" imbued social changes with purpose and meaning, movement into relatively large villages with catechists exercising newfound political influence fostered the rapid transmission of Christianity as a cultural system. The trends toward consolidation and unification evident in Christian villages (see Figure 1.2) resonate with the cultural theme of solidarity expressed in Christian moral ideals and ritual practices such as church services and feasting. The replacement of rites of ancestor propitiation by church services in village churches consolidated religious symbols and ritual (one God replacing a large number of particular ancestor spirits as the primary source of mana) just as the formation of Christian villages consolidated formerly dispersed descent groups.

Deliberate efforts at transforming social institutions are not easily explained from a functionalist perspective that views society as an integrated whole. The story of the Christianization of Santa Isabel unfolds on several levels with transformations and continuities reinforcing and contradicting one another at various points. This chapter has outlined some of the ways in which Santa Isabel Christianity is rooted in indigenous understandings about social experience, with substantial continuities between traditional socioreligious activity and Christian practices. It is ironic that an explicit ideology of change such as the "new way" of Santa Isabel Christianity ultimately derives its meaning and moral persuasiveness from some of the same principles underlying the traditional religion it is seen to replace.

3

From Heathen to Atheist on Kairiru Island

MICHAEL FRENCH SMITH

The people of Kragur Village on Kairiru Island, Papua New Guinea, have been making a place for Catholicism in their lives since the beginning of this century. But Catholicism's teachings and its place in the world outside the village have changed since then and these changes have deeply affected villagers' attitudes toward it. Villagers have seen changes in the nature of the Catholic Mission's teachings—many of which reflect the trends in Catholicism given substance by the Vatican II Ecumenical Council—and they find these disturbing. Villagers have also witnessed the diminishing importance of the institutions of Catholicism in the present world and the increasing prominence of competing ideas and institutions, both secular and religious. While many Kragur people have reacted to these transformations simply by changing the nature of their commitments to Catholicism, others have suffered more severe blows to their faith. A few profess forms of atheism and secular rationalism. This suggests that this glimpse of the metamorphosis of a novel system of beliefs and practices has furthered disenchantment with the indigenous religious tradition as well as the new religion.

In what follows, I begin with a sketch of Catholic life in Kragur, an outline of the major features of the indigenous religious tradition, and a discussion of the ways in which villagers have gone about accommodating these with Catholicism. I then describe the changes in Catholicism that villagers have perceived—changes both in the focus of its teachings and in the degree to which it dominates the outside world as seen from Kragur—and their reactions to what they have seen. I conclude with some speculations about the future of Catholicism in Kragur. It is too early to tell whether villagers' experiences with these novel ideas and institutions will incline them to regard other new arrivals with a more critical eye.

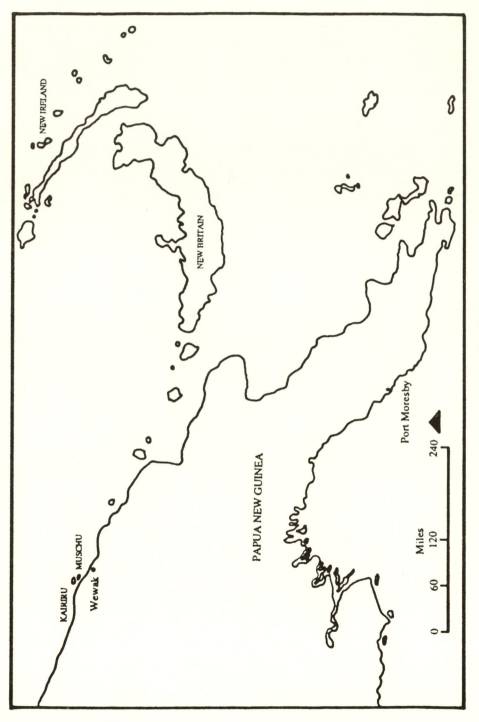

NEW IRELAND

NEW BRITAIN

KAIRIRU
MUSCHU
Wewak

PAPUA NEW GUINEA

Port Moresby

Miles

0   60   120   240

Kairiru, Papua New Guinea

ACCOMMODATING CATHOLICISM

Kairiru Island lies several miles off the north coast of mainland Papua New Guinea in the East Sepik Province. Kragur Village is located on its north coast, sandwiched between the steep slopes of the mountain that dominates the island and cliffs dropping into the sea. Its population of approximately 200 people lives in houses built from bush materials. With the exception of sporadic copra production and the beginnings of small-scale cacao bean projects, they are primarily engaged in fishing, minor hunting and gathering, and swidden horticulture. The Catholic Society of the Divine Word (SVD) Mission has been active in the East Sepik Province since just before the turn of the century and on Kairiru Island since soon after that. In the mid–1920s Papua New Guinean catechists arrived in Kragur, to begin its history of growing involvement with the Mission.

Christianity has made deep inroads in Papua New Guinea, and Catholicism has been the dominant denomination in the East Sepik Province (Firth 1975; Huber 1987). Kragur villagers speak of themselves as having been heathens before conversion to Catholicism. If I were to take full account of the perseverance of pre-Mission beliefs and their syncretic union with Catholicism I would have to conclude that this change is not yet complete. Nevertheless, at first glance Catholicism appears to have taken exceptionally firm root in Kragur, and in many ways it has. Every evening schoolchildren and adults gather for prayers in front of a small statue of the Virgin that stands in a covered altar in the center of the village. In addition, group prayers precede communal work organized by the village councillor, an elected village leader under a system originally established by the Australian colonial administration and preserved following independence. There is a small but active chapter of the Legion of Mary whose members keep track of attendance at each evening's prayer meeting. On Sundays, nearly the entire population of the village gathers for services at the village church, built from bush materials and usually kept scrupulously neat. Virtually everyone turns out for such events as the All Souls' Day observance, reciting prayers and singing hymns in the specially decorated cemeteries. In April 1976 the people of Kragur spent many days carrying sand, gravel, and cement up the precipitous track to the pass at the top of the mountain in order to erect there a near life-size statue of the Virgin provided by Mission personnel. There are many visible signs of active belief. Villagers often voice their pride in their history of close association with the Mission, and they enjoy a reputation with Mission personnel for their devotion and involvement. As one old villager phrases it, "We're number one in the eyes of the Mission."

The view from the Mission, however, is not uniform. In my conversations with its personnel familiar with Kragur and other local villages I often found little inclination to single out particular communities for either praise or criticism. Direct requests for opinions on Kragur sometimes elicited such noncommittal responses as "Well, they're not saints." But there were also spontaneous expressions of strong feelings that Kragur is a place of special merit. One priest, for example, described the village as "a real stronghold of Catholicism . . . very devout and loyal." A sister from another parish who visited the village briefly during my stay was most impressed with the religious life there, noting in particular what she saw as the villagers' single-minded devotion to the Virgin Mary.

Certainly this is not all illusion. A young Marist brother from Kragur and another Kragur man ordained as a priest in 1978 attest to the active commitment that can grow there. But Catholicism is a recent introduction and has been laid over a deep substratum of indigenous beliefs about the supernatural. A few words about the indigenous religious tradition are in order here. Before missionization the men's cult was its most prominent feature. In this, initiated males propitiated the cult's tutelary spirit or monster, known as a *tambaran* in Melanesian Pidgin, in elaborate secret ceremonial. I have little knowledge of the details of men's cult practices in Kragur, for villagers abandoned them at the behest of Mission personnel in the late 1920s. The activities of extant Sepik men's cults are intricately interwoven with other aspects of community life, and maintenance of proper relations with the tutelary beings is believed to be necessary for the community's welfare. The most vital feature of Kragur's indigenous tradition today is the belief in the intimate involvement of spirits of the dead in the affairs of the living. Villagers hold that the dead cause much illness, wreaking revenge on living persons who have angered the deads' living kin. Various magical procedures depend for their success on the goodwill and cooperation of the dead, and people routinely call on their deceased kin, particularly mothers and fathers, for assistance in such diverse contexts as disasters at sea, divination, fishing, or felling a tree they desire to fall in a particular direction. Mythology tells of a number of nonhuman supernatural beings and human or humanlike culture heroes who were responsible for the creation of features of the landscape or who provided human beings with important esoteric knowledge. Such knowledge—for example, magical spells—often figures prominently in everyday life, and some of these beings linger on in the landscape they created. Villagers, however, are more preoccupied with the spirits of the dead, for they are a more constant and immediate presence, more directly involved in the passions of living men and women.

The continuing vitality of indigenous beliefs helps account for the fact that few, if any, Kragur people approach orthodoxy in their Catholicism, though they take different paths to their heterodox syncretic formulations. Some integrate indigenous beliefs and Catholic teachings primarily by bending the latter to fit the former. Others stick closer to the Mission doctrines and bend, or even discount and discard, indigenous beliefs in order to achieve a synthesis. One stimulus to syncretism has been the problem of integrating indigenous beliefs about the recent and remote dead with Mission teachings about God. Those villagers who cling most tenaciously to indigenous beliefs assert that when missionaries speak of God they are simply referring metaphorically to individuals' dead fathers; hence, each man's dead father is his own God. In contrast, the village church leader speculates that while in the past people thought that in certain instances they were appealing to their dead kinsmen their appeals in fact went to God. In his view, to speak of the dead is to speak metaphorically of God. At the borderline of what might properly be called syncretism, some achieve a form of integration by finding continuity between the normative demands of indigenous and introduced belief systems. For example, some see the Mission teachings of the Christian ethic of brotherhood as essentially similar to the stress indigenous beliefs place on the maintenance of social harmony in order to avert illness and ensure the success of magicoreligious procedures for aiding subsistence efforts.

Not everyone indulges in such relatively systematic attempts at achieving a degree of consonance between belief systems. Some appear to avoid the problem by treating Catholicism as simply an instrumental alternative, not invalidated by or invalidating indigenous beliefs and practices. This may require them to ignore the Mission's claims to the exclusive truth of its own doctrines. Some, however, handle such claims by regarding exclusiveness as simply an instrumental necessity. They hold that the efficacy of either set of beliefs and practices depends on the degree to which it is not mixed with the other.

There are probably some who remain untroubled by simply detaching themselves from the issue. A great deal of indigenous magicoreligious activity is in the hands of specialists, and Catholicism follows the same pattern. Thus it is quite easy to leave the responsibility for the proper regulation of the community's religious life in the hands of those specialists. Some do criticize the performance of religious leaders; but by focusing their dissatisfaction on the leaders they may avoid some of the psychic discomfort they might feel if they regarded reconciling old and new religious systems as a personal responsibility.

There is no need to assume that anybody completely escapes the discomfort of confusion and dissonance. As Theodore Schwartz suggests, the strongest affirmations of belief may also be evidence of the active persistence of doubt (1968:73). In Kragur uncertainty coexists with belief. Villagers often express skepticism, ambivalence, and uncertainty quite plainly. Such attitudes are also apparent in the earnestness with which many people questioned me about my own religious beliefs or particular aspects of the Mission teachings, and the eagerness with which they presented to me and to each other their own attempts at reconciliation of indigenous and Catholic beliefs and practices. Villagers use various means to solve the intellectual problems posed by the existence of alternative belief systems and they have various degrees of success in reducing doubt, dissonance, and confusion. But belief may be strong even where alternative belief systems are only clumsily reconciled and where uncertainty and ambivalence are active and potent. In any case, despite the variability in the nature of belief in Catholicism in Kragur, belief of one kind or another is widespread. In fact it is this very variety that allows so many to proclaim themselves Catholics. And this allows the village a a whole to maintain a stance of belief despite the seeming improbability of such a full and easy adjustment.

THE CHANGING FOCUS OF CATHOLICISM

I am most concerned here with the individuals who express the strongest uncommitted attitudes toward the Mission and its teachings, and whose cases suggest a more dynamic picture of the conditions affecting the quality of religious belief in Kragur. Certainly the existence of uncommitted attitudes is not surprising. The years have not erased memories of the Mission's first militant introduction of a new and, it was hoped, exclusive belief system, and the colonial context of that first encounter. Even if the Mission appeared static and unchanging in the eyes of Kragur people, one could find many reasons for a lack of enthusiasm. But the fact is that for many the Mission has not remained a rock on which they could build their faith. They have seen the Mission radically change its orientation on certain issues. And they find that it is no longer the preponderant representative of the encroaching new way of life, having become one among many religious and secular alternatives. These transformations of the Mission are important factors in generating and maintaining uncommitted attitudes.

While there are Kragur villagers who seem to take change in stride, others are troubled by what they see as the inconsistency of the Mission's teachings. For example, some villagers report that the Mission now places much less emphasis on prayer, the activity of the Legion of Mary, and the observance of Saints' Days. Older villagers learn from younger that in secondary schools associated with the Mission, religious observance is no longer compulsory and commitment to the Catholic church is largely voluntary. Some villagers observe that the current generation of Mission personnel are less certain about the nature of God, Jesus, and the Virgin, and they are troubled by this new generation's rejection of the possibility of a concrete personal encounter with these beings. A member of the village Legion of Mary tells how in the past villagers were told that if they prayed with sufficient diligence they would be able actually to see Jesus and the Virgin. Now, however, they are told that the best they can hope for is an indirect manifestation of the power of these beings. This village Legion member thinks the Mission is abandoning the work of God and the Legion—that is, the work of diligent prayer and religious observance. Such observations puzzle some people and feed skepticism and ambivalence. Certain individuals, more extreme, interpret these trends as evidence of conscious deception on the part of the Mission in order to maintain its monopoly of the true power and knowledge of Catholicism. As one such villager says, "They want to deceive us . . . they don't want us to gain knowledge. . . . They think that we've come too close to God and it's better that they misdirect us now. . . . Before, the fathers were more truthful."

Villagers see militant campaigning against all indigenous magicoreligious practices giving way to tolerance, indifference, and even encouragement not to
abandon the "good" aspects of pre-Mission practice. A prewar training manual
for native catechists used by Divine Word missionaries on Kairiru inveighs
against the use of indigenous magicoreligious practices rather than prayer for
curing illness. Yet today people say that the Mission wishes them to abandon
only harmful magic and that practices for such positive purposes as curing or
increasing the fertility of crops, game, and fish are perfectly acceptable. An
important customary leader, a man old enough to remember his initiation into
the men's cult and the cult's subsequent demise, says angrily that the Mission
has now begun encouraging indigenous practices. Yet years ago the Mission
required the destruction of magicoreligious objects, thereby depriving him and
others of ritual paraphernalia necessary for the suggested revival. "They want
the Mission people to be the only ones with knowledge and power," he says.
"The missionaries are deceitful. Now that they've taken everything from me,
they talk about us doing things in the old way again. But with what?" Again,
among those who have noted such changes, reactions range from puzzlement
to anger at what is seen as the Mission's conscious duplicity.

Those who see deception and duplicity on the part of the Mission do not
necessarily become nonbelievers. Some are able to maintain their belief in
Catholicism despite their loss of faith and trust in the Mission. Such a solution
to the problem is one often closely associated with the typically Melanesian
form of millenarian movement known as a cargo cult. Certain villagers who
exemplify this stance most strongly had indeed been actively involved in postwar
cargo cult episodes. Though there was no organized cargo cult in Kragur during
my stay there, some villagers seem to have found employment for their millenarian energies in the intense and ritualistic pursuit of a regimen of Catholic
prayer and religious observance to which they attach extravagant expectations.

Although one might question their interpretations, villagers' observations are
not the products of their imaginations. Christianity has long been troubled by
the question of the extent to which it is necessary for people to adopt particular
social and cultural forms in order to become Christians. For European missionaries this has been a question of the relationship between creating Christians
and creating Europeans (Burridge 1978:21; cf. Webb 1986: 118–19). Part of
what villagers have observed is a trend in Catholicism toward keeping the two
more distinct, which results in greater tolerance for the indigenous culture. The
pronouncements of the Vatican II Ecumenical Council of 1963–65 have played
a role in this (cf. Arbuckle 1978). For example, under the influence of Vatican
II there has been a decline in sacramentalism in the Mission—that is, a decline
in emphasis on the inherent potency and importance of religious rites and
artifacts. The prewar training manual for indigenous catechists gives a good
example of rigid sacramentalism in a detailed description of a procedure for
baptizing sick or dying infants without the knowledge of pagan parents who will
not allow it and who thus deny their child the chance to enter heaven. The

relevant passage taken from *Skul Bilong Ol Katekist* (*Lessons for Catechists*), as I have translated it from Melanesian Pidgin, is as follows:

A catechist cannot let . . . children die without being baptized, for they will not be able to ascend to heaven. . . . If heathen men and women don't want you to baptize their children, if they're afraid that if you baptize the child it will die—you can do so as follows. . . . Take a piece of cloth and soak it in water. Now take the cloth and go into the house where the child is as though you want to wash the face of the child. Squeeze the cloth so that water falls on the child's forehead and quickly recite the formula of baptism. Once you have thus baptized the child, if it dies it can go straight to heaven. Its mother and father won't know what you did so they will not be angry.

In keeping with their obsession with the ritualistic aspects of Catholicism, early Mission personnel were often rigidly intolerant of indigenous magicoreligious practices. The decline of Catholic sacramentalism has brought with it greater indifference to indigenous practices missionaries once unreservedly labeled as things of the devil. Such greater tolerance is also associated with the increasing mood of national self-consciousness, from which the Mission has not been aloof, which prescribes not merely tolerance but cultural revival (cf. Beier 1975).

Vatican II also emphasizes a more voluntarist attitude toward individual commitment to the Catholic church. Current Mission personnel are less zealous than their predecessors in the pursuit of individual conversion as an end in itself, and they deplore prewar mass baptisms on Kairiru. The Mission is placing increasing stress on what it calls the building of Christian communities. This involves more participatory structure, more grass-roots involvement, and the movement of Papua New Guineans into positions of responsibility and authority. All these innovations are a marked contrast with the past form of the Mission as a body of persons of other races and cultures relating hierarchically to a passive population. Here also the growth of national self-consciousness has stimulated such changes—changes of a type also occurring in Protestant missions in Papua New Guinea.

Concerning the Legion of Mary, which plays such an important part in Kragur religious life, there is some truth in the contention that it is being abandoned. Those Mission fathers principally responsible for establishing and nurturing it on Kairiru have been gone from the area for several years, and current Mission personnel with whom I spoke show little interest in it. Some dismiss it as primarily a phenomenon of pre-Vatican II sacramentalism. Others voice concern that village people may easily misunderstand the ritualistic nature of its organization and activity and that this might contribute to the development of cargo cult ideologies and episodes.

THE DECLINING PREDOMINANCE OF CATHOLICISM

Villagers have not only seen changes in the nature of the Mission's teachings; they have also seen Catholicism lose its position as the virtually undisputed representative of the European world and, as many seem to have assumed, its magicoreligious basis. In the early years of European contact, many villagers probably saw the beliefs and practices promulgated by the Mission as an essential part of the European way of life and its impressive wealth and power. This was due not only to the predominance of the Mission in those early years, but also to the focus of the indigenous religion on the material well-being of the living and the belief that success in important material endeavors—such as hunting, gardening, fishing, and production of other significant material goods—must have a magicoreligious component. Currently, some villagers identify Catholicism with the positive aspects of the outside world. For example, one firm believer, an adolescent at the time of World War II, remarked that some of the Japanese who occupied the island must have been Catholics because they were good men, not cruel or harsh like others. The kind of association villagers find between Catholicism and the outside world, however, often goes deeper than this. Some see Catholicism as associated not simply with the positive moral aspects of the outside world but with its full sociocultural and material trappings.

Such a view is highly consonant with and based on the typically worldly orientation of Melanesian religions. P. Lawrence and M. J. Meggitt write (1965:18) that religion in Melanesia is "a technology rather than a spiritual force for human salvation." In accord with such a worldly orientation:

the realm of the non-empirical is always closely associated with, in most cases part of, the ordinary physical world. It is supernatural only in a limited sense. Its most important representatives . . . are generally said to live on the earth, often near human settlements. Although more powerful than men they are frequently thought to be able to assume the same corporeal form. . . . Occult forces are conceived as purely terrestrial (1965:9).

The beings who are believed to share the world with living men and women in Kragur may be petitioned, propitiated, coerced, feared, and even held in awe and respect; but seldom if ever do they represent some principle of supreme, abstract good. In whatever roles they play as enforcers of morality, reward or retribution are immediate and concrete. Performance in terms of a moral or ethical code has no relevance to the fate of the dead or the quality of any personal essence. All villagers have now heard of heaven and hell, and the principal leader of the village's Catholic religious life backs up most of his moral admonitions with reminders of the promise of heaven and the threat of hell. Yet most resident villagers with whom I discussed this admitted they found it puzzling. Many could repeat what they had heard of the nature of heaven and hell—heaven as a place of ease and plenty and hell as a place of endless toil or tortures straight out of Dante. But few seemed to find either the threat or the promise particularly compelling. At least one villager goes beyond being puzzled and indifferent by claiming disbelief and speculating that the Mission taught about hell merely to scare people into recognizing its secular authority or to prevent its clientele from defecting to one of the other missions which entered the Sepik area later. As he phrases it, the missionaries thought that "[they] must give power to all [their] principal words so that people will be afraid"; that is, they invented the vivid accounts of the fire and pain of hell so that people would feel compelled to listen and obey. Even those few who speak of heaven and hell with apparent certitude, however, devote much of their attention to the benefits to be derived in this life from proper religious observance. Schwartz writes:

Safety, longevity and wealth are the expected results of Melanesian religious practice. . . . In one sense, perhaps they should not be termed religions at all, if this term is defined as a framework for devotion. . . . Religion and magic are virtually coterminous, based on the use of supernatural instrumentalities for the attainment of the welfare of the living (1968:101).

This could easily describe religion in Kragur. I would stress, however, that religious belief and practice in Kragur cannot be adequately understood without taking account of the inextricable interpenetration of moral and material issues (Smith 1978). Material welfare is the most obvious concern of belief and practice—much of which focuses on curing illness and ensuring success in subsistence efforts and other material endeavors. But material success depends in large part on maintaining good social relations, while villagers see material plenty as an important condition of good social relations (cf. Smith 1982, 1984, in press). Both of these intertwined goals, however, are worldly ones. Such a worldly emphasis is apparent in Kragur Catholicism as well as the more or less intact aspects of indigenous magicoreligious practice. For the large majority of villagers devotion to the Christian God, Jesus, and the Virgin is unambiguously aimed at the fulfillment of needs and desires in the here and now, and they conceive of fulfillment in worldly social and material terms. Kragur people live at close quarters with the beings who are the focus of indigenous religious attention and feel them as a real and relevant presence. But mystical or ecstatic experience of the kind that constitutes communion with the supernatural in Christianity appears to have no precedent in the indigenous religion, nor is it an element in the current syncretic system. Those who desire to achieve a direct confrontation with Jesus or the Virgin through diligent prayer do so, I would guess, not in the hope of spiritual transformation or transcendent peace but in the hope of bettering their material lot in the world of the living.

Thus what many originally hoped for from Catholicism, and some continue to hope for, is the rapid transformation of their way of life, with a major emphasis on its material transformation. Kragur villagers very likely saw early Mission personnel as the magicoreligious specialists of the materially impressive European society they desired to emulate, from whom they could acquire the necessary ritual expertise. The Mission was the most salient aspect of the encroaching outside world, and villagers probably perceived it in terms of indigenous religious conceptions as the essential magicoreligious basis of that new world.

In many ways the continued vitality of the Mission presence is more notable than its attenuation. Nevertheless, whereas it once blanketed the face of the outside world as seen from Kragur, the Mission has gradually had to make room for other denominations, institutions, and ideas, and this also has affected the quality of attitudes toward it. Many of the first men to leave Kragur for paid employment went to work for the Mission. Until World War II the majority of men who went to work outside the village worked for the Mission on copra plantations, in lumber mills, as builders, as crewmen on its vessels, as cooks, as mail carriers, and as general laborers. After the war Kragur men also began to become involved in the work of teaching and preaching, being trained as catechists to teach in Mission primary schools throughout what was then the Trust Territory of New Guinea. But more and more, men now went to work for employers other than the Mission. Even for the handful of women who went out to work, the Mission no longer monopolized the scene. The war, of course, thrust upon much of Papua New Guinea myriad new experiences of the world beyond its borders.

Schools on Kairiru did not begin to increase in number until after the war. At first they were run by the Mission. But as in paid employment, in education the Mission hegemony also has weakened. While training for the priesthood or membership in a Catholic order is still a route to higher education, primary schools now teach a standardized government curriculum. In the nearest high school, although founded as a Catholic institution and still staffed in large part by Marist brothers, the curriculum is also that approved by the government and participation in religious observance is optional. And at the national university in Port Moresby and the teachers' colleges and technical schools some young Kragur villagers attend, the atmosphere is as secular as that to be found in such institutions anywhere. Many view these developments only from second hand. Even at the village level, however, there is now more information available about the outside world, for example, through Melanesian Pidgin radio broadcasts.

The advent of self-government and more recently full independence has also emphasized the discreteness of the secular political sphere. I grant, however, that these achievements have had so few tangible effects on the lives of Kragur villagers that they have done little to further the idea that secular action and not religion is the high road to a new way of life.

Both within and across generations there is increasing awareness of the extent to which the Catholic Mission is not the sole or principal representative of admired societies of the outside world. There is also increasing awareness of the extent to which it is not the sole representative of the religious institutions of the outside world. In the period of initial European contact the Catholic Mission must have been identified as the sole religion of the dominant foreigners. As a result of wider experience of the outside world, aided by the dissolution of comity agreements between missions, many Kragur people have now become aware of the existence of many Christian and non-Christian religions. One young villager, for example, tells of his investigations of a diverse assortment of Christian religious groups while away at technical school, including Lutheran, Anglican, Baptist, Jehovah's Witnesses, and Gospel Light House missions and congregations. Whereas in the first period of contact villagers would have as-sumed that a white person was Catholic, now persons of all ages will ask to which mission he or she belongs. Younger villagers might even ask for one's opinion on the news that certain learned men in Europe or America have said that there is no God at all.

For many of those old enough to have seen the Mission shrink in relation to the outside world as a whole, this experience may moderate unrealistic expec-tations that Catholicism will bring them all the wealth and power of that world and disillusion those whose faith may have rested on such expectations. Some older villagers, however, remain deeply committed to the view that Catholicism represents the essential magicoreligious component of the desired aspects of the outside world, in terms analogous to indigenous beliefs concerning the magi-coreligious component of material endeavors. For these, it is probable that no demonstration of the fallacy of this position would prove adequate to shake their faith—not faith in the Mission itself but in the potential of Catholicism if revealed in its wholeness.

But others are less committed to such hopes and many young villagers are less steeped in indigenous beliefs and more heavily influenced by introduced beliefs, secular as well as religious. For at least one young Kragur man whose exposure to the increasing variety of experience of the outside world has been through schools, both Catholicism and indigenous belief systems have given way to a professed secular rationalism. According to one of his teachers, one young Kragur student at the area high school in 1976 claimed to see the alleged truths of religion as no longer necessary to him because human reason provided him with a better tool for the explanation and understanding of the world. A few villagers, slightly older and less educated than the rationalist student, are puzzled by the Mission's reorientation, aware of the many secular aspects of the modern world, willing to entertain the notion of the basic error of Mission doctrine, but not able to return wholeheartedly to a self-sufficient pre-Mission set of beliefs. Among these there are some who have heard that scientists and other learned men have announced that there is no God. They profess to find this plausible, even probable, the secular origin of the pronouncement doing no damage to its credibility in their eyes. But their lack of a developed rationalist or other doctrine to fill the gap leaves them in a state of puzzlement.

CONCLUSION

The Mission has been transformed and such a transformed Mission—less the preeminent bearer of the new social order, more participatory, more voluntar-istic, more humanistically and less ritualistically oriented—is a great change from the Mission that first entered the Sepik area at the close of the nineteenth century. Many of those who have witnessed most or part of the process of change have found it difficult to come to terms with, and their commitments to the Mission and to Catholicism have become more problematic and uncertain.

Yet it would be greatly overstating the case to say that Catholicism is on its way out in Kragur. Despite undercurrents of disaffection there is little or no public display. Certainly there is social pressure to conform; but there is also, I believe, reluctance to make a public commitment to an anti-Mission or non-Catholic position for other reasons. As I discussed above, those who are most disillusioned with the Mission are not necessarily ready to abandon belief in Catholicism. Nor are puzzled and skeptical villagers necessarily unwilling to be convinced or eager to burn their bridges. Even for confessed doubters, severing the tie with Catholicism could be painful. The association with the Mission continues to provide tangible benefits as one of the village's most stable and reliable links to the larger outside world. To be a Catholic also provides a source of both individual and collective identity. For Kragur villagers it provides a source of distinction from the non-Catholic or the less devout. As a source of identity Catholicism is an end in itself rather than a means that might be easily discredited and discarded.

If there is a demise of devotion to Catholicism, as distinct from the Mission, it is most pronounced in the younger generations, particularly among those with better education, wider experience, and firmer roots in the outside world. Such as these are more likely to adopt a more secular viewpoint and place less value on the identity Catholicism provides, for the religion has lost some of the aura of the revolutionary and the avant-garde that it bore for their elders. Similarly, those who are more conversant with the ways of the wider world have a greater opportunity to forge other, perhaps stronger, links with it.

Though many members of these younger generations do display clearly different attitudes toward Catholicism and the Mission than do their elders, there is no large-scale or clearcut drift toward rejection of Catholicism. A very few do claim such a stance, but it is more likely that younger villagers will gradually relegate Catholicism, and the religious sphere in general, to a position of less sweeping relevance. Some may compartmentalize their commitments to Catholicism and their identities as Catholics; or, following the lead of the Mission itself, they may place greater emphasis on the social and humanistic import of Catholicism.

At the time of initial contact Kragur villagers had neither a synchronic nor a historical overview of the Mission and the wider world of which it was a part. The passage of a few decades has brought increasing awareness that the Mission constitutes only a small part of that wider world. The events of those years have also revealed the Mission's doctrinal inconstancy, although they have not enabled people to see that in the context of a long history in which change in varying degrees has been the norm. The decline of Catholic Mission hegemony has shaken many villagers' notions of the place and the necessity of Catholicism and the Mission in the new world that surrounds them; and many villagers have been angered and troubled by the changes they have seen in the Mission's teachings. (In this latter respect they resemble many Catholics elsewhere in the world who have been perturbed by the trends codified by Vatican II.)

Some of the older villagers who are still mired in the more extreme forms of conversion expectations and those who have not had the opportunity to achieve a broader view may never extricate themselves from the conundrums of doubt, belief, and ambivalence. Yet neither is the issue settled for those who have come to see Catholicism and the Mission in a larger synchronic and historical perspective. These villagers face the question of what this new Catholicism and this new Mission can mean to them as an institution and a moral and intellectual guide in the present social world. They must view Catholicism's merits in comparison with those of a growing number of competitors. Perhaps their experience with this early incursion from beyond the bounds of the precolonial world will lead them to expect less constancy and more infallibility from later arrivals.

4

The Apotheosis of Father Marino: Foundations of Tobian Catholicism

PETER WESTON BLACK

The people of Tobi, a small remote coral island in the western Pacific, were converted to Roman Catholicism in the early 1930s. This event—an en masse conversion—occurred during the brief sojourn of a Spanish Jesuit priest, Father Marino, the first missionary known to have visited the island. Apparently Father Marino made only this one short but extremely successful visit from his mission headquarters in Palau. At the time of my work with them in the early 1970s, the Tobians continued to be a religious people and faithfully adhered to the beliefs and practices of their new religion as they understood them. To all appearances, Tobian religion conformed to worldwide Catholic patterns. It rested, however, on a foundation that was highly idiosyncratic and that is revealed in seven remembered teachings of Father Marino.

If questioned about their beliefs most Tobians were able to present reasonable versions of traditional Catholic thought. They were familiar with such concepts as the human soul, divine love, hell, purgatory, and heaven. Quite orthodox explanations of the Trinity, the Virgin, the Fall of Man, and the nature of Christ's mission were also common knowledge. Young people who had attended mission school in Koror were the recognized local experts in these topics, and the older people had learned much from them. Episodes from the Bible had become part of the storyteller's repertoire, and the exploits of Adam and Eve, Noah, and various other Old and New Testament figures were often told. Each day at dawn and at dusk everyone gathered in the church to say the rosary. Every three or four months a priest came to their island for a few hours and Tobians flocked to the church to hear mass and to confess sins committed in his absence. All pre-Christian religious and magical rituals had been abandoned and the old sacred chants were heard no more. The Catholic rituals for birth, marriage, and death were thought to be of great importance and were performed with enthusiasm. The high festivals of Christmas and Easter were the focus of much preparation and enjoyment. A number of women belonged to sodalities,

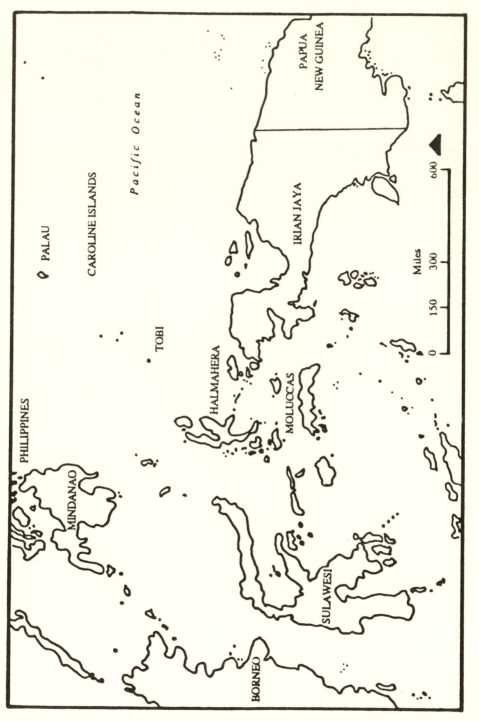

Tobi Island, Western Micronesia

special church organizations that required dietary restrictions and extra prayer. In general, Christian prayer marked many kinds of behavior. Meetings were begun and ended with prayer, as were formal meals. Individuals could often be observed sitting apart with hands clasped and heads bowed silently in prayer. Sundays were marked by an absence of work and a more elaborate church service, attended by the people in their best clothes. In short, the conversion of the islanders seemed to have been strikingly successful. The perception shared by the Tobians and their priests of the island as a Christian place seemed to be quite accurate.

Why was Father Marino, in the absence of either force or prior missionary activity, so successful? Why did people continue to be so conscientious in the practice of their new religion? These questions involve issues of importance to anthropology as well as to an understanding of the missionary enterprise. The religion of a given people is seldom, if ever, an isolated phenomenon. It is instead a part of their culture and as such is at least in part a response to the exigencies of their situation. From this perspective, aboriginal Tobian religion was Tobi-specific and, like Tobian culture, can be seen as one of many local adaptations of a general, pan-Pacific pattern. Roman Catholicism, inasmuch as it can be said to be unitary, is one of several adaptations of the Judeo-Christian pattern. Aboriginal Tobian religion probably traced its roots back to neolithic Southeast Asia and was influenced in its development by events summed up as "the peopling of the Pacific." It reached its full development on a tiny island isolated from political and economic centers of power. Roman Catholicism is a worldwide religion, and its history is interwoven with the history of various European power centers and, more generally, with the development of Western culture over the last two thousand years. The differences between the two religious forms are the result of two discrete cultural traditions lived in two very different environments.

The symbols of a religion are one of the ways private psychological states and public social forms are united into a more or less coherent whole. Religious symbols are channels through which private meanings flow into shared forms and, conversely, order is offered to the individual in assigning meaning to private states. Both the private and the public poles are, in part at least, determined by experience. Thus whatever the origin of the religious impulse, the symbols used in its expression must be shaped by the physical, social, and historical environment in which they were formed. Why then would a people exchange their indigenous religious symbols for a set that arose in radically different circumstances? Specifically, why did the Tobians replace the miniature canoe and wooden phallus of their old religion with the crucifix and sacred heart? The same question could be asked about the Tobian acquisition of other aspects of Catholic religious life. The shallow acquaintance the islanders seem to have had with Roman Catholicism before they adopted it makes the Tobian case particularly interesting, as does Tobian Catholicism's subsequent resistance to change. The Tobians seemed to have made an alien religion their own without significant modification, and to have maintained a close involvement with those unmodified forms.

When Father Marino stepped ashore on Tobi, he encountered a people who had recently embarked on an experiment in secularism. They had abruptly dropped the practice of all their communal religious ritual. Although scattered individuals may have continued to interact with supernatural forces, the islanders no longer acted as a community vis-à-vis the sacred. Even the buildings in which communal ritual had taken place were destroyed, along with all the religious paraphernalia they contained. This attempt at secularism failed, and the Tobians became firm Catholics.

The background of the attempt at secularism is important for three reasons: its failure to meet certain needs of the Tobian population was probably the most important reason for the speed and success of the original mass conversion; people's feelings about the attempt provided some of the most compelling reasons for their adherence to Catholicism; and the complex of cultural beliefs, personality attributes, and sociological factors that gave rise to both the attempt and its failure continued in play and gave Father Marino's teachings their special Tobian meanings.

PROLOGUE TO SECULARISM

In an earlier publication, I have recounted in some detail what I have been able to recover of Tobian postcontact history (Black 1978). The overall theme of this history is a rising tide of Western influence and the simultaneous ebbing of Tobian confidence in their indigenous religious and political institutions, but there were several distinct phases. In the first, early in the nineteenth century, Tobians began to interact with powerful strangers who arrived in ships. As an island with neither lagoon for safe anchorage nor commodities of any special interest, Tobi was never more than a brief stop for passing ships until well into the twentieth century. Despite the transient nature of this contact, Tobians saw enough of the size and complexity of the vessels, the extraordinary materials on board, such as metal and cloth, and, of course, the weapons they commanded to be overwhelmed with wonder. Early encounters of Pacific low-islands populations with European vessels are, from the perspective of the islands, strikingly similar in this regard to contemporary tales of encounters with extraterrestrial beings.

In the second stage, an attempt was made to control the strangers and their vessels. A group of sorcerers emerged specializing in the mystical ability to call ships to the island and detain them for trading purposes. The sorcerers used this claimed ability to extract a hefty percentage of the wealth that flowed onto the island in the form of metal, cloth, and tobacco. This enterprise lasted until the nonmystical nature of the foreigners was conclusively demonstrated. In 1832 the remnants of the crew of a shipwrecked American whaler were cast away on Tobi's beach (see Holden 1836). It rapidly became apparent to the Tobians that these people were mortal, powerless, and, in fact, rather ignorant. Never again would Tobians view the West with quite the same astonishment and wonder. In fact, the brutality with which these castaways were treated indicates, perhaps, an attempt to deny the power of men who come on ships.

A more realistic approach to dealing with the outside world emerged as Tobians began to learn ways to exploit the strangers for their wealth. This took two main forms: the development of products for trade (especially locally produced cordage) and the exchange of labor (especially as sailors) for goods. But the experience of working on the ships revealed to Tobians the extent of the discrepancy between the scope and power of their institutions and those of the Westerners; thus the next stage, which can be characterized as one of submission. This stage and the next require a more extended treatment.

In 1909 a German ethnological expedition arrived at Tobi (Eilers 1936). The scientists set up their headquarters in the main spirit house, the building where the chief performed the rituals associated with his office. These rituals centered on the chief as spokesman for and, in some senses, a personification of the entire Tobian community. It was here that people came to participate in the communal rites, and now it was here that they came to have their skulls measured by the anthropologists. A census was conducted and it was found that 968 people were living on the island. The area of Tobi is only fifty-nine hectares; thus the population density at this time was 16.4 people per hectare, which even for the Pacific is quite high. This figure is even more striking when it is compared with an estimate of two hundred Tobians when the remaining castaways escaped from the island seventy-five years earlier (Holden 1836). Even if we allow for a considerable margin of error in that estimate, it is apparent that the island had experienced a dramatic population increase.

This upward trend was soon reversed. An epidemic broke out after the visit of the German expedition, and six months later, upon the arrival of a German government vessel, it was found that 200 people had died. The doctor on the ship attempted to evacuate the island, but the people hid in the bush and he was able to convince only fifty-one men and one woman to go with him to Yap. Tobians remember the epidemic but do not recall the doctor's "rescue" of fifty-two people. Possibly this is the same event that lies at the core of a story relating how the Germans took hundreds of men from the island to work in the phosphate mines on Angaur, a Palauan island. Although the mines were opened in 1909 (Grattan 1963:351), I have found no documents to substantiate the Tobian claim. The need for mine workers may explain the imbalance in the sex ratio of those "saved" by the Germans in the same year the Angaur mine opened. In any case, it is certain that some Tobians went to Angaur at this time because the report of the ethnological expedition contains several photographs of Tobian men there.

The Tobians say that when the Germans ordered the chief of Tobi to accompany the men to Angaur, he delegated some of his functions to a younger man who remained on the island. This assistant was forbidden by the departing chief to carry out at least one of the important rites, but disobeyed his instructions and did so anyway, thus causing the death of the absent chief. The younger man then assumed the chieftainship. This is a crucial event in the evolution of modern Tobian society. It precipitated political quarrels and gave rise to two parties—the descendants of the original chief and those of his assistant. Everyone agrees that these events took place but there is disagreement about their interpretation.

The factionalism arising out of these events is a key element in all that followed, including the attempt at secularism, the conversion to Roman Catholicism, and the interpretations of some of Father Marino's teachings. The argument between the two parties hinges on the legitimacy of the assistant's links to the chiefly genealogy. The assistant occupied the office of chief for only a few years and his title then passed to his son. When that son died, the title went to a descendant of the chief who had died on Angaur. This person was the chief at the time of my research, while the passed-over grandson of the assistant was the contender for the title. The chief described the assistant as a usurper who committed acts that he knew would lead to the death of the "true" chief hundreds of miles away on Angaur. The contender claimed that his grandfather knew that the chief was already dead at the time he took over the title.

There is no way at this point to reconcile the three versions offered of this one event: the Germans said that there was an epidemic and a rescue; the current chief said that the title had been usurped by the assistant; the contender said that there had been a legitimate but incomplete succession. Yet in certain fundamentals the versions agree. For some reason the Germans did remove a number of men from the island. The chief accompanied them and later died without passing on to his heir in the prescribed manner the esoteric lore attached to his office. The present chief draws a link between these facts and the island's depopulation, claiming that the illegitimate succession cursed the island by disrupting the flow of *mana*. There probably is a connection between depopulation and the flawed succession, but the order is most likely the reverse of that claimed by the present chief. The chaos surrounding the rapid depopulation demanded a response. Leadership was necessary and the assistant attempted to provide it.

In the aboriginal order the chief performed a number of rituals through which the community related to the supernatural, and the sacred and secular worlds were inextricably connected. Most profane behavior had a "religious" aspect, and even the most arcane of rituals was thought to have important effects on the course of everyday events. This pragmatic aspect of ritual life is quite clear in the minds of the islanders. The overall function of religion both then and now is to protect the island and its inhabitants from disaster, and the islanders would certainly have resorted to ritual when faced with the epidemic reported by the Germans. Perhaps to them it appeared better in that time of crisis to have an imperfect chief than no chief at all. This decision may have eased the psychic distress of the Tobians but it did nothing to halt the population decline, which continued until recently. The nature of the decline did change, however, and that change played a certain role in the events that followed. There was never again a murderous epidemic. The next population crisis was much slower in becoming apparent.

The Germans lost their Pacific island possessions, including Tobi, during World War I. The island passed to the Japanese along with the rest of Micronesia. Sometime in the 1920s Yoshino, an agent for a Japanese commercial company, came to live on Tobi. He was the first outsider to live on the island for an extended period of time since the castaways of 1832, and the circumstances of his stay were quite different from theirs. Yoshino arrived on a Japanese government vessel with the full weight of the vigorously expanding Japanese imperial order behind him. The Tobians had experienced a century of intermittent contact with the power of men who arrived on ships and thus it is not difficult to understand the profound discrepancy in the fates of the two parties. The castaways had undergone an ordeal from which few emerged alive, whereas Yoshino was treated with great respect and Tobians submitted to his influence.

Yoshino drew into his orbit the chief who was the son of the ex-assistant and a landless Tobian named Johannes, who had recently been returned to the island from Yap by his departing German master. With their support, Yoshino forced a division of a sacred parcel of chiefly controlled land into separately owned plots to place more land into production, despite considerable opposition. Once more, Tobian society accommodated itself to outside pressure through submission. Forces were at work, however, that would call forth an active response. Foremost among those forces were demographic processes.

Apparently the demographic decline had halted by this time. The epidemic of 1909 had run its course and the population had stabilized; however, probably unknown to the islanders, a new and equally dangerous threat had appeared. Just as the Germans had brought a "plague" (probably influenza), the Japanese brought venereal disease (most likely gonorrhea). Though not fatal, this disease led to barrenness in the women. Thus the stability of the demographic structure in the early years of the Yoshino era was only illusory. From about 1925 onward the birth rate plummeted until only one woman was bearing children by the time Father Marino arrived. The illusion that further disasters had been averted also must have been shattered by then.

By the early 1930s a Tobian community had been established in Palau. The Spanish Jesuit mission there had successfully converted several Tobian families, one of which subsequently returned to Tobi. This family included a young man who explained to the chief—Yoshino's ally—the power of the Jesuits. The factionalism surrounding his legitimacy must have played some role in the chief's agreement to what followed. Armed with the chief's blessing, the young man joined with the youths from a school established by Yoshino and Yoshino's friend, Johannes, and on a dark night they burned down the chief's spirit house, the women's menstrual house, and the sorcerers' canoe house—the entire set of buildings with religious associations. This event, rather than the conversions that took place a year or two later, marks the end of the traditional Tobian order. The old rituals were scrapped, the chief abandoned his exclusive rights to certain foodstuffs, and the great majority of prohibitions associated with everyday life were no longer observed.

A new stage in the Tobian response to Western influence was about to begin. The burning of the sacred structures was, in a literal sense, a clearing away of the debris of old and apparently inadequate forms so that the incorporation of Western forms could begin. The subsequent acquisition of Christianity was the first act in a process that continues to this day: the creation of neo-Tobian culture through the integration of Western forms into a Tobian setting.

The motives of the people involved bear some examination because it is through them that we can distinguish the historical processes that had been gathering force for some time. Several of the young men who participated in the burning were still living in 1972, and I have talked with them about their activities on that night. What emerges from their accounts is that they, and others of their generation, had come to view the many restrictions or taboos that hedged their activities as onerous. This was especially true of the food and sexual avoidances associated with many types of fishing. These taboos were essentially religious, and by doing away with the religious structures on the island the young men hoped to liberate themselves from them.

The young man from Palau died during World War II, so we can only speculate about his motives. No doubt he also felt the taboos to be a burden. He had lived in Palau for a number of years, in the ferment and excitement of the creation of a new Southwest Island community. The prohibitions upon his behavior he found when he returned to Tobi must have seemed even more difficult and meaningless to him than to the other young men. Perhaps he hoped that destruction of the old order would allow him access to land and other resources. His genealogy shows that he was only marginally integrated into Tobian society. Finally, of course, there is the motivation mentioned in the story. Perhaps the religious practices of the island seemed especially futile to him after his exposure to the political and economic power of the Catholic mission in Palau.

We can also only speculate about the motives that led the chief to give his blessing to the destruction of the sacred structures. Perhaps the same factors that led to his agreement to the division of the sacred parcel of land operated here. It should be remembered that the chief and his opponents were all agreed that the flow of ritual power had terminated with the death of the old chief on Angaur. The sacred buildings were unusable because the ritual knowledge and power associated with them had been lost. The chief's attempt to use the buildings was bound to be both clumsy and presumptuous; yet failing to use them while they stood was a reminder of his irregular rise to power. More generally, the ongoing demographic crisis was inescapable evidence that traditional religious forms of behavior were no longer protecting the island; they had become empty as well as burdensome. This withdrawal of confidence led to their abandonment and the destruction of the structures and equipment associated with them. This break was not accompanied by radical transformations of other areas of the Tobian order. Life apparently went on much as before but without the ritual underpinning that had given it meaning.

The secular experiment by the Tobians failed and led to great anxiety. The fortuitous arrival of Father Marino a year or so later offered the people a chance to relieve that anxiety by adopting a new religion. Tobians believed that communal religious behavior has consequences for society as a whole. The most important of these is the prevention of disaster, and the failure of the rituals to prevent the catastrophic depopulation was probably one reason for abandoning the aboriginal religion. Ritual is thought to function in the prevention not only of physical disasters such as depopulation and typhoons but also supernatural disasters, especially the activities of ghosts or *yarus*, the most feared of supernatural manifestations. Ghosts are the essence of malicious evil and are hated and feared as a constant threat. Tobi and its surrounding seas are thought to be infested with them, but the correct performance of ritual can render the ghosts powerless.

Tobian belief in ghosts serves the same functions of displacing antisocial aggression and focusing free-floating anxiety as belief in beings called by a cognate name serves on the distant but culturally and linguistically related atoll of Ifaluk (Spiro 1952). In an environment in which forced intimacy is unavoidable and the ethics of nonaggression and cooperation very highly developed, the Tobians, like the people of Ifaluk, displace aggressive feeling onto supernatural beings. Ghosts offer both peoples an acceptable focus for anxieties that have as their actual cause consciously unacceptable drives. With complete approval by both the self and others, a Tobian can hate and fear ghosts. By abandoning the aboriginal rituals, however, the Tobians denied themselves power over those ghosts. They were caught in a psychosocial trap of their own devising.

Social and intrapsychic tensions were almost surely at a high point during the year or so of the secular experiment on Tobi. The recent population decline seems to have given rise to a great deal of covert conflict. Each family tried to expand its holdings by moving into the vacuum left by extinct groups. Land claims were made by reference to genealogical links, but in many cases two or more groups with equally tenuous grounds claimed the same estate. In some cases there were still one or two members of the original group whose title to the land was clear but who could not mobilize sufficient support to defend it. There were other sources of tension, too, making this an extremely uncomfortable period. The establishment of the Tobian settlement in Palau, the acquisition and retention of new forms of wealth, the continuing failure of the women to bear children—all were important factors.

Because belief in ghosts had not been abandoned, all these antagonisms and anxieties contributed to a high rate of ghostly activity and a great number of ghost sightings. And since the Tobians had lost faith in the ability of traditional religion to control these hated and feared apparitions, the sightings in turn gave rise to more anxiety. A vicious cycle had developed that was not broken until Father Marino was able to offer an escape through new prophylactic ritual.

It is possible at this point to provide a rough answer to two of the questions posed at the beginning of this chapter. Father Marino's success derived from the frightening and powerless state the Tobians felt themselves to be in due to the absence of control over ghosts; he offered them an alternative. The conscientiousness with which the Tobians practiced their religion was a result of their understanding of the connections between religious ritual and disaster. Father Marino gave them mechanisms for preventing disaster, and they dared not abandon them lest they again be overwhelmed by either physical or supernatural catastrophe. Thus it is not surprising that, despite all the time they spent praying, the Tobians seemed remarkably unconcerned about their ignorance of the literal meaning of their prayers.

Catholicism was appropriated to play the role of the discredited old religion; therefore there was no need to transform or even to think very much about the elements that make up Catholic belief and practice. The beliefs were simply subscribed to and the practices simply followed. In fact the elements became resistant to transformation because their success in preventing disaster lay not in their inner meaning but in their correct performance. Change, generated either internally or externally, was potentially disastrous. Once the Tobians became convinced of the utility of Catholicism, their self-perceived task was to learn the correct rituals and practice them.

THE TEACHINGS OF FATHER MARINO

If cultures are functionally integrated, then the acquisition of an institution as fundamental as religion must be accompanied by transformations in that institution so that it fits with the rest of the borrowing culture. The ethnographic literature is rich with examples of precisely this process. The Islam of some sub-Saharan Africans (Greenberg 1946), the Catholicism of some of the Yucatecan Mayans (Vogt 1964), and the Protestantism of some of the native American groups around Puget Sound (Barnett 1957) are end products of such transformations—the syncretic results of adapting the borrowed religion to local needs and understandings. Tobian religious behavior, however, did not appear to exhibit this dimension. The great bulk of their specifically religious beliefs also appeared to be quite orthodox. One of the key institutions in neo-Tobian culture appeared to have almost no Tobian coloring. If, however, we do not examine the religious beliefs and practices of the Tobians per se, but rather inquire into the islanders' beliefs about religion, then "Tobianness" begins to emerge. The functional orientation toward Catholicism, for example, is clearly a carry-over from the pre-Christian past; religion must be practiced in order to keep ghosts and other disasters at bay.

Marino arrived at Tobi on a Japanese government steamer. At that time, Japanese imperial policy was to encourage, within strict limits, the Christian missionaries in Micronesia. Marino was accompanied by a Spanish-speaking convert from Merir—an atoll 240 kilometers north of Tobi with a similar language and culture—who acted as his interpreter. Also accompanying the priest were several of his Tobian converts from Eang, the settlement in Palau. All surviving witnesses agree that Father Marino baptized all the people on the island and that he attempted to bring all existing marriages into line with Catholic law. These are the only acts that are universally attributed to him. It is generally held that Marino made four statements—a threat to raise the dead, a promise that he would be their judge in heaven, a warning that they should not give credence to any outsider who came to the island claiming to be a priest unless he was wearing the Roman collar, and a pronouncement that marriage within a clan was incestuous. The chief and his allies claim an additional statement was made, involving the destroyed spirit house. This is virtually all that was remembered about this crucial event that occurred some fifty years ago. There are no traditions about the responses of the chief, Yoshino, the young man who had burned the sacred buildings, or any of the other people who had been so important in shaping the course of Tobian events up to this time, though some of the narratives do contain hints of Tobian response. Here a sorcerer or shaman challenges the priest, there a woman tricks him into agreeing to her marriage to her lover. Yet these few scraps do not make possible a confident reconstruction of the full history of the conversion.

Father Marino, as an evangelist, must have said and done more than is remembered. Nor are the seven things that are remembered entirely congruent with what he would have stressed as fundamental. Christ, the Trinity, and the Virgin are all absent from the remembered teachings. Moreover, some of the teachings seem to be quite improbable. Finally, it is apparent from internal evidence that the baptism probably did not take place as the Tobians described it. In other words, the preservation of the seven teachings is a result of a process of selective retention in which there has been some distortion. Perhaps, then, the transformation that the notion of functional integration tells us to expect took place not in the borrowed religion itself but in the words and deeds of the man who brought it. The words and deeds of Father Marino have been subjected to systematic pressure over the last fifty years to make them congruent with Tobian culture. The most direct test of this proposition would be to compare the actual deeds and words of Marino with what is remembered today. Since the only source for his deeds and words is the remembrances themselves, this procedure is impossible. The approach taken here is to examine carefully each of the remembered teachings for the meanings they convey to Tobians. It will be shown that these meanings are congruent with other Tobian beliefs and values. It will then be shown that the memories of Marino are not merely bits and pieces but a coherent corpus that will repay analysis.

Baptism

While only vague outlines of the mass baptism are remembered, it is possible to reconstruct a more detailed picture from other sources. For example, census data show that two of the Merir converts from Palau who accompanied the priest stood as godparents to all the initiates. However, this fact was only confirmed in response to direct questioning; it was never part of the narrative itself. The initial baptism was usually recounted as follows: *"He called the people together and they were baptized."* Some of the younger people could explain this rite in orthodox Christian terms, but their knowledge came from postwar mission schools in Palau and is not an interpretation that survived from Marino's time. The fundamental and for many people the only meaning of the baptism involved the notion of the island as a whole becoming a Christian place. Emphasis was placed on the collective nature of the ritual. Marino sanctified marriages during his visit, a process that necessarily took place after the baptism of the partners. Baptism involved assigning new Christian (that is, Spanish) names to each individual. Apparently in the interest of symmetry, married couples received similar names (Juan and Juana, Terso and Teresa, Marino and Marina). This symmetry in the Spanish names of the newlyweds can only be explained by assuming that Marino knew who was to wed whom before he baptized them. From this it follows that he must have done the genealogical research necessary for making "good" marriages before he christened them. It is difficult to imagine that the sequence Marino followed was investigation of all potential spouses, mass baptism, and then marriage. It makes more sense to posit an individual sequence for each couple, including individual baptism. The distortion that led to the baptism being remembered as a single collective rite is probably based on a similar event in which all children and those few adults who for one reason or another did not wish to be married were baptized together. Such distortion supports the hypothesis that a key meaning of the original baptism lies in its total nature—it included all those actors in the Tobian sociocultural system who called themselves Tobians and thus, in a sense, the system itself. The fact that the christening of each convert with a new name was not stressed, and seldom even mentioned, indicates that the individual aspect of the baptism was not important. If it is seen as speaking to the nature of the sociocultural order, then it is necessary to inquire into the content of the message as understood by present-day Tobians.

The word used in Tobian for "baptize" usually refers to bathing (both swimming and washing), but it has two other meanings—one for the traditional cure for insanity, the other for a traditional disciplinary measure. Fathers punished their misbehaving sons by taking them to the sea and holding their heads underwater until they lost consciousness. Shamans chanting incantations used a similar technique to treat the insane. This similarity of treatment illustrates one of the fundamental Tobian concepts of behavior: the similarity between "crazy" and "bad" behavior.

It is no accident, I think, that the word for these techniques was extended to cover baptism. When people discussed the pre-Christian era, and especially the years immediately preceding the coming of the priest, it was commonly said that people were both crazy and bad. In recent times, the brief attempt at secularism after the spirit house was burned and before the arrival of the priest has been viewed in an extremely negative light even by the men who helped instigate it. The times were perceived as having been out of joint and Father Marino was viewed as having acted to put things right. Combining the role of father, because he insisted that he be called by this term, with that of shaman by reciting ritual formulas, Marino linked together in one rite the cure for insanity and the punishment for transgression, thus putting the system back in order through the ritual of baptism. It is also notable that the two traditional techniques involved rendering the subject unconscious through near drowning, whereas Tobians say the baptism involved merely tracing a watery cross on the penitent's forehead and pouring a little water over his head. The former experience was undoubtedly terrifying; the latter, especially in contrast, was not. From that contrast emerged the perception of Marino as the good father-shaman whose corrective abilities embraced a whole society but involved no unpleasantness.

The baptism thus emerges as a fundamental event and its retention in the corpus of remembered teachings becomes understandable. As a communication it has two messages, one of which deals with the contrast between pre-Christian Tobi and the present and the other with the nature of Father Marino.

Remarriage

Pre-Christian Tobian marriage patterns were characterized by a wide variety of arrangements. Men were permitted a number of wives and women could have one or two husbands. Cross-cousin marriage was preferred and serial polygamy with frequent divorces was the rule for both sexes. Since all these practices are frowned upon by the Church, one would expect that Marino would have acted to eliminate them. All that is remembered, however, is that he forced each married person to go back to his or her earliest living spouse and then sanctified that marriage. A number of points of interest arise in this connection.

It is only in stories surrounding this incident that the Tobians are seen as more than passive targets of some item of priestly behavior. This fact is due to the impossible nature of the task Marino apparently set himself. While newly christened Roberto may have been Fausta's first husband, for example, she could well have been his second, third, or even seventh wife. The opportunities this created for the type of manipulation at which the Tobians are so skilled were not lost and many people succeeded in marrying their lovers, who may have been neither a previous nor current spouse. More important, no one was forced to marry someone he or she detested. This proved to be highly adaptive since the marriage ceremonies performed by Father Marino wrote finis to the aboriginal pattern of frequent divorce and remarriage. Tobians typically said: *"He made everyone who had been divorced go back to their first spouse."* That this was their only interpretation of his behavior brings us to a seeming anomaly.

If the body of stories about Marino is in fact the locus of the processing Catholicism has undergone at the hands of the Tobians, we would expect each story to speak to important issues facing the islanders. We would also expect that most serious sociocultural problems on the island would be reflected in the stories. It is this latter point that is at issue here. Why did the corpus of remembered teachings not deal with changes in such practices as cross-cousin marriage and polygamy? From Marino's point of view the unions that existed prior to his visit were not marriages at all. It is quite likely, therefore, that the recollections were accurate and he did not deal directly with these practices in the limited time at his disposal. However, if these changes were viewed later as significant one would expect them to be reflected in the stories, whether based on fact or not. From the observer's perspective these changes certainly seem to have contributed to a major dilemma facing Tobian society.

In recent times a Tobian, especially a man, had a rather narrow range of options concerning marriage. Church prohibitions against polygamy (especially polyandry) and divorce and remarriage contributed to this restriction, but the fundamental problem was demographic. Only a few women of recent generations have proven fertile. Moreover, most of these women have given birth to many more males than females, leading to a disparity in the sex ratio that would have been unlikely in a larger population. On Tobi, however, the fate of the predominantly male children was to compete for the few available women. The situation was made worse by the fact that a male remained in the marriage market much longer than a female and so there were a number of widowers also searching for mates among the young women. The combination of Church marriage regulations with the retention of pre-Christian rules forbidding clan endogamy exacerbated the problem. This was quite apparent to the Tobians who ponder these matters. However, the most significant of the Church's marriage prohibitions seemed to be the one against divorce. This is particularly striking because divorce, in the usual sense of the term, did occur on the island.

Marriages did break up, and some spouses set up or joined separate households or even formed semisecret liaisons with third parties. The liaisons could not be sanctified, however, nor could they result in the joint households characteristic of Church-sanctified unions until the legitimate spouses of the lovers were deceased. The rule seemed to operate as follows: no one could remarry until his previous spouse had died. The factors that led to the instability of marriage in the pre-Christian era were still operative, yet the expression of those tensions (frequent divorce and remarriage) was no longer a possibility. Objectively, prohibiting remarriage while a previous spouse is still living created the most difficulty, and can also be seen as an indirect prohibition of polygamy. It stresses the exclusive nature of the marriage tie between a man and woman.

Cross-cousin marriage is not spoken of in the story of the remarriages. In recent times there have been no people on Tobi who would be eligible mates even if the rule against cross-cousin marriage were to be waived. Therefore, although a significant change had taken place with respect to the cross-cousin rule, that change was not an issue, and was not reflected in any of the stories told about Marino.

At this point it might be asked why a story had not been invented to revalidate the aboriginal practice of frequent divorce and remarriage. As we shall see, this is evidently what happened with respect to clan endogamy. But the priests who have followed Marino refused to preside at second marriages when the first spouse was still living. It was not possible for people simply to set up joint households without the Church's blessing. By concerning himself with marriage in the way that he did, Father Marino firmly set the instruction of marriage within the realm of the sacred, in marked contrast to aboriginal unions.

Power over Ghosts

While walking through the cemetery Father Marino is supposes to have said, *"My power is from Dios and it is true. Shall I call the dead people here in this ground to stand up?"* The cemetery had only recently come into use, as a result of Japanese pressure. Previously the dead had been set adrift. The cemetery is located at the northern end of the island, within the bounds of the old sacred grounds. This continuity in the spiritual geography of the island may or may not be accidental, but the fearful attitude of the Christian islanders toward this plot was probably similar to that of their ancestors. At night the area was avoided if at all possible. If a visit was necessary, as during turtle hunting season, people only went there in parties of three or more. The area was dangerous and frightening because it was the haunt of ghosts, and there is no reason to suppose that the situation was different in Marino's time. The setting in which the words were spoken thus conveyed to the minds of the islanders an aura of supernatural power.

Among the several versions of this story the most widely accepted had the missionary uttering his words in response to a challenge from a shaman. There was unanimity on two points: the wording of the phrase quoted above and the response of the audience. Everyone took Marino's utterance as a threat, since in the Tobian view a resurrection of the dead would be an unmitigated disaster for the living. The newly risen would not be mortals bound by the physical and moral restraints of the normal world but Lazarus-like beings who had passed beyond that world and returned, eerie and frightening. Whatever Marino's intentions when he uttered these words, they are felt to have been designed to impress the people with his power and the dire consequences in store for any who would not follow him. He did not, so the stories go, actually have to raise the dead since people, in begging him not to, conceded his power to carry out the threat.

This leads to an important message contained in this saying: the unique and liminal position of Father Marino. Clearly the resurrection of the dead is no task for an ordinary mortal; only a man in close touch with the supernatural could do that. The claim of power to raise the dead is a claim over the processes of life and death. The statement makes clear the source of that power. The emphasis is on the concrete and the immediate. It is not a vague statement about the omnipotence of Marino's god, but a claim to be a channel through which that power can enter the affairs of this world. The theme of Marino's special spiritual abilities runs through most of the stories told of his visit. To a people accustomed to the idea of human-ghostly dialogue, as in the pre-Christian trance states of the shamans, Marino's assertion of the power to call up a whole new population of ghosts did not appear farfetched. The claim was plausible but awe inspiring, representing a level of spiritual power unparalleled in Tobian thought.

The second message contained in the statement is that ghosts exist and, furthermore, that there is a close connection between ghosts and religion. The threat can be paraphrased: "Do what I say or there will be many ghosts on the island." The first half of this warning can only refer to the necessity of conforming to Roman Catholicism; the second half refers not only to ghosts as such but, by inference, to all disasters that are likely to strike the fragile Tobian ecosystem. And finally, the statement is congruent with the traditional Tobian notion of religion as a set of techniques necessary to ward off disasters in general and ghosts in particular.

Power to Judge the Dead

Father Marino was said to have made the following statement as he was about to leave the island: *"Don't forget that I am in charge of you and when you die I, and no one else, shall be the one to decide where you go."* When questioned about its meaning, informants argued that Marino was saying that he, and not Christ, was the one to decide whether heaven or hell would be each Tobian's ultimate destination. Obviously this statement strengthened Marino's unique cosmological position vis-à-vis the islanders. Of all Marino's remembered acts and sayings, this one speaks most directly to that point, and it does so via an idiom of power, that is, the concept of *hosuar*, "in charge" (Black 1982).

In the Tobian view of things, the only true adults were men between middle age and senility. They alone fully possessed the prime virtues of self-restraint, competence, and independence. Females and other males were thought to be capable of exhibiting these characteristics only in varying degrees. People without self-restraint and competence lost the third virtue, independence, by having someone, usually an adult male, placed "in charge" of them. All major decisions were made only with this person's consent; he had the power of reward and punishment over his wards, especially if they were children.

Tobians said that in pre-Christian times the chief, who wielded political power and acted on the island's behalf in exchanges with the spiritual world, was "in charge" of the whole island. Marino's claim to be "in charge" is a similar metaphor. As a metaphor it implies that the population of the island as a whole is deficient in the three prime virtues and a superordinate must interfere in its affairs. Marino's claim is considerably more extensive than that attributed to pre-Christian chiefs because it is thought to transcend both his and his congregation's morality. Although Father Marino was beheaded by the Japanese about ten years after he converted Tobi, thirty years later it was thought that he was still in charge of the island and watched from on high the behavior of its inhabitants. The belief that Marino would judge the dead firmly established his unique position in Tobian cosmology. The islanders' belief that they would be either rewarded or punished according to their earthly conduct was an important moral sanction that acquired its force from Tobian attitudes toward authority and, ultimately, the father.

The Tobian father was a remote and threatening figure in the life of the child. Stories told about childhood commonly included beatings by the father and stressed the respect and fear in which he was held. This attitude had been institutionalized in the custom of avoiding, where possible, the mention of one's dead father's name. When this was not possible, as for example during some of my interviews with them, Tobians made a great show of whispering the name into the listener's ear.

Evidence that this attitude extended to other figures was not hard to find, especially among the old people. Traditional behavior toward the chief was also apparently marked by fear and respect, as was behavior toward Americans or Palauans invested with some power over the islanders. No human figure was more frightening to old people, especially old women, than the Palauan policemen occasionally called to Tobi to investigate some problem.

This fear of authority was seen as highly functional by the more thoughtful people on the island. It was conventional Tobian wisdom that only fear keeps people, particularly those who are not fully autonomous adults, from dangerous and antisocial acts. This conception was demonstrated during a meeting held to determine the culprit in a possible homicide attempt. The question arose as to whether the matter should be reported to the administration in Palau. An affirmative consensus was quickly reached on the basis that no one's life would be safe and the island would be uninhabitable unless the young people were given an immediate object lesson by seeing the criminal brought to justice and punished. A policeman was sent to the island on the next field trip some months later but was unable to make any progress in his investigation. Commenting on this, one young man made a statement that clearly expresses the shared belief in the importance of Father Marino in sanctioning moral behavior. "Maybe that guy who did it," he said, referring to the person who attempted the murder, "is really proud and happy now, but when he dies and meets Father Marino I think he will be very sorry."

Other Missionaries

Father Marino's person was firmly embedded within the structure of Tobian theology. The beliefs that endowed him with this status made it extremely difficult for exponents of other versions of Christianity to make any headway at all among the Tobians. The source of their difficulty can be found in the third statement Marino was alleged to have made: *"If any person comes here and tries to say mass but is not wearing the same thing around his neck that I am, do not listen to him."* This statement was related to me in an anecdote about the first priest to visit the island after World War II, who as a navy chaplain was wearing a uniform without a Roman collar.

The statement is a part of the corpus of remembered teachings. Everyone was aware of it and there was no disagreement about its authenticity. It seems preadapted to the possibility, of which the people were keenly aware, that a non-Catholic missionary might visit the island. Since this was not a current issue the saying did not form part of the active narration, though in a negative sense it was of current importance. It was felt to be a warning against falling away from the religion revealed by Marino. It is important to note that it is primarily a warning against non-Catholic missionaries and not a direct admonition to pay heed to the other Catholic priests who over the years have followed Marino to the island. This accounts for the ease with which teachings of subsequent priests were ignored when they contradicted Marino's word. It is notable that the Marino corpus was structured in such a way that the process of ignoring more recent Church teachings in order not to violate the corpus did not in itself contradict a teaching of Marino.

Clan Incest

The next saying attributed to Marino conveys a limited message. It forbids clan endogamy, but it does so in an elliptical manner. The actual wording is as follows: *"It is as impossible to marry a clan sister as it is to marry an angel."* The wording was that given by Tobian English-speakers, some of whom have achieved a fair degree of fluency. If one talked to an old person who had been present at the crucial meeting when Marino is thought to have said this, he would quote a statement that can be rendered: "Intercourse with a sibling of opposite sex is like intercourse with a ghost. You cannot." The problem of interpretation lies in the fact that the words translated by the English-speakers as "marriage," "clan sister," and "angel" can with equal accuracy be translated as "intercourse," "sibling of opposite sex," and "ghost."

Tobian clans were named, unranked, matrilineal, exogamous groups in which genealogical connections between all members were felt to exist even though they could not be traced by any one individual. In recent times clans were the only recognized structural unit between households on the one hand and the collectivity known as "the people of the island" on the other. Exogamous clans have apparently existed on Tobi since shortly after the initial settlement. They possess a mythological charter in the epic that tells of the island's discovery, having been constituted by the original ancestress. If we assume that the clan exogamy rule was felt to be so important that it required supernatural justification, it is not surprising that the original pre-Christian charter had been reinforced by one bearing Marino's stamp. This was the only instance in which a pre-Christian rule had been revalidated in such an overt manner.

The simile expressed in the statement that marrying a clan sister is like marrying an angel acquires its force from the Tobian notion of an angel as a kind of benevolent ghost. Ghosts were frightening because they could flout with impunity the laws governing the normal world. Angels shared this characteristic and thus aroused the same reaction of horror in Tobians. The use of the word "angel" instead of the usual word for ghost was primarily a device to give the statement a Christian cast; the benevolent aspect of angelic nature is beside the point.

Acting like a ghost and being crazy were forms of behavior that shared important attributes: both were dangerous, uncanny, unpredictable, and gave rise to a great deal of fear. One important difference between ghostly behavior and insane behavior was that the fear of the former was directed outward while fear connected with insanity was directed toward the self. This is summed up nicely in the conventional wisdom that ghosts were harmful to other people whereas the insane were prone to suicide. The unknown person who was thought to have attempted murder was said to be a ghost; a man who repeatedly tried to kill himself was said to be insane (Black 1985). The fear of insanity and subsequent suicide was an important component of the sanctions against clan incest, and Marino's teaching speaks to this point by drawing attention to the ghostly nature of such an act. To a Tobian, what seems ghostly in others must seem to be insanity in the self. Recognizing the immense social pressure brought to bear on anyone attempting an incestuous match, a Tobian was likely to feel that he would have to be crazy to try such ghostly behavior.

Violation of the incest regulations, then, produced a rupture in the fabric of the normal universe as dramatic and shocking as the flouting of the laws of the physical world by a ghost. Both acts were beyond the capacity of normal men but well within the power of ghosts. Thus it is not surprising that in the only two instances of clan incest I know of, both men were described as ghosts. The fact that only the men were so described is a product of the Tobian view of adulthood discussed earlier. The belief that people are capable of anything and that only fear keeps them from behaving in immoral ways formed a counterpoint to this attitude. A normal man was one who was, among other things, sufficiently afraid of the consequences of immoral acts. In the two attempts at endogamous clan marriage of which I am aware, the primary reaction of the people seemed to consist of a mixture of wonder and horror. Wonder seemed to arise from the perception that a fundamental law had been flouted; horror originated from the people's feelings about incest. They were aghast.

In both cases the men were treated, within limits, as ghosts. People did not run shrieking from their presence, but they were avoided as much as was consistent with the obligations of civility, which minimally require a cheerful response to any social initiative of another. Eventually, they were pressured into leaving the island. The gossip that continued to swirl about these two marriages stressed the men's frightening boldness and their untrustworthiness. These men were referred to directly as ghosts. This was, of course, a metaphor; everyone recognized that they were human. However, it was a metaphor that contained a strong element of truth for the people of Tobi, since these two men did indeed act like ghosts.

Part of the strangeness of the statement when viewed from a Christian perspective is that it does not speak directly of morality; marriage to a clan sister is not said to be evil but rather impossible. To Tobians, however, the word "impossible" pointed to a greater truth about men and morality—the notion that there was essentially no difference between certain moral and physical laws. In the Western tradition the two were clearly distinguished, primarily on the basis that violation of moral laws, although bad, is possible, whereas physical laws are such that their violation is impossible without supernatural intervention. In this sense moral laws are less absolute in the West than are physical laws. In the Tobian view of things the two are indistinguishable along this axis. The word "impossible" in Marino's teaching is congruent with the Tobian idea that men are as bound by incest regulations as, for example, they are by gravity; neither can be violated by a normal person.

There is one final point to be made in connection with this statement. The word translated as "marry" refers both to intercourse and to marriage, depending on the context in which it is used. The fact that the English speakers chose the former and not the latter is significant. Sexual intercourse with a clan mate (providing that the genealogical connection was no closer than first cousin) was forbidden but aroused no great reaction when it became known. It was expected that young people would make love as often as possible and with very little regard for the amenities, and while it was bad for clan mates to sleep together, there was usually a good deal of resigned tolerance for what was perceived as weakness of the flesh. Parents or guardians would try to break up such liaisons and ensure that the act was not repeated. It was only when the parties tried to formalize the union that the full complex of wonder and horror, ghosts and insanity, was triggered. The dramatic difference in the reaction to incestuous intercourse and endogamous clan marriage lies in the nature of Tobian marriages, which involved the establishment of long-term economic exchange relations between spouses and, to a lesser extent, among their families. Marriage involved the formation of a household, the fundamental unit in Tobian society, and it involved the filiation of children to the mother's and father's kin in different ways and for different ends. Embarking on such a project with a woman of the same clan publicly flaunted one's immorality, suggesting disregard for the respect of others and for the conventions that govern the conduct of normal men. These are the actions and statements of a ghost or a madman.

Chief and Church

The final remembered teaching of Father Marino differs from the others because the Tobians were not unanimous about its authenticity. This fact provides an important clue to the workings of the entire Marino complex. Referring to the chief's spirit house, the priest was alleged by some to have said, "*It is too bad you burned this place down. It would have made a good church.*" Before the collapse of the old order the chief exercised ultimate spiritual and political power, and his spirit house was the site of most of the important rituals. This statement was an attempt to charter a role for the chief in the new religion.

The chief and his allies began a campaign some time ago to infiltrate the church's activities both on the island and in Palau. They achieved a degree of success in certain minor areas, but overall direction of the church remained firmly in the hands of the Mission. The chief's objective was to be recognized formally as leader of the congregation, especially for the rituals (novenas for the dead, for instance, and twice daily *rosarios*) that constituted the religious life of the island, except for the services held by the priest on the four or five days a year that he visited the island. The chief also would have liked to be the sole intermediary between the people and the priest on all matters pertaining to church business and ritual. Although the Mission treated the chief with great respect, it refused to fall in with his plans. The American and Palauan priests were unimpressed with his appeal to the authority of Marino, but it was obvious that the islanders understood the implications of the statement that the chief and his partisans attributed to Father Marino (Black 1983).

This, then, is all that is remembered about Father Marino: out of a much wider range of potential memories the Tobians have chosen these seven items. There is no way to tell at this late date whether they are grounded in fact or fantasy, though it is certain that they all contain particularly Tobian meanings. The understandings that arose about them were remote from orthodox Catholicism but fit with the rest of Tobian culture. Transformation took place not in the borrowed religious practices, but in the words and deeds of its conveyor.

Further analysis reveals that these seven items formed a coherent ideological complex with definite properties. The complex was nonfalsifiable, possessed a certain dynamic, and had both positive and negative functions for the people who used it. It was also an idiom that expressed certain Tobian truths about man, society, and the supernatural. The system had two major tenets: first, religion is necessary, and second, Tobian religion must be Father Marino's. The former is supported by the baptism and by the threat to raise the dead, which teach that society is bad and crazy without religion and further that religion is necessary to prevent disasters. That the religion of Tobi must be Marino's is supported by belief in his special powers over ghosts, over the individual soul, and over society. These beliefs derive, at least in a cognitive sense, from Father Marino's remembered teachings. His power over ghosts is spoken of in the threat to raise the dead; his power over individual souls is asserted in his claim to be their postmortal judge. His power over Tobian society is taught in the baptism, in the statement about being "in charge," and in the threat to raise the dead.

The other four items—remarriage and statements about clan incest, other missionaries, and the chief's spirit house—perform a different function. They speak to specific issues that have been given a religious coloring. These teachings are adhered to because Marino's power to dictate them is validated by the major tenets about religion and his place in it. On a more general level, the whole corpus of Father Marino's teaching can be seen as a revalidation of the entire Tobian ethical and moral system. Acts ranging from hoarding to murder were thought to be evil both before and after the conversion. Since then, they have also been taken to be sins that Father Marino will punish.

For both sides in the succession dispute, the argument about whether Marino actually made the statement was the only argument that mattered. It is a property of this system, and perhaps of all ideological systems, that once an issue has been framed in its terms only those terms are relevant. Arguments based on other grounds, such as personal interest or pragmatism, simply did not apply. This did not mean that the solutions it offered were permanent, but it did mean that as long as the two general tenets were accepted, change in the solutions required change in the Marino corpus. Those solutions were adjustments made to cope with past realities. When those realities changed, the solutions became maladaptive. This led to considerable tension and pressure to modify the system. A number of factors made this a difficult and slow process.

This intrinsic resistance to change could be most clearly seen in disputes over clan endogamy. A young Tobian might wish to marry a clan sister. He could point out his present unhappy, wifeless situation. He could assure the girl and her guardians of his deep love. He could offer the guardians tobacco and money and tell them of the land he owned or stood to inherit. All these arguments based on his, the girl's, and her guardians' personal interest would tempt but not persuade those guardians to give their blessing to the match (a blessing that was absolutely necessary if the young man was to succeed). He could raise the argument to a more general level and point out the scarcity of eligible women on the island and the dearth of babies. He could also claim that he and his followers would have to seek non-Tobian spouses if the rule was not waived. The guardians would agree that this was a shame and might even complete his arguments for him, pointing out the relatively large number of such marriages that had already taken place, resulting in many children with no Tobian clan. At this point someone was sure to say that if this kept up eventually there would be no more Tobians but only half-caste Palauans (most non-Tobian wives are Palauan). This was not a compelling argument, however, and the guardians would still not agree to let their ward marry within the clan. Their refusal would be framed in terms of the Marino ideology: *"It is as impossible to marry a clan sister as it is to marry an angel."* The young man could counter this by telling how he was taught at the Catholic mission school that the Church does not forbid clan endogamy. He could even remind his elders of the many sermons the American priest had preached on just this topic during his visits to the island. The guardians would probably respond along these lines: "You know what the Americans are like. They are very nice but they want everyone to like them. The priest just tells us that to make things easy for us. But we are strong enough to follow the true law, the one of Marino."

Tobians operated in two other social systems besides that of their island. One of these was the community that grew up in Eang, composed of people from all four of the Southwest Islands. These people were but one or two generations removed from their natal islands of Sonsorol, Pulo Ana, Merir, and Tobi. They created a village and a social system based on linguistic and cultural similarities, and like the people of Tobi were all Catholic. The other social system in which Tobians operated was that of Palau. Although there was religious diversity in Palau, one of the strongest elements of Palauan social organization was the Catholic church, which had considerable economic and political power. Tobians used their Catholicism as a major dimension of identity in their interactions with both Palauans and other Southwest Islanders. As fellow communicants of a universal church, they had a basis for meeting with these people that is not founded on invidious distinctions. This was particularly true of their interactions with Palauans. Just as a reasonable existence on Tobi demanded the cooperation of one's kinsmen, a reasonable existence in Palau depended on overcoming the prejudice some Palauans exhibit toward Southwest Islanders. Education, health care, and employment were concentrated in Palauan hands. The Catholic church was virtually the only institution in which people from the Southwest Islands could make meaningful contacts with the people who controlled the levers of power and service. The church also directly bound the Southwest Islanders to herself by providing employment and education and by helping them when they ran into difficulties with Palauan institutions. All these factors meant that a young man wishing to marry a clan mate could not simply take her to Eang and marry her outside the church. He needed his identity as a Catholic to function adequately in the greater society in which Eang is embedded.

In effect young men had no option but to comply with the clan exogamy rule. The old people controlled both the women and the priests. As trusted elders of the congregation, they could convince the priest that the proposed match was inappropriate. In recent years, as the priests gained more familiarity with the islanders, guardians resorted to camouflaging their efforts by using agents to explain why the priest should not marry their ward to her clan mate. That their control of the priest was slipping was evidenced by the recent completion of one of the two intraclan marriages attempted since Marino's visit. However, this was not really a very hopeful precedent for the young men; it took a number of contention-filled years for two middle-aged clan mates to persuade the priest to marry them. They then moved to Palau and had very little to do with any of their relatives. None of the specifics of this case was likely to be repeated soon. Indeed, the total dependency of this couple on the husband's meager cash income became something of an object lesson for the young people. The problem of maintaining the clan exogamy rule thus hinged on the motives of the old. Why did they persist in enforcing this rule when by doing so they threatened the extinction of the very institution it was designed to preserve?

There was no great commitment on the part of any Tobian, young or old, to the integrity of Tobian society. People were interested in their own fate and, to a lesser extent, that of their families. The future course of their society was a matter of little concern. Therefore, when the young men pointed out to a clan mate's guardians the number of Palauan women who married into Tobian society and the fact that their children had no Tobian clan, their arguments carried little weight. A girl's guardians knew that she would eventually marry someone, so commitment to family was not a factor either. Finally, as people already in control of the island's resources, there was not much that a girl's guardians stood to gain personally from allowing their ward to marry a clan mate. Indeed, for these firm believers in Marino's word, they stood to lose paradise, the only reward ahead of them. As people close to death they were much concerned with their fate after death. And Marino not only ruled out clan endogamy but also proclaimed himself the judge of that fate. The young men were armed only with statements from current, unmythologized missionaries, who could offer no arguments powerful enough to counter those drawn from the Marino corpus. Change in the marriage rule required change in the Marino corpus, and, as survivors of the original conversion, the old people controlled that corpus. It was their memories upon which it was based. And these memories were a resource in the struggle between the generations just as surely as the women, land, and specialized knowledge were also controlled by the elders.

It should be pointed out that the preservation of the clan exogamy rule has certain unique characteristics. The observation that the clans would become extinct if foreign women were continually incorporated into the population was a truism for the Tobians, yet does not appear well founded. The continuity of a clan depends not on the social identity of the women married by its men but rather on the production of female children by its own women. Further, it must be noted that even if all the clans were to become extinct there would be few if any repercussions. The clans functioned only in the regulation of marriage, and as such were complemented by Catholic incest regulations. Clans have had no other function in recent times, regardless of the role they may have played in the past. The clans had no estates and no significant role in the ritual life of the island.

If clan exogamy were not unique in these ways the dispute over its maintenance might have been considerably different. Changes in the Marino system and the behavior it justified depended on the survivors of the original conversion. If they decided, either consciously or unconsciously, to remember things differently, then the system could be adapted to meet changed circumstances. Failing that decision, change awaited their death.

CONCLUSION

The questions of why the Tobians converted so rapidly to Catholicism, why they appeared so orthodox in their observance of Catholicism, and why they were so active in its practice are three aspects of but a single question: Why is contemporary Tobian religion as it is?

Past events reveal the fundamental and increasing pressures to which the Tobians have been subjected. Their world view helps to explain their response to those pressures. The religious nature of the reaction to depopulation follows from the islanders' definitions of both disasters and religious ritual and the connection assumed to exist between them. This combination of history and world view promoted rapid and unanimous conversion to Catholicism.

The apparent orthodoxy of current Tobian religious behavior can best be understood as an epiphenomenon. The meaning of these behavioral forms is to be found not in their content but in their status as validated procedures for preventing disasters and maintaining Catholic identity. Mourning rites provided the single exception to this. They were Christian in that they were the occasion of endless prayer and at least three church services, but they did not follow orthodox Catholic practice. From the canoe in which the deceased was buried and the elaborate food presentations after his funeral to the rigorous year-long taboos placed upon his close female kin, these practices seemed to be an amalgamation of aboriginal and Catholic ritual. It is not surprising, considering what we know about Tobian ghosts, that the one area of ritual activity where syncretistic forces have clearly been at work is that concerned with death.

Validation of this and other (less transparently hybrid) ritual is provided by the precepts of the system constructed out of the remembered work of the evangelist, Father Marino. Each fragment conveyed meanings to the Tobians. They created a system that justified and even compelled close adherence to the new religion in an unmodified form. This adherence extended to the frequency with which religious ritual is performed—a result of a combination of ideas about the function of religion with faith in the Marino system.

In both behavior and belief there were some departures from the faith propagated by the Vatican. To understand these differences it is necessary to distinguish between knowledge of religious beliefs, personal commitment to those beliefs, and beliefs about religion. Tobians had knowledge of most traditional Catholic beliefs. They knew of the Virgin, the Trinity, papal infallibility, and other Roman Catholic dogma. They had little personal involvement with those beliefs, and in this sense they were different from many other Catholics. Such involvement as they did show is as much an epiphenomenon of the Marino system as the constant attention to prayers, the words of which also conveyed no meaning to them. Tobians also had a set of beliefs about religion not shared by most other Catholics. These ideas about the nature and function of religion led them to give great weight to those several idiosyncratic beliefs they did not share with other Catholics. Their faith in Father Marino as a personal savior with power over ghosts is obviously out of line with mainstream Catholic thought, but is basic to the Catholicism of the islanders. The highly personalized view of the church held by the islanders, which was so evident in the manner in which they dismissed the American priest's efforts to withdraw church sanctions from the clan exogamy rule, made any attempt to force a change in their beliefs a contest between the present missionaries and the ever-present Marino. The islanders' refusal to grant the American priest equal status with Father Marino rested on their failure to grasp the institutional nature of the church. To them any contradiction of the Marino system by a missionary could be resolved only by weighing one priest's words against another's. Even with the support of a considerable segment of the Tobian population, missionaries have failed to modify behavior based on the Marino system. This was particularly striking in the use of the Marino system to validate the prohibition of marriage between clan mates, thus perpetuating a rule felt to be a burden by some and a blessing by no one.

Father Marino was an agent of change for the Tobians. He converted them to Christianity by offering them an escape from the dangers and anxieties of formal secularism without a concomitant secularization of world view. Yet by mythologizing him the islanders created new difficulties. In constructing an ideology out of his teachings, the Tobians invented a system that responded only minimally to change and made of Father Marino an agent of conservation. By choosing to ground solutions to pressing social problems in a supernaturally based ideology, Tobians traded anxiety for security, but in the process gave up the flexibility to meet new and equally pressing problems in the future.

5

Personal Faith or Social Propriety: An Interpretive History of Christianity in a Korean Village

GRIFFIN DIX

Do not think that I have come to bring peace on earth; I have not come to bring peace, but a sword. For I have come to set a man against his father, and a daughter against her mother, and a daughter-in-law against her mother-in-law; and a man's foes will be those of his own household (Matthew 10:34).

In the years Kemyo (1603) and Kapchin (1604), Christianity became popular with a certain class of young men [in Korea] who contended for it, saying that God Himself had come down to earth, and given His commands through angels. Alas, in a single day, their hearts were changed, and turned away from the writings of the Sages! It was like the boy who graduates in the Classics, and then comes home to call his mother by her first name, a sad state of affairs indeed! (An Chung-bok 1795, quoted in Clark 1961:227).

Christianity had been introduced to the village of Ye-an (a pseudonym), Korea, almost ten years before I came there to do anthropological fieldwork in 1974. At that time, the Christian "church" in the village was a small room in the home of a widow. One other widow, the wives of two broad-minded and unusually sympathetic men, and the wife of a notorious village drunk and debtor met there several times a week. These women also brought their children to most church meetings on Sunday, when a seminary student from the city an hour away came to preach. Many more village women wanted to attend, but were prevented from doing so by their husbands.

The women participants were vehement in their denunciation of the nonbelieving "sinners" in the village, and most males were as adamant in their opposition to the church, which they saw as a threat to their Confucian ideals. Despite its small attendance, then, the Christian church had created considerable controversy. Gossip became increasingly hostile, hamlets and families

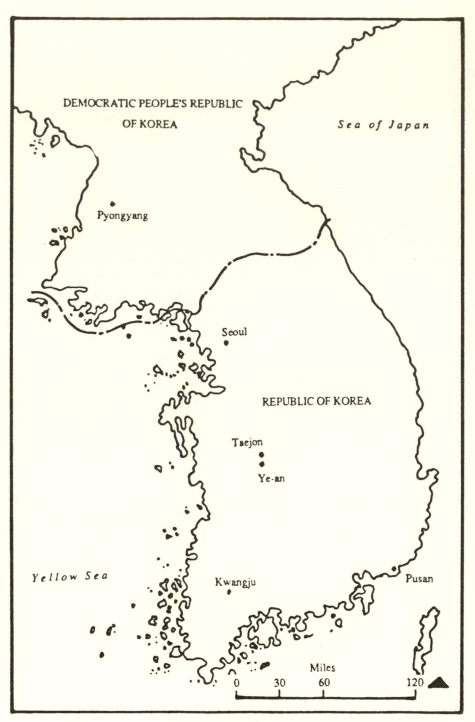

DEMOCRATIC PEOPLE'S REPUBLIC
OF KOREA

Sea of Japan

Pyongyang

Seoul

REPUBLIC OF KOREA

Taejon

Ye-an

Yellow Sea

Kwangju

Pusan

Miles

0   30   60   120

Ye-an, Korea

were divided, violence was threatened, and finally policemen were summoned from the city to settle a dispute. This chapter is an attempt to interpret this controversy by examining the relationships between rural Korean Confucian social principles and the implicit meanings of Christianity as presented to the village.

Although complex church doctrine was not understood by villagers, they recognized a number of differences between Christianity and traditional custom. It was not Christian doctrine per se that mattered, but rather its social implications. Christianity has to date failed to gain many converts in this village because it makes a new set of demands and requires fundamental changes in the standards for evaluating and adjusting human relationships. Christianity and Confucianism are perceived by villagers as positing contradictory views of fundamental social obligations. In particular, Christianity is seen as conflicting with Confucian "propriety." The essence of "propriety" (*yeŭi*) is the idea that social relationships are to be regulated by the application of sets of rules coming principally from ancestor worship and lineage organization (Dix 1977).

A place to begin is Max Weber's dichotomy between "piety toward concrete people" and being "bound to a sacred cause or an idea."

Mencius rejected the universal "love of man" with the comment that it would extinguish piety and justice and that it is the way of animals to have neither father nor brother. In substance, the duties of a Chinese Confucian always consisted of piety toward concrete people whether living or dead, and toward those who were close to him through their position in life. The Confucian owed nothing to a supra-mundane God; therefore, he was never bound to a sacred "cause" or an "idea." . . . The great achievement of ethical religions, above all of the ethical and asceticist sects of Protestantism, was to shatter the fetters of the sib [lineage]. These religions established the superior community of faith and a common ethical way of life in opposition to the community of blood, even to a large extent in opposition to the family (Weber 1951:236).

Weber does not completely deny that Confucianism has a religious "cause," but suggests that the "idea" is relatively more bound to particular social relationships and therefore provides less "leverage" for altering or disregarding those specific relationships in the name of some other cause or principle. Weber pointed out that Christianity—in its Western manifestations—is an unusual combination of ideas. It is inner-worldly (it aims to change social relationships) but ascetic (it emphasizes self-denial). Also, rather than being a collection of specific rituals for particular ends, it is a long-term plan for the life and afterlife of an individual. Its purview is less the solution (through ritual action) of particular mundane problems, such as sickness or the inability to bear a son, and more the ongoing inner life of the person. Accordingly, Christianity minimizes ritual and the significance of behavior per se, and emphasizes intentions, love, internal faith, and other mental attitudes of the individual.

The true Confucian, however, would answer Weber that Confucian "propriety" has an equally comprehensive life plan, but one in which all social activities should be part of an expanded realm of ritual. Much of the difference hangs on whether a religion gains more "leverage" by using externally visible ritualized action to guide internal beliefs and feelings or does so by using internalized faith and commandments to control external activity. This is the first theme of the analysis.

Weber also pointed out that social and religious change is not usually a gentle, even process, but rather involves conflict between the "status situations" of various types of people. The second theme concerns the new status situation of women in rural Korea and its implications for the interaction between Christianity and traditional religious meanings.

The next section of this chapter gives background on social changes, the "status situations" of women, and the arrival of Christianity in the village. Then compatibilities and contradictions between Confucion "propriety" and Christian principles are discussed. The compatibilities led many villagers to be interested in Christianity; the contradictions led widows and other women to accept Christianity as an alternative to ancestor worship and "propriety." The contradictions that are discussed help interpret the resistance to Christianity exemplified in the conflict described in the final section.

BACKGROUND

The most important religions in rural Korea are Confucianism and shamanism, the first the religious speciality of men, the second that of women. As practiced in rural Korea, Confucian ancestor worship involves belief in supernatural spirits of departed ancestors in the male line, to which one has ritual responsibilities (see Janelli and Janelli 1982 for a description of Korean ancestor worship). The idea that Christians should not participate in ancestor worship immediately made Christianity unacceptable to most males, but females have no place in ancestor worship. They are not permanent members of the lineage since they marry out and become attached members of the lineage of their husbands. Women are thus without a place in the most organized and regular religious collectivities in rural Korea. On the other hand, shamanism is practiced primarily by and for women (cf. Harvey 1979; Kendall 1985). Their shamanistic religious activities are irregular and done for specific purposes: a sick child, mental illness, persistent misfortune, and so forth. However, now that modern medicine is available at city pharmacies, the shaman's exorcisms seem less effective. With decline in belief in the efficacy of these rituals and a desire for more frequent social and religious activity, Christianity appeals particularly to women.

Over many decades the position of women as defined by Confucian precept and rural practice has been changing. There are now more alternatives to the traditional view that a respectable woman must obey her father before marriage, her husband in marriage, and her son when she grows old. Among the reasons for and expressions of this fact are the decline of Korean *yangban* ideology, which defined social strata according to ancestry and behavioral approximation to Confucian ideals; new opportunities for gaining wealth and family security outside of local control by the village elders; modern education even for women (while I was in the village the first village girl ever to attend high school was still a student); government propaganda against "wasteful ceremony" that often excludes women; "women's clubs" that promote a new role for women; a few "love marriages" rather than arranged marriages; and a decline in the tyranny of the mother-in-law. Signs of the change in women's status are everywhere. For example, most young women used to eat their meals in the dark of the kitchen after their husbands and parents-in-law had finished. Now they usually eat with the rest of the family. While I was in the village a group of women took their second trip to a beautiful temple to sightsee, dance, and even drink together, something unheard of in the past.

These two factors—the improvement in women's status and the decline of belief in the efficacy of shamanism—have combined to create a profound religious search in rural Korea. It is led by women groping for some systematic framework within which to affix their familial goals and cope with the difficulties of poverty, poor health, rapid social change, and a feeling rural women have of being left behind by modernization. Men too, confused by the inability of the Confucian vision of society to contain new developments, are creating hundreds of new religions across rural Korea. But women, so often the proletariat of religious uprisings, have taken the lead in accepting Christianity and rejecting ancestor worship.

Not all women of the village have done so, however. Like most Korean villages, Ye-an is divided into hamlets. Two of the three natural hamlets, Yang hamlet and Upper hamlet, maintain a more traditional atmosphere, with strong lineage and community control over deviant behavior. But Yin hamlet, which has in the past twenty years grown to be the richest and most progressive, is astir with the religious search. The women of Upper and Yang hamlets criticize those of Yin hamlet as nosy, gossipy, busybodies. They say, "Why don't those women stay home and take care of their families?" The Yin women are involved, for example, with plans to collect money from every household to treat a nearby army base on New Year's Day. They occupy themselves with the village women's club and with a government "modernization" plan in which every household is to set aside one spoonful of rice every meal and put that savings in a village bank account. Their involvement with Christianity and other activities fits into their busy search for alternatives to traditional custom.

The women of Yin hamlet were the most interested in Christianity when it first entered the village around 1965 in the person of a young student from a theological seminary in the city who began coming once a week to visit village households and explain Christian doctrine. The men of the village were hostile to him. They soon learned that Christianity made claims in opposition to their religious activities such as ancestor worship. The theological student was persistent and managed to interest many of the women in Yin hamlet. His best audience was, not surprisingly, a small group of widows who were cut off from male ancestor worship and who did not have to contend with the hostility of males toward Christianity.

He began to have weekly prayer meetings in the home of one widow. This woman had been the wife of a leading man of the village, a relatively wealthy and scholarly man. But the family had come onto hard times. First the husband's father contracted tuberculosis and lay in his bed for years becoming more and more helpless. His daughter-in-law had shown exceptional devotion to him. Daily she would wash his wasted body, clean his excrement, provide him with clean clothing, and wipe the tuberculin sputum from his mouth. She was so devoted that the village chief recommended her to the sub-county (*myŏn*) office; the vice-*myŏn* chief came to the village and in a public ceremony presented her with a prize for the female counterpart to filial piety. Eventually both her father-in-law and her husband died of tuberculosis, and her children all contracted the disease. The strain on this woman was enormous. She had to manage the family as best she could and care for her two sons and two daughters. She began to sell land and tried to do as much agricultural work as she could, renting the rest of her land to tenants. People say that the prize for filial piety was not a help to her but a burden. "Once you have received a prize like that you cannot act like a normal person. You cannot show anger or release your pent up desires. She could not live under such a burden." The woman had a mental breakdown and at some time during her tribulations was converted to Christianity. Her home became the meeting place for the new congregation.

Gradually the number of people attending the services in her home grew to more than thirty (half of them children). Included in this number were about five men, all in some way socially peripheral or psychologically troubled. For example, one man was a very poor tenant from a lineage that had only two households in the village. He had been deeply in debt for years and tended to squander whatever money he could get on drink. His wife insisted that he start attending, and he complied. For a time, he gave up drinking, in accord with the demands of Korean Protestant Christianity. Another man who attended was from a minor and distant branch of the dominant lineage of the village; his son had been sick often and he had been told by a fortune teller that the boy would not live long. He was desperately searching for a way to save his son's life, and tried attendance at the Christian meetings as well as devout offerings at a nearby Mountain Spirit shrine. A few other men attended out of a mixture of curiosity, pressure from their wives, and a felt need for a new set of principles.

Unfortunately for the church, the widow at whose house they were meeting had another mental breakdown. Her symptoms took on a shamanistic aspect. She began speaking as if possessed by a spirit and became totally out of control. She would curse anyone who came near her, let forth with the wildest stories and disconnected fantasies, and then go into a withdrawn trancelike state. Such spirit possession is not altogether foreign to some forms of Christianity brought to rural Koreans. The preacher and his most devoted disciples, for example, believed that if someone refused to accept the word of God it was because an evil spirit (*makui*) possessed that person and blocked him or her from the truth.

Competition between religions in rural Korea is often phrased in terms of power: a religion and its gods ought to demonstrate power particularly in protecting supplicants. The Christian preacher attempted to manifest the power of his God by exorcizing the spirit from the widow. He held a long prayer vigil for her, but nothing worked. Finally he lost his temper and tried to beat her into compliance. He hit her head against the ground and beat her unmercifully until she was so hurt that she had to be hospitalized. She was sent off to a hospital in Pusan, far from the village, at the expense of the church. The preacher was never seen again in the village.

Although minor violence against a possessed person is common in Korean shamanism, the extreme brutality of the preacher was unacceptable to the community, and the number of villagers interested in hearing the Christian message declined sharply. Nonetheless, Christianity was not finished in the village. The church was reduced to its core of a few widows and wives, all of whom were having some kind of serious social or psychological problem. The church gained back some degree of respect when the injured widow returned from the hospital, forgave the preacher, and set up the church room in her house again. A new preacher began coming to the village and visiting houses, but the original hostility of the males was now hardened and the number of people attending the church rose only slightly.

This incident provides a background for understanding Christianity as an issue in local affairs in the 1970s. The underlying causes for female status inferiority had been diminishing. Modern economic and social currents were no longer contained by the common channels of male-dominated ancestor worship and female shamanistic curing. Village women were attracted to the power of a foreign dogma that rejected ancestor worship and undermined other male prerogatives, such as alcoholic excess. Due to their shamanistic traditions, the women were predisposed to accept the occasional failure of a powerful God to exorcise a possessing demon. Paradoxically, male resistance to Christianity was strengthened by the excess of a partially trained theology student whose brand of Christianity shared certain beliefs with shamanism. At this point, let us examine in more detail some of the consistencies and contradictions in old and new religious ideas. The contradictions between Confucian and Christian principles help in interpreting the strong reaction that males had to the Christian church.

COMPATIBILITY AND CONTRADICTION: NEW AND OLD IDEAS

I have mentioned several ways in which traditional shamanism seems to have carried over into rural Korean Christianity. It would be surprising if such socially significant and individually meaningful approaches to life as those in religion did not carry over into a new religion when first adopted. Some of the influences of shamanism are (1) the concern with power, and the attraction of a God who can dominate other spirits and protect human protégés; (2) the hope of tangible results from faith in Christianity, just as shamanism was often a religious means to specific familial, medical, or financial objectives; (3) the belief in ubiquitous and potentially dangerous spirits. This last is manifest among the Christians, for example, in their conviction that group hymn singing (a new religious activity in rural Korea) will keep away dangerous spirits. Spirits are also seen as influencing a potential convert's acceptance or rejection of Christianity; an evil spirit (*makui*) may invade a nonbeliever and keep Christ out, on the one hand, but when rural women gain faith, they often do so quite suddenly in an experience analogous to that of becoming possessed by a spirit in shamanism. As indicated earlier, exorcism of spirits is also an accepted ritual in rural Christianity. The overzealous exorcism of the mentally ill founder of the local Christian church by the neophyte preacher is not the only example of such an exorcism. I once saw one of the women perform a Christian exorcism. When a poor believer was sick, four other Christian women went to her house and sang hymns to drive away dangerous spirits; then the leader stood over her head making motions in the air, and hissed "shshshshsh" until she thought the demon had been exorcized. Kim Harvey (1987) points out many other relationships between Korean Christianity and shamanism. The religious division of labor by sex is a tradition in rural Korea, and female interest in Christianity continues that tradition. (See Dawnhee Janelli, 1986, on the relationship between women and male ancestor worship.) Most adult males do not communicate with any supernatural beings but their own ancestors.

If shamanistic beliefs and practices intrude into rural Korean Christianity, however, we might also expect the rural elaborations of Confucianism to have some effect on the new believers. Confucianism was the highly esteemed and publicly acknowledge world view of Yi dynasty Korea (1392–1910), and Confucian terms came to dominate religious and cosmological language as well as thought. Given the tenacity of traditional beliefs, the Christian preacher who came to Ye-an was forced to make himself understood in the dominant Confucian mental configuration using Confucian terms and Confucian beliefs.

For example, once when I attended the service in the village, the essence of the preacher's sermon was:

Praying is the same thing as doing ancestor worship because you have received fortune [*bok*, "blessings"] from your ancestors. Sunday is the day that God gives us *bok*. We can gather every Sunday to receive fortune. We thank God and he gives it to us. Vacations are given by the people with governmental authority but Sunday is given by God for his believers to rest. Unbelievers are slaves to *ch'oi* ["sin," but see below for precise meaning]. Unbelievers are slaves to authority [*kwŏllyŏk*] and to ghosts [*makui*]. If we believe, God controls and protects us [*chukwan*; perhaps "supervise" or "has charge of" is closer to the original bureaucratic meaning]. The ghosts cannot do with us as they want. Believers live for five things: (1) eternal life; (2) God's word; (3) true principles [*chinli*]; (4) freedom; and (5) material welfare. Most people start with number 5 and go to number 1 in order of importance, but we need them in the order 1 through 5. People usually spend most effort trying to get material well-being. We want eternal life the most. Because God forgave our sins we thank him. If God did not live, there would be no Sunday so it is proof that he lives.

The preacher's sermon contains several themes that relate to the Confucian world view. First of all, this interpretation of Sunday is of interest. The calendar is of course a major concern of peasant folk religion and Confucianism. The preacher argued that the existence of Sunday as a special day (in the cities) is evidence of the power and existence of the Christian God. But he contrasted God's power with the authority of the political world, the leaders of which grant trivial vacations. In folk religion, the traditional king's authority was fitted to the power of the cosmos, each an expression of the other. All citizens were dependent on this one specific temporal person, the king, and many rituals of "propriety," including ancestor worship, restated that dependence (Dix 1979). The preacher seems to have retained some belief in the connection between cosmos and kingdom. He argued that the existence of Sunday demonstrated the power of the Christian God rather than being due purely to political and historical circumstance.

Although phrased in the concepts of the folk-religious world view, the preacher's sermon contains as much contrast with folk belief as similarity to it. For example, his emphasis is on eternal life rather than material or social welfare. The preacher also mentions *ch'oi*, an idea much closer to our meaning of legal guilt than of sin. The idea of original sin, that man is guilty from the start of sin against heaven, is a new one to Korea. A missionary account of the conversion of a Confucian scholar shows the impact of the new idea of sin and faith. The scholar is quoted as saying:

The men who preached to us spoke so much about sin. It all sounded very silly to me. I knew nothing of sin. I had kept out of jail, and thought as long as I had been that successful I certainly was all right. You know . . . there is nothing in the Chinese classics about sin. I know the classics from beginning to end. . . . While for some time it all seemed silly, yet as I continued to listen I began to grow uncomfortable. I saw myself in a new light. . . . At last my conscience was awakened; I saw that I was a sinner. . . . But what could I do? There certainly was nothing in the Chinese classics telling me how to get rid of sin. . . . Then I saw the secret. . . . As I look back I can see that the Holy Spirit was working. When at last I saw myself a sinner, undone, by faith I saw the Son of God, Jesus Christ, taking my place on the cross, bearing my sin. I could not define it, but I knew that something had taken place in my life, a great transformation had occurred; my sense of sin and guilt was gone, and while I cannot fully explain it even now, I know that I passed from death unto life (Chisholm 1938:14–15).

Christians had to adopt the term *ch'oi* to mean their idea of sin even though it means specific crime and guilt. The lack of a distinction between internal sin toward a God's commandments and external crime against political and legal authority was a problem for the translation of Christian belief into Korean. But the closest idea is Confucian: that man, the son, is inevitably guilty against specific members of his family, particularly his parents. When they die, for example, the son is said to be responsible. People say, no matter how diligent he was, that the son should have worked harder to find a way to keep them alive. He is also guilty because he was unable to repay the huge debt (*unhye*) owed to his parents for bringing him into the world and nurturing him.

There is a degree of similarity between the Confucian attitude toward the father and the Christian attitude toward God, but the father and God are associated with two different ideas of heaven. The Confucian idea of heaven is a very fatalistic one, and internal sin has little effect on one's destiny. Instead, heaven and fate are closely connected to the calendar and to one's parents. As the cosmos changes by its own internal order and at its own pace, human fate is determined. Attempts to represent these hourly, daily, monthly, yearly, and millennial cycles are to be found in the almanac used in rural Korea for choosing propitious days (Dix 1980). But to a son his father is said to be "Heaven." The father is thought to be important to the fate of his son not only because he created the son but also because the two are cosmologically connected. When the father dies it is *chong ch'ŏn chi sa*, "the end of Heaven." In the funeral, the son, a criminal (*ch'oiin*), traditionally wore a huge hat so he could not look up to heaven. People told me that the phrase used in ancestor worship toward one's male ancestors should be interpreted to mean "my grief is as broad and endless as the Heavens." The Korean idea of heaven tied one to specific consanguineal "concrete people whether living or dead." This concrete connection was the point of ancestor worship and all the intricate rules of "propriety."

Finally, when Christians searched for a word to translate the idea of their one God, they chose the work *Hanŭnim*. This word has a long history in Korean religions. *Hanŭnim* is a traditional god who is above other gods, but it is also associated with *hanŭl*, heaven.

These are all thus *partial* resonances between native belief and Christianity that manifested themselves in the translation of the religion into Korean. To reiterate: (1) The Confucian heaven is cosmic fate, which determines man's life and death. In Christianity, heaven is the fate one hopes to attain. (2) Heaven is associated with the father in Confucianism, and God, the Father, is in heaven in Christianity. (3) The Confucian son is a "sinner" toward his father for having caused the father's death. Man is a sinner in Christianity for having disobeyed the word of God and for putting to death God's only son, Jesus. (4) Confucian sons owe a debt (*ŭnhye*) for the gift of life and nurturance from their parents (cf. Bellah 1970 on the comparison between God and the father). Of course, that God should so love the world that he would give up his only son to be murdered by mankind in order to bring his word to the world has a strong meaning for rural

Koreans who place such value on sons. Mankind owes a debt to God for his grace (*ŭnhye*), which is the gift of eternal life. In other words, although there are certainly differences in the meaning of each, there is also some similarity in the way these important religious symbols are connected in each tradition.

We have been discussing compatibilities and contradictions between rural Confucianism and Christianity, but over the hundreds of years they have been associated, Confucian ideas and Korean shamanism have developed their own compatibilities. This larger system has a place and a time for a great many traditional practices and for the customs associated with the different seasons and particular statuses. It is a loosely organized conglomeration of beliefs in sharp contrast with the take-it-or-leave-it rigidity, regularity, and constant demands Christianity makes even on the *internal* thoughts of "the faithful." Some traditional beliefs carry over into rural Korean Christianity and some incompatible ones (such as the strictures against ancestor worship and the consumption of alcoholic beverages) have been added. But the demand that one have internal and exclusive faith in a distant God who is only fictive kin is a very new idea.

Faith is not an issue in Confucianism or shamanism. The spirits in Confucianism are remembered ancestors. These spirits are kept comfortably in their place not by faith but by proper offerings and—more generally—by the continuity of the male line. The ancestral spirits, though important, are not omnipotent, so injustice raises less of a problem of doubt.

Although the existence of ancestral spirits and the myriad spirits of shamanism does not go unquestioned, the issue of doubt is combated by numerous "miraculous" occurrences during a seance, including spirit possession itself. The shaman's spirits do not demand faith; they demand gifts, treats, bribes, and deference. Whereas ancestors demand constancy above all else, relationships with the spirits of shamanism are extremely fickle. As soon as the harm they cause disappears, most people ignore them.

Faith in the Christian God must be constant and internal, but in rural Korean Christianity, faith is believed to guarantee the faithful power and protection. One of the Christian women was the wife of a very highly respected village leader. He had studied the Confucian classics in a cottage school for about four years and was considered a scholar. This man was clearly an opinion leader in the village and soon after I left was selected as the village chief. But his wife had various psychological problems and still occasionally would fall into a swoon, overcome with her worries. Her husband once told me, "After I got out of the army my wife had many diseases and problems. There was no wall between our house and the next and she was so sick that I had to cook my own rice. I was ashamed and did it secretly. [Men never go into the kitchen and cook.] She prayed and began to go to church often and she got better." And his wife said,

I don't know how I came to have faith. I was sick often and anxious. I could not live. I was going to "sell" our son to a shaman at a temple. They said that if I did, by purchasing the shaman as a powerful surrogate, ritual parent, the child would live long, but that was a trick. Some children said to come to the church. So, not knowing anything, I did. When the preacher first came into this village he said it looked like a "ghost place" and I guess it was. But I began to pray and soon I gained faith. To begin to believe is to receive a huge *ŭnhye* ["grace," an outstanding gift, such as the gift of life].

Your spirit [*yŏnghon*] has to be able to see God but he can't if there is a ghost there. Chong-Ik's mother [the widow who has given the church a room in her house] lost her husband and from then she could not hear very well. She began to pray and light came down on her. She received *ŭnhye*. She fell over and saw twelve pigs come down from the mountain. [These were ghosts. The number twelve is important in shamanism. There are twelve gates to the shamanistic other world, for example.] When they came down she prayed harder so the ghosts died and she believed. And she lost her various diseases [*chap pyŏng*].

Christianity is often seen to be in a power struggle with shamanistic spirits, but it was the gift of grace that made this woman able to conquer the ghosts and begin to have faith in God. It happened all at once and from then she believed. This idea of sudden belief with accompanying personality changes and the acquisition of new powers resembles the rapid psychological changes that occur when a spirit possesses a woman. The scholar, a man of patience and wisdom, was very impressed with the effects of this faith on his wife. He told me,

If I go to Tang valley I am afraid and I cannot go at night. This is because someone hung himself there. There are ghosts there that say things to people and the people will become "surprised." ["Surprise disease" is common in rural Korea, and many deaths especially of children are attributed to it.] There are many child-ghosts [*ajang*] there. Once a pottery salesman came into the village by truck. He saw a tiger there and got "surprise disease" and fell over and had to go to the hospital. It is a very bad place. If women are carrying something on the head there it will fall off. When I walk by there I put stones in my pocket and walk slowly and warily. I once saw a woman there walking toward me but she never got closer and then she became a tree. Some years ago I went with Chang-Ik's father to catch crayfish. When we went by there we heard the voices of about twenty children from the top of the mountain. Then there was a lone cry and the voices stopped. Chang-Ik's father said it was ghosts. When kids die we just bury them without a full funeral and we put stones over the grave because animals would dig it up. In that valley where Kim T'ae-man has melons he built a small hut on stilts to guard them. He made a mosquito fire under the hut and then went to sleep there at night. When he woke up the child ghosts were warming their hands by the fire under his hut. The amazing thing is that my wife will go by there even on a rainy night. She and the other Christians don't mind at all. They think the ghosts will not get them. When there is thunder and lightning most people think "Is there something I've done wrong so I'll be punished?" But people with a God are not afraid.

The demand that people have faith is a truly new idea in rural Korea. That faith in a god could bring constant inner conviction against fears and temptations is not an idea easily combined with Confucian propriety. Confucian ritual is a staged short-term display characterized particularly by its boundedness; it should become a model for ordinary, profane activity. Although the Confucian classics argue for taking that respectful display into every mundane activity, there is no god judging internal commitment or faith. Faith is difficult to maintain, but if it can be maintained it may provide more "leverage" than extending Confucian ritual into mundane, nonsacred occasions.

Another issue of contrast in rural Korea concerns male prerogatives and the family finances. Ritualized drinking sessions have important functions in the male political world. Male drinking is often a great burden on family finances and the woman usually does not have the power to limit it as much as she would like. Males usually drink in all-male groups where there is a great deal of attention to social relationships. Drinking (and smoking) have become rituals of exchange. Status and social obligations are expressed and manipulated in these rituals. When a Christian woman opposes drinking, she is opposing the expenditures of maintaining a pattern of ritualized relationships in the male world, just as when she opposes ancestor worship she is opposing (among other things) expenditures for maintaining proper relationships with the ancestors of the male line. Faith in Christianity implies a more frugal household economy and a more ascetic life-style, but may provide an opportunity for the growth of capital. The opposition that Weber noted between "piety toward concrete people" and Protestant Christianity is not lost on rural Korean women. Christianity comes to Korea from a very wealthy country. Protestant Christianity as it is brought to rural Koreans contains the ascetic message, but it also implies the possibility of attaining wealth.

When the preacher or his converts talked about Christianity, one problem to which they often returned was, "Why has Korea fallen behind?" "Why is Korea now a small underdeveloped nation that has to depend on other nations for support?" The answer given was that the West had adopted belief in a more powerful God than the Korean spirits. The preacher told me, "The West is wealthy. Korea is poor. If Korea would only adopt faith in God it would become as rich as the West but we have wasted our energies on superstition and ceremony instead of putting ourselves in God's care." The small but vocal group of Christian women often returned to this line of argument.

Much of the Christian work down in Korea has been by Western missionaries with Western funds. In the eyes of rural Koreans, these missionaries are enormously wealthy. They live in huge Western-style houses; they drive their own automobiles; they finance large universities; they build huge churches, which they often have trouble filling with believers. Missionaries are associated with wealth in the eyes of rural Koreans.

On the other hand, several people expressed shock that a collection is taken at regular church meetings. The rural Korean is willing to offer sizable sums of money and food to spirits on special ritual occasions in order to show a sense of obligation, or for protection or in hope of a cure for sickness. But the idea of *regularly* donating money directly to a wealthy church surprises him. He suspects the church of greed and trickery. The regularity of Christian meetings and the collection relate to the distant, nonspecific but constant and demanding nature of Christianity. Most Koreans find this difficult to accept.

INTERNAL CONVERSION OR "PROPRIETY'"

The elements of similarity between Christianity and Confucianism were not lost to my informants. I used to enjoy listening to a somewhat scholarly Confucian neighbor argue with his wife over the relative merits of their two doctrines. For example, one day just after the assassination of the Korean president's wife, I was sitting on their porch with them listening to the news on the radio. He said, "In the old days there would have been a huge funeral and they would have made a large tomb for the king's wife. If there was a 'national funeral' [kuksang, at the death of the king or his family] all citizens wore a white mourning hat [paeknip] and did a memorial service [Ch'udoshik] like an ancestor worship ceremony for the dead." His wife said, "Ch'udoshik? That comes from Christianity." The scholar replied, "That is Chinese and it has a deep meaning that you do not understand." (As usual the Christian term for a mourning service had been a Confucian term the Christians had to adopt in order to convey their meaning.) The scholar said, "All people live for God. I think there is something of value in all religions. They are all saying much the same thing. Isn't the God of Christianity called the Father?"

But his wife had a different idea: "Even though they beat God's son, he worked for God. He opened people's eyes to God." (Here is real filial piety.) The scholar turned to me and said, "I sometimes read the Bible in Chinese characters [hanmun]. There is much that is of value in the Bible, much that is worth learning. I cannot stop smoking and drinking and you have to get up early in the morning to go to church [the church bell is rung at about 4:30 or 5:00 A.M.] so I have not become a Christian, but there is much of value in it. I understand the Bible better than my wife does. She used to believe in many spirits and now she believes in only one and she does not have so many illnesses as she once did."

Incidentally, this man is suggesting that his wife is illiterate in Chinese characters, and can only read the version of the Bible written in Korean script (hangul), and so because of the homonymic nature of Korean, does not get the full semantic associations that Chinese characters invoke to a scholar. This is an important part of the sociology of religious knowledge in rural Korea. A scholar was traditionally respected in part because only he was literate enough to interpret classical wisdom to villagers. Christianity, by translating the Bible into hangul, sometimes referred to as "women's writing," is now challenging this monopoly on literacy. It is still an unwritten rule that all contracts, all offertories to the mountain spirit and the dragon rain spirit, and those in ancestor worship must be written in Chinese characters.

The scholar accepts the Confucian image of the world, and although he seems to believe in the spirits of shamanism and Christianity, his primary criterion for measuring the value of a religion is still social. He respects Christianity for the changes it has made on his wife's mental and physical state, and for the determination, group cohesiveness, diligence, and courage it gives to the local Christians.

But this scholar and village leader has not become a Christian. He once told my assistant the following story to explain why he would not do so. In interpreting this incident one should remember the great emphasis placed on harmony and propriety in Confucianism. Village scholars and leaders are responsible for harmonizing conflicts, and they often become involved as arbitrators in trying to bring kinsmen and neighbors back to a relationship in which they are willing to treat each other with at least the outward respect that Confucian "propriety" demands. A common saying in a village such as this (and a fundamental principle necessary for understanding the lives of these poor peasants who have few alternatives) is "We *have to* live together." Here is what he said:

Im Chong-shik's wife wanted to go to the church but her husband was violently against it. Every time she would go he would beat her. One day he got drunk and went over to the church room which is next door to his house. Many people in the village object to hearing the church bell several times a week so early in the morning, and he thought he would put an end to it. He burned the rope which supports the old pressurized gas container that is used as a bell. When the preacher heard about this he reported it to the police [something no villager would have done]. The police came and called upon many villagers living nearby in order to get evidence. Im Chong-shik came to me and we went to see the preacher who was with another younger preacher then. Im Chong-shik asked to be forgiven. The preacher said, "If only on the outside you ask for forgiveness and on the inside you do not think you did wrong, I cannot forgive you." They had already discussed what they would say if Im came to them. We had gone to visit them in the city and we all took a taxi to the police station. I gave the police a small amount of money for their "cigarette fee" [a common expression for what Westerners think of as a small bribe] and asked the preacher to ask the police to forget it. He said, "We are trying to get rid of that kind of thing [giving bribes] and I will not ask them to forget it." He did not say anything good though he could have easily settled it. It was not such a large offense. Im Chong-shik paid the fine but from then on I did not think well of those people [Christians]. If the church asks for forgiveness they should forgive but they do not, even though I went with Im. So I was angry after that. One day while I was teaching my son Chinese characters the preacher came to our house and said, "You do not need those any more. All you need is the Bible." Before that I used to listen to all that the preacher said and only nod my head but I could not accept this and I said, "We need to know all we can." And I opposed him and got angry with him so he just went away.

By their insistence on internal repentance, by sticking to principle and not accepting the outward forms of "propriety" in Im's half-hearted plea for forgiveness, the Christian church in this village had lost its one best hope for a convert who had the respect of the community. (See Fried 1987 on Christianity's lack of tolerance as a reason for its failure in China.) It is not an exaggeration to say that if this confession of guilt had been accepted in a way more sympathetic to traditional Korean "propriety," the history of the Christian church in one village might have been very different. But in the end, such a conflict between the ways of propriety and the Christian insistence on internal repentance was to be expected.

CONCLUSION

Max Weber pointed out that a major contrast between Christianity on the one hand and folk shamanism and Confucianism on the other was the difference between being "bound to a sacred 'cause' or an 'idea' " and "piety toward concrete people." The rulers of a Confucian society were determined to set a carefully devised, externally visible ritual pattern for social relations, one that would harmonize and stabilize society. Relations between any two people could be fit into this plan; the superior person must exhibit paternalism and restraint, the inferior must outwardly exhibit deference. The rules of ritual were to be extended into every context in order to shape society in the pattern of ritual.

The Confucian choice "among a finite set of possible developments away from magical realism" was toward the idea of "propriety," an elaboration of outward offerings of respect toward particular categories of elders and ancestors and "those close to one through their position in life." We are only now coming to understand how this could have such powerful impact on social life (Fingarette 1972). But certainly the Confucian idea of "propriety" by itself would not be viable as a religion in rural Korea. Combined with folk Confucian beliefs and shamanism, however, the idea has been powerful indeed. The combined folk religion of rural Korea also has answers to such questions as the problem of meaning (why do the good sometimes die young?), salvation, and so forth. Males believe they are saved from death by an endless line of descendants properly offering food to them as their spirits survive in the other world. Christians believe they are saved from death by their exclusive, internal faith toward their one all-knowing God.

Conflicting interpretations of sin/guilt, the proper role of women, the need for faith, ritual, literacy and knowledge, male drinking and exchange of alcoholic beverages, fear of myriad ghosts, the curing of disease, religion as a means to wealth or afterlife, repentance, minor bribes (gifts), and social harmony are all the results of a fundamental difference in the central premises of these two ideas of life. In Confucian ideology, people were to associate with each other by following a pattern of ritual performances enacted between different generations in the line of male descent. The great weight of belief and religious elaboration supports this pattern and if it is broken it must be mended so that social life will not remain permanently disrupted and chaotic. Christianity makes new demands on its believers and provides them with new ideas about social life. Once they have faith, they believe they are constantly protected and supervised by an all-seeing God who demands that their actions be right regardless of social disruption and external form. The few in the vanguard of the new religion no longer fear ghosts, and they no longer abide the social courtesies involved in the exchange of cigarettes and drinks. They no longer labor to keep relationships with their ancestors right by ancestor worship. Their God seems to have replaced the proper pattern of particular social relationships toward concrete others with his own fatherly demand that each person internalize faith and single-minded obedience to his word.

The Confucian father is not a god before whom each individual stands alone. He is a surrogate, a representative of the whole lineage, and the pattern of relationship with him is easily conceived to extend in varying degrees to particular others. Males reject the Christian God because he would disrupt this ideal of continuity and social harmony through male-dominated ritual. Females take an interest in Christianity for exactly the same reasons, but (for those same reasons) few can disobey their husband and become Christians.

The central difference, the difference that seems to make the difference, is the one mentioned in the two quotes that preface this chapter: the difference between a God who has "not come to bring peace but a sword" and who states that "a man's foes will be those of his own household" and the Confucian scholar writing in 1785 who is outraged at the young men whose hearts were changed in a single day. The scholar objects not to anything they believe, but rather to improper ritual action. These bad young men are "like the boy who graduates in the Classics, and then comes home to call his mother by her first name, a sad state of affairs indeed!"

6

The Origins of Revival, a Creole Religion in Jamaica

WILLIAM WEDENOJA

Revival is an Afro-American religion that emerged in Jamaica in 1860 and is still practiced on the island. It is a descendant of several slave cults and movements that were based on African religions, but it was also heavily influenced by Protestant missionization in the early nineteenth century. A unique combination of beliefs and practices from many sources and periods, the cult is the product of a complex and dynamic history of religious transformations. The purpose of this chapter is to trace the course of religious evolution in Jamaica, identifying the origins of elements of present-day Revival, the historical events and social conditions leading to religious innovation, patterns and processes of religious transformation, and the social and cultural consequences of religious change.

Jamaican religion evolved in response to a number of factors—the oppression of slavery, the multiethnic composition of the slave population, the poverty and deprivations of plantation and peasant subsistence, famines and epidemics, and a system of social stratification based on color—and it played an integral role in the development of an indigenous or Creole culture by fusing African and European traditions and reducing stressful cultural dissonance. Cults, sects and movements, prophets, healers, and sorcerers have been prominent in every period of Jamaican history. Each stage in the development of Creole culture was first expressed in cult innovations, and syncretic movements have been a major vehicle for cultural transformation.

CONTEMPORARY REVIVAL

Jamaica is an extremely religious and largely Christian society with a Protestant, fundamentalist, congregational, millenarian, salvationist, evangelical, and charismatic or "spirit-filled" orientation. There is, however, a wide range of variation, on a continuum from African traditions to Euro-American sects and de-

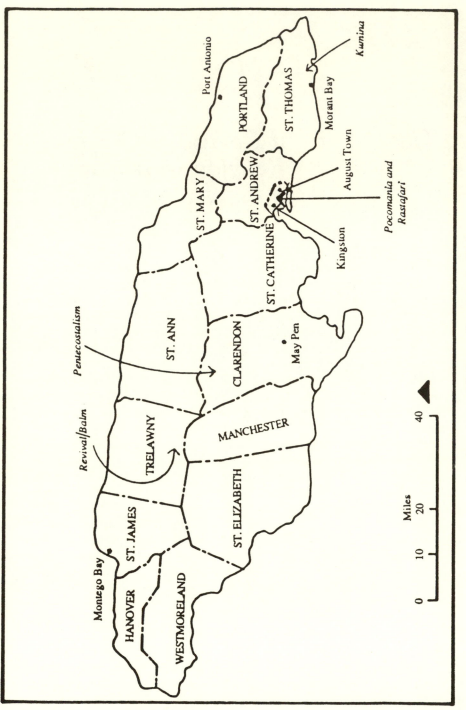

Jamaica: Areas of Religious Concentration Today

nominations. The most African tradition is an ancestor cult called Kumina, which is still popular in the parish of St. Thomas (see map of Jamaica). Belief in Obeah or sorcery, which developed during slavery and is based on African notions, is very widespread. Baptist, Anglican, Methodist, Presbyterian, Moravian, and Roman Catholic churches are at the orthodox Christian end of the continuum. They are found in every area of the island and, for the most part, were introduced by English missionaries during the early nineteenth century.

Between these two extremes there are several syncretic, indigenous traditions with a strong African influence that developed in the latter half of the nineteenth century. Balm or "spiritual science" is a form of folk healing practiced throughout the island, and it is often allied with Revival cultism, particularly in the highlands of Trelawny, St. Elizabeth, and Manchester parishes. Pocomania is a kind of Revival cultism found in the city of Kingston, although the word is also often used in a derisive way to refer to Kumina, Balm, and Revival. Rastafarianism and De Laurence are syncretic traditions with less African influence, and developed in Jamaica during this century. The Rastafarian movement is essentially an urban ghetto phenomenon, and most of its followers are young men. De Laurence or "Science" is a modern version of Obeah involving the selling of "guards"—charms, powders, candles, and prayers—by individuals known as "scientists" or "professors," and is based on a magic catalog from a mail-order house in Chicago.

There has been a rapid growth of fundamentalist, evangelical, and pentecostal sects in recent decades (Wedenoja 1980), beginning with the Adventists and followed by several varieties of the Church of God, which is especially strong in the parish of Clarendon. Many of them are affiliated with American sects, but some are exclusively Jamaican, and in either case they are largely under local control and have taken on a distinctively Jamaican character.

Most of my ethnographic research has been in the central highlands of northern Manchester and Clarendon, where I located thirty-three orthodox, eleven evangelical, thirty-three pentecostal, two Jehovah's Witness, and twenty-seven Revival churches in a sixty-square-mile area in 1976. In addition, there were two balmyards and several "scientists" and obeahmen, but no Kumina or Pocomania groups and few Rastafarians. The following description of Revival focuses on a cult that I will refer to as Gilead. It is one of the larger and more active cults in the area, and I have made a detailed study of it (Wedenoja 1978).

Gilead is in a large concrete building with a mosquelike dome at the back, situated on top of a prominent hill in the center of a peasant hamlet. It is surrounded by a fence, which has cloth "banners" with "spirit writing" (written glossolalia) and biblical quotations over the gateways. There are also five banners on a flagpole erected to attract spirits called "angels" and to guide "pilgrims" and healing patients to the church. Orange segments and glasses of water containing a healing plant called "Leaf-of-Life" (*Bryophyllum pinnatum*) sit on several wooden columns, and these "seals" are used to attract and feed "angels" and to remove evil or "destruction" from visitors. Behind the building there is an "office" where the leader sees patients and another room where an assistant bathes them.

The inside of the building resembles a Christian church, with rows of pews facing an elevated section at the front, where there is a pulpit, an altar, and seating for the leaders and choir. There are, however, some distinctively Revival features too. A polka-dot ball and a vase of flowers sit at the base of a seal between the altar and the pews, on a circular chalk drawing with cabbalistic designs, resembling a Haitian "vever" drawn by a woman in a state of visionary trance. The altar is made up of a golden cross with the blade of a penknife in the top to represent the punitive "sword" of God, a vase of flowers "to entertain the angels," and open Bible to ward off demons, a clock "because time is running out," a silver candleholder, a kerosene lantern ("because the light of the world is Jesus") that wards off evil spirits, a collection tray, and a world globe to symbolize prophecy. The walls are decorated with banners, a table with a pitcher and glasses at the front is used to dispense "the medicine" (water with Leaf-of-Life in it) during healing services, and a shepherd's crook and a cross, which are carried in processions, stand in two corners.

The leader of Gilead, who is referred to as "Mother," lives with several of her assistants or "workers" and some "patients" and boarders in a large, three-story house near the church. She is a black, middle-aged woman from the hamlet, who was sickly and suffered from typhoid fever and malaria as a child, and later went to live with a sister in Kingston where, at the age of twenty-five, she became a parlormaid. One morning, when she was twenty-seven, she was "struck down" and stunned by "a flash of light" and felt "confused" all day. That evening, she saw a vision of Jesus and fell unconscious, and after waking felt compelled to "warn" others of the imminence of Judgment Day. This was the first of several spiritual experiences that led her to consult a balmist, who told her she possessed a spiritual gift. Later, she went to work as a servant of the British ambassador in Washington, D.C., but in her first year there she was "crippled" with paralysis in the limbs and hands and had a visionary calling to return to Jamaica and start a ministry, which she did in 1950. She gained a large following, achieving particular fame as a healer, and in 1960 was ordained a minister in a black American sect, the National Baptists, which she left in 1970 to affiliate with a spiritualist sect from California.

Gilead currently has about sixty active members, 77 percent of whom are women. The average age is forty-eight, and 49 percent are married. They are largely poor and black, and make their living at farming. It is a tightly knit group, held together by strong devotion to the Mother, who has total control. She has a group of "workers," resembling the "hunsis" in Haitian Voodoo, who work full time for the church under the supervision of a middle-aged woman called the "Armor Bearer" or "Secretary." Some of the workers are also "Leadresses," who are responsible for ceremonial roles such as preparing the medicine, bathing patients, and leading the congregation in songs. The Mother, Armor Bearer, and Leadresses wear ornate and colorful turbans and dresses, which are embroidered with symbols and have lace and epaulettes. The workers and other women wear white gowns and turbans to services, and men generally wear dark suits. Most of the men have honorific positions, such as the elderly "Captain" or senior deacon and younger "Bandsmen" or junior deacons, and their responsibility is limited to preaching and taking up the collection. In addition, there is a pastor whose main responsibility is to officiate at weddings and funerals.

Revival ideology stresses the Old Testament and emphasizes submission and dependence on a punitive and demanding God who provides protection and security in exchange for worship and obedience. Revivalists value humility, self-sacrifice, mutual support, and passive contentment, and they often proclaim "we are the despised and rejected," "the meek and the lowly." In recent years, however, there has been an increasing emphasis on pentecostal, New Testament themes such as moralistic self-perfection, identification with Jesus, spiritual cleansing and personal "rebirth," love and happiness, and rejection of worldly ways and worldly people.

Revivalists believe in and interact with many spirits, particularly "angels"—which include Old Testament prophets and New Testament disciples—who serve as intermediaries with a distant God and protect them from demons, fallen angels, and "duppies" (malevolvent ghosts). Angels deliver "warnings" in the form of dreams, which are interpreted by the cult leader. A wake, called a "set up" or "Nine-Night," is held to pacify the soul of someone who has died and render it harmless, and this is usually followed by a tombing ceremony and annual memorial services.

Dedicated members of Gilead gather for prayer at 5:30 A.M. every weekday and come to a fasting service on the first Thursday in the month. There is a "Divine Worship" every Sunday, and Communion is served once a month. An annual "Convention" and quarterly "Rallies" are held for fellowship with other groups and to raise money. Additional calendric rites include an annual "Flower Service," a Good Friday service, a "Watchnight" on New Year's Eve, and an Easter program.

Revival cults occasionally hold a feast called a "Table" or "Board." Gilead has a "New Year's Table," a "Physician's Board" or "Patients' Table" in April, an "Atonement Board" or "Thanksgiving Table" in August to honor the Mother, and a "Tabernacle Board" or "Members' Table" in November. The seal at the front of the church is replaced by a table, which is set with candles, bottles of soda and wine, oranges, bananas, a tall cake, vases of flowers, Leaf-of-Life, Bibles, hymnals, whistles, and plates for each of the twelve disciples. During a Table, which begins at noon and ends at midnight, goat meat and rice are served.

The structure of Sunday services is a mixture of Anglican and Baptist formats. The beginning and end of other services follows the Anglican order of service, but the middle is markedly "African." A service begins with prayers, readings from the Bible, and slow, monotonic "Redemption Hymns," followed by "testimonies" from members and sermons from leaders, which are punctuated by rhythmic "choruses" with a quick tempo. Participants sing and dance to the beat of tambourines and two goat-skin drums, while some of the workers and leaders perform a variety of rituals to remove ill will and evil spirits ("destruction") from the church, to "entertain" the angels, and to "get in the Spirit."

The high point of a Revival service is ritual trance, an altered state of consciousness, which they regard as a "manifestation of the Spirit" or Holy Ghost. It varies from simple trance states and spasmodic jerks to rapid dancing and even jousting with demons, and sometimes involves possession by angels, who deliver messages from God through "visions" and "tongues." Revivalists often perform an ecstatic ring dance called "shouting" or "laboring," which ensues after someone "cuts and clears" destruction from the church by swinging a wooden sword, dancing in a whirling motion, and bursting bottles of carbonated soda in the corners. Several workers then form a "band" and dance in a counterclockwise circle, rhythmically stamping the floor and hyperventilating in unison until the angels depart.

One of the central concerns of Revival is to combat "destruction," which refers to illness, misfortune, and malicious behavior caused by supernatural forces. Rituals are performed to attack duppies and demons, to protect people from these forces, and to remove destruction from individuals. Some revivalists operate balmyards where spiritual healing is a full-time business, and about half of all Revival cults offer regular healing services.

Rural Jamaicans often blame illness and misfortune on supernatural forces. Duppies are said to cause madness. Ghosts punish their descendants for failing to perform proper burials or hold regular memorial rites, and they haunt people who owe them money. God punishes Christians who fail to live up to his precepts. Successful people are fearful of envy and worry that someone will go to an obeahman and "set hand" against them in spite or to "bring them down." It is said that obeahmen capture duppies or ghosts at gravesites and silk cotton trees and set them on others in the form of frogs, lizards, and birds. They also supposedly use magical spells and mixtures of leaves, roots, water, blood, and grave dirt to do harm. However, people usually go to obeahmen for "guards" to protect them or to influence events such as court cases and love affairs.

There are many folk remedies to ward off duppies, such as carrying a Bible or garlic and lime and wearing a tape measure, but people often turn to Balm when these measures fail. Every Monday Gilead conducts a lively healing service "to cheer up the spirit" of patients, and the shouting ritual is performed to remove destruction from them. Consecrated water containing Leaf-of-Life is served, and patients are individually bathed in water with healing leaves. Each patient is then privately "read" by the Mother, who receives guidance from an angel while in a state of trance. She always offers moral counseling and usually prescribes herbs or "bush" and patent medicines. Her special "gift of the Spirit" is to "draw" a patient's suffering into her own body and "set them free." Sometimes she does spirit writing on a sheet of paper in a state of trance and tells the patient to wear this amulet, which is a prayer to God, under their hat or shirt. She also rubs patients with mauve-colored alcohol and gives them candles and prayers.

PRECURSORS OF REVIVAL

There were perhaps 60,000 Indians in Jamaica when Columbus landed in 1494, but they did not survive the brief period of Spanish occupation. The island was taken by the British in 1655, and several thousand sugar, cotton, pimento, ginger, cattle, and coffee estates were developed. Labor for these estates was provided by black slaves, who greatly outnumbered whites, and over 500,000 Africans were brought to Jamaica before the slave trade was abolished in 1808.

The foundation for Revival and other Jamaican religions was the pragmatic and this-worldly but communal and intensely spiritual tribal religions that were brought to the island from Africa. They had a belief in a supreme and benevolent creator, but he was distant and generally uninvolved. Spiritual interactions focused on a pantheon of intermediary deities, associated particularly with natural but also cultural phenomena, and the "living dead" or ancestor spirits, who were the guardians of custom. The living had to praise, obey, and offer sacrifices to these spirits and carefully attend to burial and memorial rites for their ancestors because they often intervened in human affairs, and the cost of neglecting or offending them was illness, death, or misfortune. Worship of the gods involved singing, drumming, and dancing, and they communicated with the living through dreams, oracles, visions, and ceremonial possession states. The priests who served the gods were also called on to expose witches and sorcerers, who were often blamed for problems, and to provide charms and medicines for protection and healing.

The Church of England was the official church of Jamaica during slavery but, in the words of a clergyman, it left the slaves "in heathen darkness" (Gardner 1909:199). There were only twenty Anglican churches in 1800, and they were staffed by generally untrained and sometimes disreputable characters who were frequently indifferent to their charge. The Anglican churches were established for the exclusive use of the whites, who were hardly devout and often lived "a life of riotous debauchery" (Gardner 1909:379). Little if any attempt was made to Christianize the slaves during the first 150 years of English settlement. The size of the clergy was insufficient and they showed little interest in the task. The planters often claimed that slaves were incapable of understanding Christianity, but they were particularly anxious to avoid the awkward moral and legal questions that Christianization would raise.

This situation favored the preservation of African religion, and an average annual influx of over 43,000 new slaves from Africa also helped to keep it alive. On the other hand, many African traditions were destroyed or transformed by slavery and the mixing of Africans from different tribes, ethnic groups, languages, and cultures on the plantations. An indigenous religion and culture that was based on a synthesis of many African traditions and adjustments to slavery began to emerge among the slaves.

European culture had a very limited influence on slaves and the early development of Creole culture. Only about 10 percent of the population was white, and most of them regarded their residence as temporary: "England was always their home, and Jamaica merely a place out of which the most was to be made" (Sewell 1862:237). The slaves made creative and productive use of every opportunity to develop their own social and economic institutions and culture. Many of them grew their own food on "provision grounds," and they established an internal marketing system that also fed the white population. Slaves gathered at Sunday markets to hawk produce and craft goods and also to sing, dance, and share experiences. On holidays such as Christmas and Easter, they were allowed to visit other estates and participate in indigenous celebrations such as "John Canoe," a pantomime with colorful masks and costumes.

The slaves were prohibited from performing religious rites or organizing religious groups, although music and dance were permitted, so slave religion had to be practiced privately, secretly, and in disguised forms such as holiday celebrations and dances. Funerals provided a regular occasion for religious observance. They were often joyous affairs because the deceased had escaped slavery and it was thought that his spirit would return to his ancestral home and kin in Africa. The corpse was carried by everyone's home on the way to the grave, and if there were any outstanding debts or grievances it was drawn to the door for reconciliation before moving on. The wake involved a feast, drumming, dancing, horn blowing, praise songs, and libations. Food was left by the graveside for the spirit of the deceased, which would wander for forty days, at which time a final rite was held (Brathwaite 1971:216–17).

The African idea of multiple souls persisted in a tripartite model of body, soul, and "shadow" (Patterson 1973:186–205). The shadow or dark side of a person's character was said to linger at the grave as a malevolent duppy or ghost unless it was rendered harmless by a ceremony or caught and buried. The slaves faced a life of constant oppression, deprivations, a high rate of mortality, and many debilitating or life-threatening diseases, and they often blamed their suffering on duppies.

An indigenous practice of divination, healing, and sorcery called "Obeah" developed to deal with duppies and a wide range of other problems. Obeahmen filled calabashes or gourds with items such as "bits of red rag, cats teeth, parrot feathers, eggshells, and fish bones" (Long 1774:420), and these "obi" were buried at the doors of houses to harm the inhabitants or hung on trees in provision grounds to prevent theft. They made potions and charms to influence an overseer or a loved one, and took people's shadows so they would waste away and die. They administered herbs, retrieved lost shadows, and extracted objects such as glass bottles, snakes, and other reptiles from the skin to heal the sick. The obeahman was a powerful, feared, and respected figure in slave communities.

The planters were amused by Obeah at first, but the problems it caused soon led them to outlaw it. Obeahmen were skilled in poisons and occasionally used them on whites. Fear of Obeah among the slaves sometimes led to work stoppages on the estates. A notorious desperado called Three-Finger Jack carried an obi to make him invulnerable. Obeah also figured prominently in numerous slave revolts. It was said to have enabled Tacky, the leader of a revolt in 1760, to "catch the bullets of the soldiers and throw them back" (Gardner 1909:133). Obeahmen rubbed the bodies of Tacky's followers with a powder to make them invulnerable, and they administered a sacred oath and had the rebels mix their blood with gunpowder and grave dirt and drink it to ensure their secrecy, commitment, and solidarity (Long 1774:473).

The first Creole religion, a secret society known as "Myalism," emerged after 1760 as an outgrowth of the role of obeahmen in organizing revolts. Its most conspicuous element was the Myal Dance, in which an obeahman administered a drink that seemed to kill a person, then squeezed a juice of herbs into the mouth of the corpse. While this was taking place, his assistants danced "hand in hand . . . in a circle, stamping the ground loudly with their feet to keep time with this chant" until the initiate was resurrected (Lewis 1834:354). Myal cultism apparently united slaves from many ethnic groups and plantations into a common body (Schuler 1979:67), greatly increasing their revolutionary potential, and it led to numerous revolts between 1760 and 1776.

The failure of these revolts was accompanied by demoralizing events such as devastating hurricanes from 1766 to 1786 that led to famines and epidemics, a cut-off of food imports from 1775 to 1787 because of war, and economic depression from 1783 to 1793 that ruined several estates. The resulting despair transformed Myalism from a nativistic to a thaumaturgical cult, but creolization may have been another factor: by 1789 Jamaican-born slaves made up 75 percent of the population (Schuler 1979:68).

Myalists were sometimes employed as "doctors" at estate infirmaries because of their knowledge of herbs, and Myal cults came to specialize in healing. They offered protection from duppies and Obeah, exorcised spirits, extracted obi from victims' bodies, located buried obi, recovered lost shadows, and captured duppies. The Myal Dance was performed under silk cotton trees where shadows and duppies were through to linger. It became a divinatory possession ritual, a way to locate obi and lost shadows through contact with spirits.

Slaves in the American South were exposed to Christianity long before missionaries came to Jamaica, and it was an American freedman, George Lisle, who brought Afro-Christian religion to the island. Lisle was born into slavery in Virginia and, after converting to Christianity, was freed and granted a license to preach. In 1775 he organized one of the first black churches in America near Savannah, Georgia. After the Revolutionary War Lisle joined a contingent of Loyalists who sought refuge in Jamaica. In 1784 he established the Jamaica Baptist Free Church, commonly known as "the Black Baptists," in Kingston (B. Brown 1975).

The covenant of Lisle's church included the practice of baptism in a river, foot washing, praying over the sick and anointing them with oil, and a strict code of behavior. Lisle's evangelists organized converts into "classes" and appointed class leaders. This fostered a rapid, cellular-like growth of his movement, but it also encouraged fragmentation and innovation as he had little contact with or control over them. Myalism was regularly mixed with the Baptist teachings of Lisle, and class leaders often broke away from his church to form "Native Baptist" cults. One leader made his candidates go into the "wilderness" and pray until they received a dream or vision before being baptized. Another sacrificed fowl and pigs and had his followers fast at least one day each week. This syncretism proved to be very popular because Myalism could be carried on under the guise of a Christian veneer that made it more acceptable to whites, but it was a very significant step away from African tradition toward acculturation and creolization.

The Native Baptists imbued Christianity with the spiritual and pragmatic, this-worldly orientation of African religion. They were generally illiterate and sought knowledge and guidance from dreams, visions, and possessions induced by the Myal Dance. Their leaders, who were known as "Daddies" or "Mommas," claimed to have spiritual gifts such as the ability to foretell the future. They interpreted the dreams of their followers and healed the sick by rubbing their heads with oil. John the Baptist was their highest deity, and baptism was practiced to wash sin and sorcery away. Native Baptist cults also contributed to the social organization of slave communities by establishing church courts to enforce their codes of behavior and settle disputes without having to turn to the law and authorities of white society.

The first missionaries were Moravians, who arrived in 1754. They initially worked on five estates in St. Elizabeth owned by two English converts and received an allowance from the proprietors. After these allowances were terminated, they supported their work by farming an estate they had acquired, but this compelled them to own slaves. The Moravians' concern for slaves was limited to their spiritual welfare and they never openly challenged or even questioned slavery. Instead, they strove to demonstrate that Christianization made for a better slave: "more diligent, more reliable and loyal" (Furley 1965:15). Moravian missionaries sought to stamp out African "paganisms," imposed puritanical standards of morality on the slaves, and had stringent criteria for membership. Consequently, they were often disliked and made few converts.

The first truly influential missionaries were the Wesleyan Methodists, who came to Jamaica in 1789. They concentrated on the towns, where they appealed particularly to the "free coloreds" or mulattoes. Like the Moravians, they were neutral on the issue of slavery and preached patience and obedience. But Jamaican whites were fearful of the nearby revolt in Haiti, wary of the growing power of the free coloreds, and suspicious of "schismatic" or "dissenter" sects, so the Methodists encountered white hostility and the legislative Assembly of Jamaica charged them with communicating "dark and dangerous fanaticism."

George Lisle appealed to the British Baptist Society for assistance in his movement, and a missionary was sent out in 1814. The Baptists concentrated almost exclusively on estate slaves and expanded rapidly by continuing to follow Lisle's leader-class system. They quickly became the most popular and influential mission, and this was due in large measure to their concern for the material as well as the spiritual welfare of the slaves.

Jamaican planters tried to counter the influence of the "dangerous" Baptists by calling for missionization from more conservative churches. The Assembly began to pay Anglican curates for the instruction of slaves in 1816 and it provided an annual grant for missionaries from the Church of Scotland who arrived in 1819, but these churches had far less success with the slaves than the Baptists. Their form of worship was too staid or unemotional, their requirements for membership were too stringent, and they were too closely allied with the white power structure.

There were many reasons for conversion to Christianity, such as the group support and fellowship provided by classes and the prestige and influence of being a class leader, but one of the most important was a desire to identify with white society. The free colored, in particular, hoped to gain respect and acceptance from whites. Reading and writing could be learned in the mission schools, and literacy often led to occupational and social mobility. An especially strong value was placed on the rite of baptism. After this "rebirth," a convert could take a new name and expect to be treated differently. Baptism was also seen as an initiation into the cult of the masters, a way of gaining access to their power. Slaves commonly regarded it, and the membership tickets issued by the Baptists, as protection against Obeah.

Many of the converts accepted Christianity as a supplement, rather than as an alternative, to their own traditions, and freely mixed them together. Christianity took on a more pragmatic and this-worldly character in the hands of slaves with the use of the Bible, the cross, and baptism for protection from spirits and Obeah. Christian deities and biblical figures such as angels and John the Baptist were added to the pantheon of Myalism, and sectarian titles such as deacon and evangelist were adopted by cults. Sin and sorcery were equated and ceremonial possession was identified as a manifestation of the Holy Spirit. On the other hand, puritanical standards of moral conduct, avoidance of "worldly" pleasures, the innate depravity of man, and eternal damnation were alien notions that were less readily adopted. This superficial or incomplete assimilation of Christianity, characterized by syncretisms and reinterpretations, has persisted to the present because the popularity of mission Christianity was short-lived, and waned not long after emancipation.

Missionization coincided with a period of economic decline on the estates, many of which had to be sold to cover debts. An act of England's Parliament brought the slave trade to an end in 1808, and the Crown embarked on a program of "amelioration" or reform to improve the lot of slaves. Jamaican planters were angered by these changes, which they saw as threats to their fortunes and livelihood, and strongly resisted reform, fearing that it would incite revolts and lead to emancipation.

In 1823 the Baptist and Methodist churches decided to support the antislavery movement, and this led to a rapid growth in the number of converts as their missionaries frequently interceded on behalf of the slaves. The slaves' expectation for change was greatly increased, and they seized on Christian ideology as a religious rationale for their freedom struggle. Slaves could easily identify with the suffering of Jesus at the hands of Roman conquerors and readily equate their bondage and servitude with the Hebrew captivity and deliverance from Egypt, but the most appealing notions of Christianity were the brotherhood of all men and the equality of everyone before God.

Missionary support for the antislavery movement led the planters to insult and abuse them, bar them from their estates, and punish converts. In addition, the Assembly passed several laws to restrict missionaries. During the 1820s gangs of white rowdies broke up sectarian services and damaged chapels. The slaves' hopes and the planters' fears were heightened by the granting of full civil rights to the free colored in 1830 and by the progress of emancipation legislation in Parliament in 1831. Jamaican whites held public protest meetings across the island, with some advocating an alliance with the United States to preserve slavery.

During 1831 there was a rumor among the slaves that the king had issued a "free paper," which was being withheld by their masters. A Baptist deacon and Native Baptist "Daddy" called Sam Sharpe preached that God was the one true master, and that Jesus said, "No man can serve two masters." Gambling that the king's troops would not oppose it, he used the missionary class system to organize a general strike of estate slaves. Sharpe's followers swore on a Bible that they would not return to work after the Christmas holiday until they received freedom and fair wages, but others took military titles, organized regiments, and gathered arms (Reckord 1969).

The strike quickly turned to serious revolt in the western parishes, involving 20,000 slaves. Estates were raided and burned and several skirmishes were fought with the militia, but lack of communication and coordination among the slaves allowed the militia to speedily regain control. At least 207 slaves were killed and many of their houses burned. Afterward, 626 slaves were tried and 312 of them executed. Then the whites turned their ire on the missionaries, blaming them for the "Baptist War." Several missionaries were arrested, and vigilante groups led by an Anglican minister waged a nightrider campaign against the Methodists and Baptists, destroying seventeen chapels, hanging missionaries in effigy, and firing volleys into their homes at night.

The excessive white reaction to the revolt hastened emancipation. Baptist missionaries met in Kingston in 1832 to formally declare their opposition to slavery, and then sent representatives to England, where their stories of planter atrocities and persecution led to public outrage that helped to move Parliament to pass an Emancipation Act in 1833.

The slaves were to endure six years of "apprenticeship" before receiving full freedom, but abuse and exploitation of slaves was widespread during this period, and even though Parliament brought it to an early end in 1838 the problem continued. The freedmen had to work on the estates and pay often exorbitant rents to retain their homes and provision grounds, which were sometimes destroyed, and many of them were evicted. A third of the sugar estates went under by 1847, resulting in increasing unemployment and declining wages. Some freedmen left the estates for the towns, but there were not enough jobs in trade or industry to accommodate them, and the towns were soon overcrowded, ridden by disease and malnutrition, and occupied by "dissolute idlers, loafers, and vagabonds" (Sewell 1862:203).

However, as many as 30 percent of the freedmen took up small-scale cultivation, often in the mountainous and largely uninhabited interior, where a prosperous and independent peasantry quickly developed. According to one observer, they could earn as much in a month's work on their own properties as in a year of labor on a sugar estate (Sewell 1862:176). The geographic separation and economic independence of the peasants from white society also led to a separate society and culture. As Philip Curtin (1955:116) has noted, "There were more clearly than ever two different Jamaicas—the planters' Jamaica of the coastal plains and inland valleys, and the settlers' Jamaica of the mountain freeholds."

The planters viewed the development of a peasantry as an economic and political threat, so the Assembly passed a number of oppressive laws between 1838 and 1865 to drive freedmen back to estate labor. Peasants were burdened with taxes and harassed by the police, freedmen received excessive punishments for minor offenses, flogging and the treadmill were reintroduced, and tax requirements were used to reduce the number of black voters, but these measures only served to further alienate freedmen from white society (Knox 1977).

There was a dramatic increase in converts during the decade after freedom because of the churches' support for emancipation. A Toleration Act gave missionaries greater freedom to evangelize and their persecution generally ceased. They worked hard on the freedmen's behalf, intervening in wage disputes and conflicts with employers, lobbying for black civil rights, and establishing medical and educational facilities. However, as Table 6.1 indicates, their popularity soon waned. Converts were lost because the missionaries imposed increasingly demanding moral expectations and they refused to give converts greater control over their congregations. In addition, the increasing geographic and economic separation of black and white probably encouraged religious separatism. As the special alliance of the missions with their black population wore thin, many freedmen turned to their own religious leaders and syncretic traditions.

Between 1841 and 1865 over 8,000 Africans who had been taken from slave

Table 6.1
Membership in Dissenting Sects, 1800–1865

	Moravians	Methodists	Baptists	Presbyterians
1800-04	938	520		
1805-09		832		
1810-14	2,282			
1815-19		5,487	2,000	
1820-24	2,300	7,060		
1825-29		12,000	5,246	70
1830-34	4,496	13,000	10,380	
1835-39	9,913	20,000	14,000	
1840-44	5,000	27,000	33,658	7,000
1845-49		21,176		
1850-54	4,182	19,554		
1855-59		16,636	19,300	
1860-64	4,460	17,575		
1865		18,105	22,000	5,124

(Data from Brathwaite 1971, Gardner 1909, Hastings and McLeavy 1979, Patterson 1973, Phillippo 1843, Robotham 1981)

ships by the British were brought to Jamaica as indentured servants. Because they resisted acculturation to Creole society and maintained a separate identity, their religion, Kumina, persisted and it is still widely practiced in the parish of St. Thomas today (Schuler 1980). Kumina is an ancestor cult or family religion, and membership is based on inheritance. The indigenous traditions of Obeah and Myalism, and more recently, Revival, have had a small influence on it, but it is still largely an African rather than a syncretic tradition. Kumina ceremonies focus on the dead, particularly in burials and memorial rites, where ancestral spirits or "nkuyu" are entertained with music and dance and fed in exchange for their knowledge, guidance, and power, which are transmitted through ritual possession (Brathwaite 1978; Ryman 1984). The introduction of Kumina at a time when freedmen were turning from the missions could have served to reinfuse the African element of the evolving Creole religious tradition.

The 1840s and 1850s were decades of despair. Severe droughts ruined peasant harvests in 1839, 1841, 1844, and 1846, and hundreds of sugar and coffee estates closed. Indentured servants began to arrive from India in 1845, competing with black labor and driving wages down. The percentage of gainfully employed blacks declined from 62 percent of the working age population in 1844 to 42 percent in 1871. Public sanitation was virtually nonexistent, and the poor and rural populations had very little access to physicians. Serious diseases were rampant, with cholera killing up to 30,000 in 1849–50.

The widespread misfortune of the times was blamed on Obeah and duppies, and fear of them reached epidemic proportions. There was a resurgence of Myalism, with more Christian elements, as people returned to their thaumaturgical traditions to cope with distress. The Myalists or "angel men" claimed to be on a millenarian mission from God to cleanse the land of Obeah and call the people to prayer before Christ's return. They were strict and moralistic like the missions, abstaining from drink and excluding those known for bad lives. Myalists equated sin with sorcery and used the Bible as a charm to combat spirits. During the day, they would sing and dance, sprinkle a bush juice called "the weed" on bystanders to convert them, and use a talisman called an "amber" to see Obeah in the ground or beneath the skin. At night, Myalists sacrificed fowl and performed the Myal Dance until they fell into violent trances involving rapid spinning, tree climbing, self-flagellation, and running through the bush. They sought divine guidance in dreams, visions, and glossolalic utterances, and used them to recover lost shadows and identify obeahmen, who were caught, beaten, and forced to confess and repent.

Myal cultism led to an antisorcery movement on the north coast, where estate laborers refused to work until Obeah had been dug up. The "Great Myal Procession" of 1841 began when Myalists were called to an estate near Montego Bay in December to cleanse it of Obeah following some inexplicable deaths. Myalist exorcisms were held on at least nineteen more estates in St. James in the summer and fall of 1842, and the movement spread to Trelawny and perhaps Westmoreland in October. It was temporarily curbed by the arrest of some Myalists, but reappeared on an estate in Trelawny in 1845 and in Manchester and Clarendon in 1848, 1849, and 1852.

THE EMERGENCE OF REVIVAL

By 1860 the native cults had become more influential than the Christian missions. To counter this, the Baptists intensified their evangelism and held special fasting and prayer meetings, promising that God would soon visit Jamaica. The "Great Revival" began in a Moravian congregation in Hanover, from which it spread "like a tidal wave" across the island: "Men and women . . . were actually stricken down while working in their homes or fields . . . and would run to their ministers . . . overwhelmed with grief, ejaculating the one word, 'Sin! Sin!' repeatedly, as the prelude to some confession of disgraceful conduct" (Henderson 1931:104). Many couples who had been "living in sin" were married and 37,000 Bibles were sold in eighteen months. As Gardner (1909:466) relates, "Evil habits were abandoned. The rum shops were forsaken by multitudes, and thousands were added to the different congregations."

The Great Revival took on an increasingly ecstatic form in areas of Native Baptist influence, and it turned into a myalistic movement in 1861. There were processions with singing and drumming from one village to another. Angels possessed dancers, sometimes causing them to fall prostrate on the floor and giving them the powers of prophecy, divination, and curing. Obeah was dug up and obeahmen identified. The missionaries were shocked by this "wild extravagance and almost blasphemous fanaticism" (Gardner 1909:467) and rejected the movement. Many members of the missionary sects joined the Myalists and Native Baptists, leading to a new and more Christian Creole religion called Revival, which became the popular religion of Jamaica.

Revival is fundamentally an African religion. It is unabashedly spiritual, and the focus of its ceremonies is ritual possession by a pantheon of intermediary deities who bear messages and bring power from God. Revival seals, which hold offerings to spirits, are probably derived from African shrines. Singing, dancing, and polyrhythmic drumming are the key elements of worship. Mortuary rites are of great concern, and the dead must be honored and placated. There is a pragmatic emphasis on illness and misfortune, which are seen as spiritual problems, and this is reflected particularly in the practice of Balm.

The African foundation of Revival comes from Myalism, which, for example, carried on the African tradition of herbalism that is still found in Balm. The most conspicuous element of Myalism in Revival is its antagonism to duppies and sorcery. The rapid spinning of Myalists in trance during the 1850s is still common in Revival ceremonies today. Myalist syncretisms, such as use of the Bible for protection from spirits and a pantheon of Christian figures—John the Baptist, the disciples, prophets, and angels—who replaced African gods in name but not in form or function, were incorporated into Revival.

The shouting ritual, a very distinctive element of Revival, is one of many "ring dances," based on African tradition, that are still popular in Jamaica. It is probably a derivation of the Myal Dance, which was initially part of a rite of passage into rebel conspiracies and later used to bring on possession to locate Obeah and identify obeahmen. Shouting also seems to be a symbolic reflection of the field slave's experience. The Armor Bearer in a Revival cult acts as the "overseer" for the ritual, singing to set the tempo and calling out "orders" to the "bands" of "workers," who dance in unison, swinging their arms vigorously and going through stages that include "cutting and clearing," "flogging the banner," "laboring," "drilling," and "signing the orders." Similar dances were performed by American slaves, who called them "shouts," and they may have been brought to Jamaica by black Americans such as George Lisle.

The Revival practices of river baptism and anointing the sick with oils began in the Black Baptist church of George Lisle. Many elements of Revival originated with the Native Baptist cults that broke away from Lisle's movement, such as reliance on dreams and visions for spiritual guidance, a weekly fast, animal sacrifice, prophecy, the leadership titles of "Daddy" and "Mother," and the belief that baptism provides protection from Obeah. The processions of 1861 may have led to the current practice of marching and singing to the tune of drums in rural areas on Easter, but this seems to be the only specific contribution of the Great Revival.

The real importance of the Great Revival was that it redefined Creole religion—the Myalists and Native Baptists—as Christianity and led to a rather complete adoption of Christian beliefs and practices without abandoning the African foundation. Today, revivalists do not recognize that much of their faith is derived from Africa or the syncretic cults of slavery. They think they are true Christians, in fact better Christians than the members of denominations, which they refer to derisively as "nominal" churches. Gilead's building is very similar to that of an orthodox Christian church, the annual round of services is based on the Christian calendar, the order of service is derived from the Church of England, many of their hymns come from the Baptists and the Methodists, and titles such as deacon and elder are obviously Christian. Unorthodox elements such as seals and shouting are said to be based on instructions from God received in dreams and trance.

Although the basic structure of Revival was formulated in 1861, the cult continued to evolve until about 1930, sometimes as a result of foreign influences but more often because of innovative leaders and changing social conditions, and it also spawned some new movements.

TRANSFORMATIONS OF REVIVAL

Jamaican cults are basically thaumaturgical but they have a latent capacity for militancy and violence. Obeah was transformed into the revolutionary secret society of Myalism in 1760, the Native Baptist movement erupted in violence in the Baptist War of 1831, and the Myalist movement of the 1840s had

revolutionary undertones. Three decades of hard times and oppressive government set the stage for a tragic confrontation involving Native Baptists in the
Morant Bay Rebellion of 1865.

According to a visitor to Jamaica in the early 1860s, "the people . . . are not
cared for; they perish miserably in country districts for want of medical aid; they
are not instructed; they have no opportunities to improve themselves . . . ; every
effort is made to check a spirit of independence" (Sewell 1862:178). In 1865
the Baptists sent a letter to the colonial office protesting the callousness of the
island's administrators and their lack of assistance to the poor. This encouraged
peasants to write an appeal for Crown lands to Queen Victoria, but she merely
advised them to show "industry and patience."

Lack of response to several peaceful appeals led Paul Bogle, a Native Baptist
deacon in St. Thomas, to take a more confrontational approach. In October
of 1865, he marched into Morant Bay with two hundred men to observe the
trial of one of his followers, and they had to flee after one of them caused a
disruption in the court. A force of constables was sent to arrest Bogle and
twenty-seven of his men, but it was overcome by a mob. Bogle then marched
on Morant Bay, where he fought a battle with the militia and burned the
courthouse. Fifteen whites, including the custos (the chief magistrate for the
parish) and some magistrates, were killed and thirty-one wounded. Later, several
plantations were plundered and three planters killed. The governor declared
martial law and encircled the parish with troops, who burned over a thousand
homes and killed eighty-five blacks in the ten days of the uprising. Bogle and
354 others were executed and six hundred were flogged.

The Assembly abolished itself in 1865 to prevent blacks from gaining elective
office, and a Crown Colony government was appointed in 1866. The brutal
suppression of the rebellion and reforms instituted by a new governor served to
prevent militant action for many years to come, but living conditions saw no
real improvement. Agricultural employment declined greatly while the population grew.

Revival, and particularly faith healing, flourished from the 1870s through the
1920s. Stewart the "Haddo Doctor" was a popular revivalist around 1880 who
claimed that Christ had given him the power to heal. Thousands came to his
balmyard in Westmoreland for healing and to participate in nightly revival
meetings, where they danced in a ring and sang Salvation Army choruses.

Salvation Army officers came from England in 1887, but fled a year later after
attacks by hooligans. Their work was carried on energetically by a charismatic
white, Raglan Phillips, who by 1894 had 123 officers and 8,000 followers. In
1906, while serving as an evangelist in Baptist churches, Phillips was involved
in a spectacular revival movement in which faith healing and speaking in tongues
were prominent. He instigated a similar revival in 1924 and established an
independent church called City Mission, which was initially a blend of the
Salvation Army, the Baptists, and Revival, but is now a local Pentecostal sect
(Calley 1965:159–60).

In 1896 Myalism reappeared in the parish of Hanover in the guise of "Convinced Doctors," who said they were called by God to deliver "the oppressed negroes of the island . . . from the slavery and oppression of the white doctors and parsons" (Elkins 1977:4). They sought out Obeah, removed spells, and cured the sick with blessed water. In the same year a revival broke out in Quaker missions in Portland, where Revival "Shepherds" were erecting "booths." Crowds of people flocked to their healing springs for "Jesus Medicine," and "bands" danced ecstatically until some fell unconscious and were cared for by Revival "nurses" (Bowles 1900:90–92).

A branch of the Christian Catholic church of Chicago, commonly called Zion, was established in 1896, and the Church of God came from Toronto in 1904. These "full gospel" Holiness churches used prayer, anointing with olive oil, and the laying on of hands to heal the sick. They promised an instant cleansing from sin through the baptism of the Holy Spirit and proscribed the use of medicines and tobacco, eating pork, wearing jewelry, and drinking alcohol, coffee, and tea.

The Holiness sects stimulated religious activity and encouraged new innovations. A nomadic group of revivalists who spoke in tongues, required multiple baptisms, prophesied doom, and called themselves "Zions" was reported in Manchester, St. Catherine, and Port Antonio in 1905. In 1909 another new revivalist group called Pocomania appeared in St. Mary. In the frenzy of meetings, they were said to tear their hair, beat their breasts, utter barking sounds, and cut their bodies with pieces of tin to gain remission from sins.

This ecstatic thaumaturgy sometimes included militant rhetoric and defiance. The Rev. Captain "Warrior" Higgins was a colorful revivalist of the 1890s who led processions in Kingston that often ended in violent clashes with gangs and the police. He used the Hope River near Kingston to baptize converts into his "Millennium Band" and gave herb tonics to patients at his "Millennium Hospital." Higgins denounced the churches, the pope, judges, and ministers. He called the Anglican bishop a "damn lazy idle dog" and threatened to marry a white lady so white people would want to cut their throats. He declared that "white men murdered the son of God" and were damned for it, and said people should only obey Christ.

Solomon Hewitt and "Doctor" David Bell were popular revivalists in 1914. Hewitt staged a mock crucifixion in Kingston and "arose from the dead" on Easter. Bell wore colorful vestments of red, green, and yellow with spangles, beads, and brilliants, and said he had been resurrected by God to preach and heal. His followers carried flags and marched to the tune of "Onward Christian Soldiers." At Bell's "Faith Healing Church of God" in May Pen there was an eternal flame, kept alive by "Vestal Maidens," and a deep pit of healing mud, which was dispensed to thousands of patients.

Bell and Hewitt preached against whites, the colonial government, and the clergy. Bell said whites were "all liars, thieves, hypocrites" and claimed the Spirit had told him to inform the king of "the misrule that is taking place in

Jamaica." Hewitt stood in front of a police station and called on God to destroy it with lightning and thunder. They preached that Judgment Day was imminent and that their opponents would be punished with fire and brimstone. Both were arrested, and Bell was committed to the lunatic asylum.

The increasingly militant tone of revivalists was echoed by promoters of socialism and black nationalism. Isaac Brown or "Prince Makarooroo" urged Jamaicans to unite and strike for higher wages and refuse to pay taxes. J. L. TaBois predicted a world revolution when "all mortgages and debts would be repudiated, the poor would take over the property of the landlords, and a heavenly kingdom would be established on earth" (Elkins 1977:63). There were several strikes and violent demonstrations between 1917 and 1919, and many unions, cooperatives, and political clubs were formed, including the United Negro Improvement Association of Marcus Garvey.

In 1917 Jamaica was a society "where extreme poverty and misery reign . . . where so many human beings are paid starvation wages and are treated worse than animals. The ruling class . . . leads an excellent and elegant social life but has . . . little interest in the welfare of the negroes" (quoted in A. Brown 1979:94). About 70 percent of the population suffered from hookworm, and 3.3 percent died from influenza in 1918 (Eisner 1974:138, 342). The popularity of religious healers was based on the poor health of the people, and their deprivation and despair were conducive to the rise of another major religious movement, led by the healer and prophet Alexander Bedward.

Bedward was working in Panama in 1885 when the "Son of God" appeared in two dreams and told him to return to Jamaica to "save your own soul and be the means of saving many others." After returning to Kingston he became an elder in a movement led by a prophet called Shakespeare, who told his followers that "a fountain would be opened in August Town, but that the man to rule it was not yet ready." Bedward received this calling in a vision in 1891, when a spirit told him to fast and pray three times a week and use the waters of the Hope River to heal the body and soul.

Bedward followed the Revival tradition but adopted some Salvation Army practices, including drumming and street meetings. He called himself a "Shepherd" and appointed "Mothers" and "station guards," which are Revival offices, but he also named pastors, elders, and evangelists and was ordained as a bishop, following the apostolic pattern of Christianity. His followers fasted from midnight until noon to purify their souls and held a Communion Table on Mondays, Wednesdays, and Fridays. On Wednesdays Bedward would preach at the Hope River, bless the water, and invite the crowd, which numbered up to 12,000 in 1893, to drink or bathe in it and be cured. In 1894 he built a chapel in August Town, and his Jamaica Native Baptist Free Church developed into a movement with about 7,000 followers as pilgrims carried jugs of his healing water throughout the island and established Bedwardite camps.

In 1895 Bedward was arrested on a charge of seditious language after saying that "the Governor and Council pass laws to oppress the black people" and

Creole Religion in Jamaica   111

calling on blacks to "remember the Morant War" and "rise and crush the white people," but he was acquitted by reason of insanity. Imprisonment made him a martyr and the trial spread his fame. People began to say "Jesus is our King and Alexander Bedward is prince," and after his release he proclaimed "the end of the law" and announced that "Jesus is going to burst the prison and mash the asylum and do away with all the churches."

Following a great earthquake and fire in Kingston in 1907, which killed one thousand people, Bedwardites paraded through the streets, the women dressed in white, saying it was a warning of the imminence of Judgment Day. Between 1912 and 1920, a series of hurricanes and the Great War served to punctuate this apocalyptic message and add momentum to his movement. In 1920 Bedward claimed to be Jesus Christ, and said he would bring the world to an end because his ministers were not allowed to perform marriages. He announced that he would ascend to heaven in a flaming chariot on December 31, but return for his followers in three days and carry them into glory before raining down fire on the world. The white race would be destroyed and there would be a new heaven and earth in which blacks would become white and Bedwardism would reign for a millennium. Thousands quit their jobs, gave away their possessions, and gathered in August Town to witness his ascent and become part of his new kingdom, but when the appointed time passed and nothing happened he told them it had been postponed. After three more tries, he proclaimed a "spiritual" ascension and said God had commanded him to stay on earth for another seventeen years. In 1921 the government challenged Bedward's land titles and ordered his eviction. He called for a six-mile march on Kingston "to do battle" with his enemies, but was arrested along the way. After his trial, he was again sent to the lunatic asylum, where he died in 1930, and his movement disintegrated.

One of the consequences of this period following the Great Revival is that healing or Balm became a major emphasis of Revival. It is practiced by at least half of the cults today, and in some cases is their only purpose. Balm is a combination of African herbalism, Myalist spiritism, and Holiness faith healing. Balmists rely on spiritual guidance, combat malevolent spirits, pray, and lay hands on the sick, and, like Bedward and Higgins, offer consecrated water and herbal concoctions. Magical powders, oils, candles, incense, fragrances, and prayers, which are inspired by an American mail-order house called De Laurence, were added to Balm before 1955, and patent medicines have also become popular in recent years.

Although the Salvation Army never gained a large following in Jamaica, it did have a strong influence on Revival, which borrowed uniforms, musical bands, marches, banners, and choruses from it. The Revival office of "Captain" may come from the Army, and revivalists also followed the Army's practice of allowing women to become officers.

Throughout the course of Jamaican history, new cults arose by combining African-derived Creole traditions with imported Christian ones, but City Mission was probably the first to be incorporated and gain legal recognition. Originally a synthesis of Revival with the Baptist religion and the Salvation Army, it became a local sect of Christianity with the right to ordain ministers, establish branches, and perform marriages and funerals. Many Revival cults have followed a similar path in recent years by affiliating with American sects and denominations such as the African Methodist Episcopal (AME) Zion Church and the National Baptists. This has had little effect on the actual practice of Revival, but it has given it greater respectability and some legal privileges. A significant new development took place in 1983, with the encouragement of the prime minister, when a national sect, the Afro-Zion Revival Church of Jamaica, was established.

Revival has given rise to some new cults, including Convince, which is probably defunct, and Pocomania, which is still being practiced. Pocomania cults have a stronger element of Myalism than Revival cults. They are often associated with Obeah because they invoke "ground spirits," including duppies and "fallen angels," and frequently engage in exorcism. Pocomania is essentially amoral, and rum and marijuana are used in services. The music of Pocomania follows different beats than Revival, and worship is more ecstatic or frenzied. There is more male involvement and the leaders, who are called Shepherds, are usually male (Seaga 1969). In contrast, about half of all Revival leaders are women or "Mothers."

Bedward is revered as a prophet by many revivalists, who share his apocalyptic and millenarian ideas and believe they are living "in the last days" before the Second Coming of Christ, which they expect in the year 2000. Some elements of Bedwardism that have been incorporated into Revival are feast tables, healing water, fasting, the symbol of a shepherd's staff, and white gowns worn by the women.

The anti-establishment, anti-church, and anti-white rhetoric of Revival leaders such as Stewart, Higgins, Bell, and Bedward is not generally found in Revival today, but it was inherited by the Rastafarians, a messianic cult that began in St. Thomas in 1933 during the Great Depression. Rastafarianism is based on the belief that Haile Selassie, the former emperor of Ethiopia, was a living god and messiah for black people and would return all "exiled" Africans to their homeland. Rastafarians believe in black supremacy and look for an apocalyptic upheaval that will transfer power from whites to blacks.

Rastafarianism is an example of "Ethiopianism," the identification of black people in the New World with their African "homeland," which has been popular in Jamaica during this century. Isaac Brown in 1904 and "Prince" Shervington in 1924 caused stirs when each claimed to be heir to the throne of Abyssinia. Marcus Garvey launched his United Negro Improvement Association in Jamaica in 1914, a "Hamitic Church" was established in 1925, a cult called the "Israelites" appeared in 1930, and several Ethiopian organizations were founded in 1933. Ethiopianism reached its height in the 1930s with the coronation of Selassie in 1930 and the Italo-Ethiopian war of 1935–36.

It is commonly believed that the founders and initial followers of Rastafarianism were Garveyites, but some of them were also Bedwardites (Hill 1983:38).
The Rastafarian belief in the apocalyptic destruction of the white race and a
subsequent black millennium was first enunciated by Bedward, and many elements of the cult, such as its music, banners, and garments, seem to be derived
from Revival cultism. Rastafarians, like revivalists, look principally to the Old
Testament for guidance, and for this reason are sometimes referred to as "Black
Jews," but they rely on the smoking of marijuana for inspiration and do not
practice spirit possession.

Rastafarianism is not really a rival of Revival, but Pentecostalism is. Pentecostalism has grown dramatically over the past three decades, and it is now the
most popular religion in Jamaica. Pentecostalism developed in an entirely different socioeconomic context than Revival—a period of rapid growth, material
progress, and independence—and it has been more successful at attracting the
middle class.

There are many contrasts between Revival and Pentecostalism. Spiritual experience is important in both of them, but Pentecostal possession is attributed
to the Holy Ghost while revivalists are possessed by "angels" too. Revivalists
recognize a wide range of spiritual experiences, but Pentecostals focus on speaking in tongues. Healing is regularly practiced by both religions, but Pentecostals
rely solely on prayer and the laying on of hands. Pentecostal ideology is also
much more Jesucentric and New Testament–oriented.

Although Pentecostalism came from America, it has taken on a different
character in Jamaica, where music and dance dominate services and build a
rhythm that leads to widespread ecstasy and communitas. This is probably due
to the influence of Revival in particular and the African heritage in general.
Despite their rivalry, which is sometimes hostile, Revival and Pentecostal congregations often meet together in church "conventions" and "rallies." Gilead's
pastor was, in fact, ordained by a Pentecostal sect.

The practice of Balm will probably persist for some time, but Revival cultism
is slowly waning and Pentecostalism is its successor. Revival cults are being
"pentecostalized": electric guitars are replacing drums, Pentecostal choruses are
quite popular, speaking in tongues is becoming more common, altar calls and
testimonies have been incorporated into Revival services, and some Revival
cults have affiliated with Pentecostal sects. Another indication of the imminent
demise of Revival is that its traditions are now commonly performed by professional dance, theater, and folk-singing groups. However, Revival has had a
strong influence on Rastafarianism and Pentecostalism, the most important
movements in Jamaica today, and it will live on through them.

PATTERNS AND PROCESSES IN THE EVOLUTION OF
CREOLE RELIGION

Although the basic structure of Revival is African and much of its content
comes from Christianity, it is somewhat misleading to simply regard it as an

Afro-Christian syncretism. Revival was actually based on indigenous transformations of African traditions, such as Obeah and Myalism, and of Christianity, such as the Black Baptists and Native Baptists, and it evolved as an adaptation to local conditions. Jamaica is a Creole society—that is, the product of a plantation colony and a master-slave relationship between white and black—and Revival is a Creole religion, a creation of Creole society.

It is also simplistic to think of religious evolution only in cultural terms, as retentions, reinterpretations, or syncretisms of various traditions. Jamaican religions are ways in which people have adjusted to—made sense of and coped with—chronic and immediate problems such as the subjugation of slavery, natural disasters, poor health, political alienation and oppression, and chronic deprivation. Many different types of cults and movements—nativistic, millenarian, redemptive, thaumaturgical, and separatist—have developed in Jamaica. They have brought hope, provided occasions for catharsis, healed the sick, unified people, and pressured governing powers.

Religious cults are often considered to be psychological palliatives, offering ritual and symbolic release and relief, and their revolutionary potential is frequently underestimated. Religion has been the main vehicle for the expression of distress and discontent throughout Jamaican history. Jamaican cults have always been the core of an indigenous black counterculture, attracting large numbers of people who were alienated from, and often hostile to, the institutions imposed on them by white society and the colonial government, and social discontent and anti-establishment views are still being expressed in Jamaican religion, particularly in Rastafarianism but also in Pentecostalism.

Most episodes of unrest in Jamaican history, until the advent of political parties and trade unions in the 1920s, were associated with religious cults, which not only met religious needs but also served as protopolitical organizations. Jamaican cults have often resulted in mass movements that challenged and disrupted the status quo, and they have also led to revolts and rebellions. The Native Baptists, for example, were the nucleus for the Baptist War of 1831 and the Morant Bay Rebellion of 1865, and the militant rhetoric of Revival leaders from the 1890s to the 1920s helped to set the stage for a great deal of political unrest in the 1930s and 1940s.

Jamaican cults are dynamic, and their character has often changed as they responded to pressing conditions of the times such as sickness and despair or reacted to events such as earthquakes and emancipation. Rastafarianism, for example, has been called a millenarian movement, a messianic movement, a nativistic cult, an "escapist-adjustive" cult, and a separatist sect and, indeed, it has been each of these in different periods. Myalism began as a nativistic society to plan slave revolts, but it later became a thaumaturgical antisorcery cult. Bedwardism was a healing cult that developed into a separatist sect, then became a millenarian movement.

Cults and movements are phases in an evolutionary process. Each Jamaican movement was born from one or more existing cult or sect, and it resulted in a new cult. Cults and sects are the nuclei from which movements grow, and movements transform cults. Cults and sects are hearths of innovation, reinterpretation, and syncretism. The multiplicity of cults and sects in Jamaica has provided a pool of variation from which new adaptations have been selected. Christianity simply added to this variation and stimulated new innovations. Widespread distress due to social conditions or natural disasters has been a catalyst for change, transforming cults and sects into mass movements. Movements have served as vehicles for the spread of cult innovations, establishing them as new traditions.

Cults and movements have been a regular feature of Jamaican society throughout its history, and most if not all of them clearly fall into the category of "revitalization movements," which Anthony F. C. Wallace (1956:265) defined as "a deliberate, organized, conscious effort by members of a society to construct a more satisfying culture." The continual transformation of cults and the frequent emergence of new ones in Jamaica is due to the fact that the society has been in a perennial state of crisis and cultural distortion.

Revitalization movements are often engendered by culture-contact situations, and one of their functions in this situation is to reduce the dissonance of conflicting traditions, either by rejecting an alien culture or by assimilating it into native tradition. For the most part, Jamaican religions assimilated Christianity even as they rejected it. Through a succession of cults and movements, an increasing amount of Christianity, and Western culture in general, has been woven into a local religion and culture derived from Africa and formulated during slavery. The evolution of Creole religion has progressively reduced the dissonance of the "two Jamaicas" of the plantation era, and it has been a central factor in the emergence of a distinctively Jamaican identity and culture.

A BIBLIOGRAPHIC NOTE

Virtually all of the information on contemporary Jamaican religion in this chapter is based on my own ethnographic fieldwork. The historical information comes from a great many sources. Direct quotes have, of course, been cited in the narrative, and references were also included if there was one major source for a particular topic, but in most cases my coverage of a subject was based on a variety of sources and it was not feasible to cite all of them in the text.

I have drawn on some overviews of Jamaican religion by Leonard E. Barrett (1974), Donald Hogg (1964), George E. Simpson (1978), and Joseph J. Williams (1932), and on African religion by Geoffrey Parrinder (1961), Benjamin C. Ray (1976), and Harold K. Schneider (1981). The main sources on Revival are Martha Warren Beckwith (1929), Barry Chevannes (1971), Edward Seaga (1969), and George E. Simpson (1956). Myalism is very thoroughly discussed by Monica Schuler (1979). There are several detailed accounts of the Moravians in Jamaica, including J. H. Buchner (1854), Oliver Furley (1965), S. U. Hastings and B. L. MacLeavy (1979), and Fred Linyard (1969). Most of the information on revivalists, cults, sects, and movements in the period 1880–1930 comes from W. F. Elkins (1977). A comprehensive account of Bedward is provided by Roscoe M. Pierson (1969).

Additional information on the topics above and other subjects such as Obeah, the Native Baptists, missionization and the Morant Bay Rebellion was obtained from Edward Brathwaite (1971), Philip D. Curtin (1970), William James Gardner (1909), Samuel J. Hurwitz and Edith F. Hurwitz (1977), A. J. G. Knox (1977), Orlando Patterson (1973), and James M. Phillippo (1843).

7

Tradition and Change in an Immigrant Chinese Church in California

LAWRENCE A. PALINKAS

Since the time of Sir James Frazer, anthropologists attempting to understand the human condition have repeatedly been drawn to the analysis of religion, that system of symbols that seems so often to form the core of a people's culture and ethos. As Clifford Geertz suggested a few years ago, religion establishes "powerful, pervasive, and long-lasting moods and motivations in men by formulating conceptions of a general order of existence and clothing these conceptions with such an aura of factuality that [they] seem uniquely realistic" (1973a:90). Religion fuses cognitive, emotional, and motivational factors in a symbolic system that often provides the foundation for meaningful life in social groups. Though there may be mystery (and mystification) in religion itself, then, there is no mystery in its significance for anthropological analysis.

Given the anthropological fascination with religion, however, there are still surprisingly few serious anthropological studies of Christianity, and especially few comparative studies of the religion as it has developed in distinct cultural contexts. This book is an attempt to meet a genuine need for more analyses of this type. In addition, we will abstract from the variety of cases presented here some general observations about the unique features of Christianity, the history of its propagation, and the dialectics of religious and cultural change.

Though now a major world religion, Christianity emerged some 2,000 years ago as a localized protest movement, a small-scale attempt to respond to the tensions of a particular historical moment and cultural milieu. The stresses that gave rise to early Christianity were generated partly in the culture conflict attendant on the spread of the Roman Empire, and partly by the internal dynamics of authority relations within the Jewish nation (Gager 1975). The content of the new religion was gradually developed, by Jesus and his followers, from ideas and symbols already extant in the Jewish tradition, from the flux of social relations in a troubled time, and from the psyches of individual actors. Rather than a static corpus of dogma, then, Christianity from its inception has

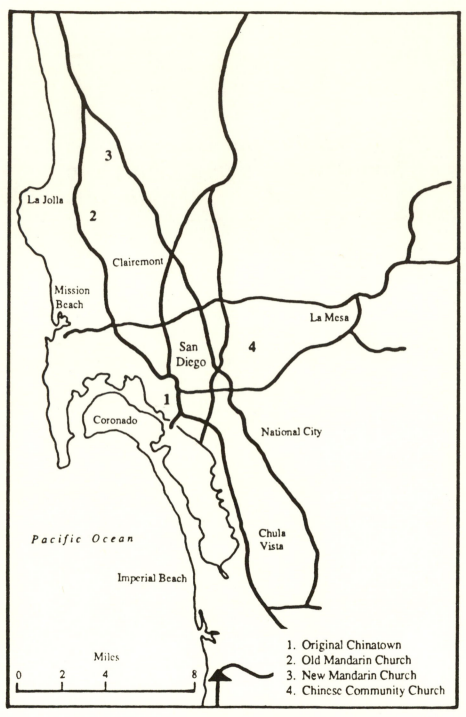

La Jolla

3

2

Clairemont

Mission
Beach

La Mesa

San
Diego

4

1

Coronado

National City

Pacific Ocean

Chula
Vista

Imperial Beach

Miles

0   2   4   8

1. Original Chinatown
2. Old Mandarin Church
3. New Mandarin Church
4. Chinese Community Church

San Diego, California

new belief system and world view. Many attend these churches for the express purpose of learning English. The emphasis, therefore, is more on adjusting to the present than maintaining continuity with the past. One would suspect, therefore, that Chinese Christian churches have historically been forces for change among Chinese immigrants.

Nevertheless, while Chinese Christian churches have been permanent fixtures of American Chinatowns since 1852, their impact on assimilation of Chinese immigrants into American society has been limited by several factors. As a focus for social interaction, the churches were overshadowed by an elaborate segmentary organization of voluntary associations. Christianity, which was deeply embedded in the cultural system of the West, was ideologically at odds with Chinese religious beliefs, a syncretic mixture of Buddhism, Confucianism, Taoism and folk religion. Many immigrants socialized under the latter belief system found it difficult to accept the tenets of Christianity. Moreover, the early Chinatown churches were dominated by white Protestant ministers, many of whom spoke little or no Chinese. Despite the good intentions of many of these ministers, the cultural differences, language barrier, and occasionally paternalistic attitude toward the immigrant combined to create a distance between pastor and potential convert. Finally, Chinese have traditionally viewed religion in pragmatic terms, worshipping ghosts and dead ancestors with the intention of promoting the welfare of the living or at least protecting oneself and one's family from misfortune. In the United States this pragmatism was extended to involvement in Christian churches. Many immigrants attended these churches to learn English but avoided attempts by ministers to convert them. To the extent that the Chinese Christian church often provided the only opportunity to learn English in a Chinatown setting, it may be considered an instrument for acculturation. Otherwise, its role in the process of sociocultural change was somewhat limited.

In the Chinese community of San Diego, California, however, we are confronted with religious institutions that approximate both the Catholic church of the European immigrants and the Christian church of the American Chinatown. The Chinese churches of San Diego present us with a fascinating case study of the transformation of Christianity to meet the needs of an immigrant community. These churches are distinguished by their seemingly contradictory roles as bastions of traditional culture, social relations, and ethnic identity and as agents for social change. They bear similarities to the Catholic churches of the European immigrants by preserving traditional forms of belief, social relations, and ethnic identity. They also display similarities to the model of the Chinatown church by providing the usual means for acculturation. In other respects, however, these churches have undergone certain transformations that are a response to the unique character of the Chinese community of San Diego. They have facilitated changes in social relations and cultural patterns by assisting in the dispersion of the Chinese community throughout the city and integrating this community into the larger society, while providing a substitute for the traditional kinship system where the social, cultural, and psychological conflicts experienced by immigrants are addressed and, to a certain extent, reduced or resolved.

This chapter examines these two aspects of the role of Chinese Christian churches in San Diego in the process of sociocultural change of Chinese immigrants. The first aspect has been chronicled in local historical records, while the second is examined using data gathered from fieldwork conducted in 1979–80 among Mandarin-speaking immigrants attending two Chinese churches. Specifically, I shall argue that Christianity has been transformed by the Chinese in San Diego in a way that enables it to be a force simultaneously for tradition and change.

THE CHINESE CHRISTIAN MISSION OF SAN DIEGO

To understand the transformations Chinese Christianity has undergone in San Diego, one must acknowledge the sociocultural context of the early Chinese Christian Mission. The Mission was called upon to play a role unlike that of its counterparts in other Chinese communities in California. I shall begin, therefore, with a brief outline of the history of the Chinese community of San Diego and its involvement with Christianity.

Although the city of San Diego has no distinct Chinatown today, from 1870 to the middle of the twentieth century the few local Chinese resided in a separate ethnic enclave in the downtown area. The first settlers of this enclave were fishermen (McEvoy 1977) who resided near the waterside in redwood shanties. The Chinese community grew considerably, however, when over a thousand laborers arrived to build the California Southern Railroad line from National City to Waterman [Barstow] (MacPhail 1977:10). Many of these laborers were involved in various construction projects in and around San Diego for the next two decades, but by the end of the century most had left and the Chinese population declined from a high of 1,000 in 1882 to 292 in 1900.

Although small in numbers, the Chinese community in the early twentieth century could be characterized as stable. In contrast to Chinatowns elsewhere, there was a small imbalance in the sex ratio of Chinese in San Diego and a greater percentage of families. In fact, by 1947, two-thirds of the community possessed the same surname (*San Diego Union* 2/16/1972:B2). Nevertheless, most of the early Chinese residents were male "sojourners." In other American Chinatowns, these sojourners would develop a hierarchy of voluntary associations (Crissman 1967; Weiss1974:146–47; Wong 1982). Two associations common to American Chinatowns and also found in San Diego were the Chinese Benevolent Association (CBA) and the tongs, secret societies modeled after the Triad society and other revolutionary organizations in southeastern China (Lyman 1974; Nee and Nee 1974). The tongs were known to have been quite active during the nineteenth and early twentieth centuries, providing protection to the sojourners and operating the gambling houses and opium dens as well as moving illegal Chinese immigrants from Mexico. The Chinese Benevolent Association represented the interests of the Chinese community to the larger society, heard grievances and settled disputes, and organized members to police the Chinatown district. Throughout its existence, the local CBA has served primarily as a social service agency as well as a political forum for the Chinese community of San Diego.

The pattern of leadership in the association and the Chinese community in general was similar to that found in other American Chinatowns in that the leaders were usually prosperous merchants. According to Judith Liu (1977:71), these men spoke English, which enabled them to interact with the non-Chinese community and represent Chinese interests. They also supplied goods and services to the Chinese, housed laborers, functioned as contractors and interpreters, and provided police services for the community. Two of the most prominent merchants and the founders of the two leading families of the Chinese community of San Diego were Ah Quin and Teung Hom. Ah Quin arrived in San Diego in 1878 and returned in 1880 as a labor contractor and foreman for a gang of Chinese laborers from San Francisco hired to work on the California Southern Railroad. He later owned a market in Chinatown and expanded into real estate and restaurant businesses (Griego 1979:324). Until his death in 1914, he was known as the "Mayor of Chinatown," a title assumed by his son, also a merchant, until his own death in 1937. Teung Hom came to San Diego from Canton in the 1890s. He was also a merchant and raised eight children. His descendants have provided the bulk of the leadership among the San Diego Chinese and one family member has even served as a state assemblyman. Both Ah Quin and Teung Hom as well as their descendants were Christians, making them "respectable" in the eyes of the non-Chinese community and putting them into contact with many of the prominent leaders of that community. Both men were able to exercise power and influence over the Chinese community in San Diego without recourse to the network of voluntary associations that constituted the power base of Chinese merchants elsewhere in the United States (Kwong 1984; Thompson 1979).

Despite the existence of the Chinese Benevolent Association and the tongs, the full complement of traditional voluntary associations was lacking. There is no record of either clan or district associations ever existing in San Diego, for example. Why this was the case is difficult to say. Judith Liu (1977) speculates that it was due to the small size of the community. The ability of the merchants to exercise leadership in the Chinese community without the support of the network of voluntary associations may also have been a factor. Perhaps the most significant factor, however, was the role of the Chinese Christian Mission in facilitating the adjustment of Chinese immigrants in San Diego and providing the necessary organization and services normally furnished by voluntary associations elsewhere.

In 1885 a local Chinese resident persuaded Dr. William C. Pond of the American Home Missionary Association of San Francisco to come to San Diego and establish a Chinese Mission school. The early Mission school provided several major services to the Chinese community. First and foremost was the opportunity to learn English and gain some insight into the intricacies of life in America. In the early days many Chinese young and old men found their way directly from China to the Mission because of their desire to learn the English language. Knowledge of English was of vital importance for anyone wishing to work for or carry on business with the non-Chinese community. The small size of the Chinese community precluded its isolation from the larger society as was the case in Chinatowns elsewhere. There were, of course, religious services as well. In addition to the regular Sunday services, which usually were conducted by a non-Chinese minister or deacon, there were devotional services every evening. All that was asked of the students was that they attend the services (Chinese Community Church Annual 1953).

The classes in English also put the Chinese into contact with the prominent members of the non-Chinese community who served as volunteer teachers. "They not only taught English but helped in solving the many problems facing the solitary and lonely men in a strange and often hostile land" (MacPhail 1977:11). In addition to aiding in the search for employment, this contact helped to minimize many of the severe consequences of discrimination and violence against the Chinese community that characterized Chinatowns elsewhere (Lyman 1970:22; Barth 1964).

Another important service provided by the early Mission was the housing of unmarried Chinese males. In 1907 the Mission moved into a new building that included a long dormitory containing tiny rooms that were rented to Chinese men. "The dormitory rooms were always filled to capacity with young men, mostly newcomers to San Diego and those recently arrived from China with no other place to go. It was an opportunity to meet other Chinese and to find employment" (MacPhail 1977:14). A new church and dormitory were built in 1927 and the Mission continued as a tong until 1959 when another new church was constructed in a different part of the city.

It was in this capacity that the Chinese Congregational Mission served as one of the major foci for social activities in Chinatown. Christians and non-Christians alike attended the many social events sponsored by the Mission. The Mission represented the interests of the entire Chinese community and could do so effectively because of its association with the prominent members of the non-Chinese community. This association also enabled the church to provide many of the community services, such as employment referrals, legal representation, housing, and food, which the Chinese Benevolent Association was unable to provide.

While many of the early Chinese in San Diego viewed the Mission school as purely a pragmatic device in aiding their own adjustment to life in the United States, there were also those who were affected by the religious message of the teachers and ministers. Several Chinese became baptized Christians as a result of their association with this Mission. An excellent account of such an early conversion experience is provided in a newspaper interview in 1899 with one Lee Hong, a local resident:

There were no missionaries near my home in China, so I had never heard of Jesus. I knew only the Confucius religion. When we went to the temple to worship, we did not ask God to give us a new and better heart, that we might love our God and our neighbors more. We did not think of God as a loving father whom we should worship, but as a far away spirit to be feared; and in His place we had many different idols, to whom we offered sacrifices and prayed for success and happiness. After I had been in California several years, I came to San Diego harbor on the U.S.S. Wolcott, and one day when I came ashore and was visiting in a Chinese store, a friend asked me to go to a mission school with him. I accepted the invitation, and when I left the ship later and remained on shore as the captain's family cook, I went to the mission school almost every day. The instructors there not only taught me English but also led me to see Jesus as the Savior, as the light of the World. The Chinese made fun of me, calling me a Jesus boy and many other names. After I was baptized by immersion they asked me if the water was wet, and many such foolish questions. I thought my father in China would not like it so I did not tell him for a long time, not until my cousin had told him. Then when I wrote to him that I was a Christian, he did not scold me. When they saw my photograph with my Queue off they called me a monk. I have now known Jesus as my Savior for five years. Before I felt the love of Him I only lived to earn money enough to return to China and make me a home here on earth, not thinking about the end, for there the mystery commences. Now I am spending all my money for an education that I may be of more service to Him. I am now in the sixth grade of the public school and my prayer is that I may earn money enough to carry me through college (*San Diego Union* 3/23/ 1899:5).

Many of the early converts to Christianity were the influential merchants and leaders of the Chinese community, as noted earlier. Even with the community's adherence to traditional beliefs and the occasional derision of converts as in the example just mentioned, the precedent set by the merchants may have made it more acceptable to attend the Mission, as it provided other Chinese with a model of successful adjustment to life in San Diego. These merchants stood in stark contrast to the merchants in other Chinatowns who preferred the leadership of the traditional voluntary associations and for the most part avoided the Christian churches and missions.

The involvement of the merchant leadership in the Chinese Congregational Mission was only one of the characteristics that distinguished the Chinese church in San Diego from its counterparts in other American Chinatowns. Elsewhere, Chinese Christian churches were numerous but their role in the Chinese communities was usually limited to providing instruction in English and a social organization for members of the community (women and children and those who did not belong to large and influential clan and district associations) denied access to power and influence in the hierarchy of traditional voluntary associations (Cayton and Lively 1955:59; Weiss 1974:95). According to Rose Hum Lee (1960:295–96), "Chinese women and children join churches more fre-

quently than males. Understandably, women join churches because they have
seen fewer possibilities than the men of attaining leadership in the Chinese
community." In San Diego, however, men were also involved in the Chinese
Congregational Mission, perhaps because of the absence of the clan and district
associations.

Another important difference is that the antipathy held by the Chinese Benevolent Association toward the Chinese churches in other communities (Cayton and Lively 1955:35) appears to have been relatively absent in San Diego.
This is most likely due to the fact that the leaders of the local CBA were usually
members of the Chinese Congregational Mission as well. This association proved
beneficial to both organizations and even today both serve as cosponsors for many
of the community activities for Chinese residents of San Diego.

Finally, in other Chinese communities, the desire to speak the language of
the host country was the predominant motive for church attendance and was
rarely transferred into a desire to convert to Christianity. As one observer wrote
in the nineteenth century: "They go to these schools solely to learn English. I
have heard Chinamen frequently say that they went to these places simply to
'catchee English.' They laugh at the idea of being converted to Christianity"
(Farwell 1885:100). While it is impossible to determine the extent of commitment to the new religious doctrine by the early Chinese converts in San Diego,
there does appear to have been a greater tolerance for and acceptance of Christian belief among the Chinese community as a whole in San Diego than was
the case in other American Chinatowns.

From 1890 to 1946 the Chinese Congregational Mission was supported financially by the Congregational Conference and was ministered by several
different Chinese pastors. In 1946 the Mission became a self-supporting church
and was renamed the Chinese Community Church to indicate its nondenominational status (MacPhail 1977:19). Services were held in Cantonese and English. A Ladies' Guild, Men's Club, Teenagers' Club, and a Married Couples'
Club were formed. Picnics and youth outings, and a vacation Bible school were
held in the summers.

Because of its transformation in San Diego as a focus for social organization,
the Chinese Community Church may be viewed as having played a major role
in the acculturation of Chinese immigrants. The dispersion of the Chinese
community throughout the city is a closely related phenomenon. While the
community at one point resembled the typical American Chinatown, it was
never a large one, either in terms of geographical area or numbers of residents.
Unlike the Chinatowns of San Francisco and Los Angeles, San Diego was never
a major point of debarkation, and economic activities within the community
itself were limited, particularly after government legislation had all but eliminated Chinese involvement in the local fishing industry (McEvoy 1977). Sources
of employment became scarce upon completion of the major construction projects that first attracted immigrants to the area, and in the first two decades of
the twentieth century a series of police raids and urban renewal measures forced

the closure of the gambling houses and opium dens, the major source of income for Chinatown itself. In the mid–twentieth century, the Chinatown enclave began to disappear as its residents moved to other areas of the city. This dispersion may be attributed to several factors, including the decline of already limited economic opportunities (Liu 1977), the small size of the population, and the relative absence of a strong network of traditional voluntary associations (Palinkas 1981), but one particularly relevant factor is the influence of the Chinese Community Church. In essence, the church prepared the immigrant for residence in the larger society. There was no need for the security and protection afforded by the Chinatown enclave. When the time came to move outward, the Chinese were both willing and able.

It is difficult to say whether the activities of the Chinese Congregational Mission precluded the development of a network of traditional voluntary associations or if the absence of such a network created a need for social organization that the Mission was able to fulfill. A case could be made for either position although the available evidence suggests the latter conclusion to be correct. In either case, the Chinese Congregational Mission was transformed into a center of the San Diego Chinese community by several factors, including the small size of the community, the number of families with women and children who normally joined such churches, the power and influence of the merchants who were baptized Christians, the lack of traditional clan and district associations, and the need for the services, especially housing and language instruction, provided by the voluntary associations. At the same time, however, it became a more effective force for acculturation and change than its counterparts in other American Chinatowns. It not only provided needed instruction in the English language and Western culture and helped to integrate Chinese immigrants into the larger society, it may also have contributed to the dispersal of the Chinese community throughout the city.

THE CONTEMPORARY CHINESE CHURCHES

Chinese Christian churches continue to provide the centers of social interaction in the Chinese community of San Diego. Today, there are six of these churches in the San Diego area. Only the two Mandarin-speaking churches will be discussed in this chapter, however, because they represent contemporary transformations of Christianity to meet the needs of new Chinese immigrants.

The two Mandarin-speaking churches cater almost exclusively to first-generation immigrants from mainland China, Hong Kong, and Taiwan as well as a number of Indochinese refugees. The older of these two churches was founded in 1970 as a fellowship group. In 1973 a church building was purchased and the first Mandarin church in the city was established. The second church actually began as an offshoot of the first. In 1979, dissatisfied with the interpretation of the Bible and the "message" of the original Mandarin church, a small group began meeting separately for religious fellowship and established themselves as a separate congregation, using the facilities of a non-Chinese church. This group also wishes to purchase or build their own facility.

Both churches claim to be nondenominational although their religious doctrines, rituals, and practices are strongly Baptist in orientation. The nondenominational label enables them to attract Chinese Christians who were not converted as Baptists. Both churches also define themselves as "fundamentalist." To be admitted into the church, converts must "accept Jesus into their heart" by accepting the Bible as the "word of God" and being baptized by immersion. Great emphasis is placed on prayer, avoidance of temptation, and "leading others to Christ," either through behavior or preaching.

The two congregations differ somewhat in composition. The old church is the larger of the two, with 114 adult "members" and 150 overall, including children. The members include older (age fifty-five and above) mainland-born Chinese, mostly from Shanghai, Kwangtung, and Hunan; younger adults, principally students from Taiwan or Hong Kong attending local colleges and universities or recently graduated from those schools; and Indochinese refugees, mostly ethnic Chinese from Vietnam. The new church includes in its membership eighty adults and thirty-three children. Its congregation is similar in composition to that of the old church with three notable exceptions. First, the average age and length of residence in the new church are greater. This is due largely to the significant numbers of college students and Indochinese refugees in the old church. Second, the new church's congregation is more prosperous despite the comparable level of education of both congregations. Among the older members, those attending the old church are usually regarded as "self-made men," while many of those attending the new church came from wealthy families who fled the Communist takeover of the mainland in 1949. The students attending the new church also come from more prosperous families than those attending the old church. Third, the new church's congregation is linguistically and ethnically more homogeneous. This is due largely to the significant Indochinese population in the old church.

Members of both churches attend Sunday services, Bible study and prayer meetings, revival meetings, and social events such as dinners and field trips. The pattern of rituals observed during Sunday services roughly conforms to that of other Baptist churches, although there is a good deal of autonomy and independence among Baptist churches in general (Lipphard and Sharp 1975). In the old church, services are conducted in Mandarin with simultaneous English translation while in the new church only Mandarin is spoken. In both churches, members participate in activities such as the choir, women's club, and youth group. Both churches also sponsor Chinese language classes for new immigrants. By far, the best attended events in both churches are the social events, including the post-Sunday-service luncheons, potluck dinners, film showings, and public lectures by visiting scholars and students. These affairs draw nonmembers as well as members and provide excellent opportunities for food and conversation.

Both churches are administered by a pastor, a group of deacons, and a church council. In the old church, however, the pastor serves only part time and receives no compensation for his efforts, while the pastor of the new church is full time and salaried. Deacons share responsibility for finances, scheduling, organization of social events, and, in the old church, for preaching.

While these two churches provide an opportunity for immigrants to join together and interact socially, they also assist the immigrant in adjusting to his new environment. Chinese immigrants, Christian and non-Christian, China-town dwellers and suburbanites, all experience to one degree or another different forms of social, cultural, and psychological conflict. The source of this conflict is the opposition of two cultural systems, one Chinese and one Western. In many respects, those who attend a Chinese Christian church are better prepared to adjust to the opposition between cultural systems. Many are well educated, able to speak English, employed in skilled or professional occupations, and reside in middle- to upper-middle-class neighborhoods. Their daily contact with non-Chinese and their ability to successfully utilize the social, cultural, and financial resources available to them enable them to adjust to the new environment much more successfully than other Chinese or Indochinese immigrants. Despite these advantages, however, these immigrants also experience varying degrees of social, cultural, and psychological conflict. The nature of this conflict and the mode of its resolution are both mediated by the arena of the Chinese Christian church.

Chinese immigrants in the United States are usually confronted with two different sets of values and beliefs. Many immigrants are forced to choose between the independence demanded by American society and the submission to authority and family demanded by Chinese society; between the high value of innovation in a capitalist society and the value of tradition and repetition in an agrarian society; and between self-expression in the form of argument and the value of "saving face" and "preserving harmony." Often, these choices differ with respect to age, education, socioeconomic status, and generation, thus leading to social conflict. One of the most common forms of social conflict occurs between the first generation, foreign born who adheres to traditional Chinese values, attitudes and behavior and the second generation, native born who adopts contemporary Western values, attitudes, and behavior. Church members are not immune to the family tensions resulting from generational differences and many see the church as a way of bringing the family together.

Another consequence of the cultural opposition confronting the Chinese immigrant in residence in a non-Chinese community is psychological stress. Immigrants in general have always been a high-risk group for mental illness (Brody 1969; Malzberg and Lee 1956), and Chinese immigrants are no exception (cf. Sue and Sue 1973; Berk and Hirata 1976). E. V. Stonequist (1937:204) attributed this risk to the culture conflict associated with immigration. Whatever its form or extent, however, one of the most important components of this psychological distress is a crisis of identity. "Migration is one of the most obvious instances of complete disorganization of the individual's role system and some disturbance of identity and self image is to be expected" (David 1969:80).

In the two Mandarin-speaking churches of San Diego, instances of extreme forms of psychopathology or psychological disorder are rare (Palinkas 1982). Nevertheless, church members display moderate levels of anxiety and uncertainty related to adjusting to the demands of their new home. Occasionally, this will manifest itself in various forms of depression, somatic complaints, and anxiety neurosis. Older members will complain of physical ailments that physicians have been unable to diagnose. Younger adults will experience problems at school or at work because they feel unmotivated and depressed, are constantly tired yet unable to sleep, and have difficulty eating regularly.

Several issues contribute to the formation of symptoms such as these. For instance, there is considerable anxiety and uncertainty about old age. In the traditional Chinese family, old age would be welcome because the elders are revered by younger family members. In the United States, however, church members often are isolated from their children and feel they are of little value to them or are unwanted by them. This anxiety becomes even more acute with the prospect of death. Old age and death are universal concerns but what makes them worthy of note here is the absence of the traditional support system—specifically the kin network and ancestor worship—that would normally assist the individual with these concerns. Kin ties have been lost through immigration and the ancestor worship has been abandoned through acculturation and religious conversion.

The absence of the traditional system of kin support entails other problems as well. One such problem is financial security. Lacking close kin to rely on in times of unemployment or financial distress, church members are often unaware of other options. Similarly, the task of finding a good job without assistance from close kin also contributes to the uncertainty and anxiety.

Another set of problems relates to the mundane but important exigencies of the new environment: language and cultural differences between the immigrant and his non-Chinese neighbors and coworkers, the endless red tape of naturalization procedures, and occasionally, the trauma of immigration itself. This is particularly a problem for many of the Indochinese members of the old church. Several of these immigrants arrived after having been forced out of Vietnam or Cambodia by hostile governments, encountering numerous obstacles, and losing several loved ones, who were either left behind or died along the way.

In the resolution of this cultural conflict and its associated social and psychological problems, Christianity has been transformed to effect two distinct processes. One is the integration of elements of a Chinese cultural system with those of the Western (American) cultural system. The second process is the establishment of distinctions between the two cultural systems. While these two processes appear contradictory, they manage to coexist by operating on different sets of elements. Integration involves elements of both cultural systems that are viewed as desirable and useful to the task of adjusting to the new environment. Distinction involves elements of both cultural systems that are viewed as undesirable and serve as impediments to successful adjustment. In the attempt to deal with the social, cultural, and psychological conflicts experienced by Chinese Christians as individuals and as a group, both integration and distinction of two opposing cultural systems are evident.

One of the most common attempts to integrate the Chinese and Western cultural systems is the comparison made between the Christian church and the traditional Chinese family. In many ways, church members refer to an analogic relationship between God and the congregation and parents and children. In both the Chinese Christian model of the unified or uplifted church and the Chinese model of the ideal family, there is an emphasis on subservience to authority. This connection was established by one speaker who quoted Ephesians 5:23: "For the husband is the head of the wife, as Christ is also the head of the church." God is viewed as a stern but loving father who is entitled to respect and obedience from the congregation. In return for these displays of piety, God protects and assists the congregation. In the absence of these displays, however, God is seen as justified in punishing his children, as an unpropitiated ancestor might do. The family analogy is also demonstrated in the use of kin terms such as "brother" or "sister" or "auntie" or "uncle" in referring to members of the congregation.

Finally, social relations within the church are governed by the standards and customs of kinship. Members rely upon each other as sources of information, assistance, emotional, and financial support. Relations are governed by respect for age and authority, the hierarchy of status, and the obligations associated with the concept of filial piety. Thus members are encouraged to "honor and respect your parents and also the elders of the church" (pastor, new church).

In addition to comparing the Christian church to the ideal of the Chinese family, social unity is promoted through the concept of an "uplifted church" (Palinkas 1984). Such a church is distinguished from other churches by several criteria. An uplifted church, for instance, has a large congregation whose members by virtue of their spirituality and activity are guaranteed salvation. Such a church is also materially prosperous and free from internal strife. It is also a place where Chinese may worship without fear of racial intolerance.

It is in the concern for salvation that we clearly see an attempt to unite a Chinese and a Christian world view. Both churches view the world or environment as hostile, immoral, violent, and chaotic. This view is consistent not only with a Chinese representation of the world as found in orthodox Buddhism, folk-religious sectarianism (Granet 1975; Yang 1961), and fundamentalist Christianity, but also with the immigrant experience, particularly for those immigrants incapable of adjusting to the new environment and especially if that adjustment entails the surrender of certain traditional values, attitudes, and behavior.

Extricating oneself from or adjusting both pragmatically and spiritually to this chaotic environment is viewed in terms of the Christian concept of salvation. However, salvation is seen both as eternal life after death and as deliverance from current environmental pressures. Both forms of salvation are achieved through a combination of faith and action. Action involves prayer, Bible study and interpretation of scripture, and preaching the "message of Christ."

The second process of resolving cultural conflict involves the use of a sacred-secular dichotomy to transform the opposition between Chinese and Western cultural systems into one mediated by Christianity. This mediation occurs through different strategies. One involves the articulation of three oppositions: between the Chinese Christian and Chinese who are not Christian, between the Chinese Christian and non-Chinese, and between Christians and non-Christians. All three oppositions are referred to as conflicts between Chinese Christians and "worldly people."

"Worldly people" are viewed as primarily responsible for the chaos and disorder in the world today. They are characterized as concerned with material posses-sions, social status, and temporal pleasures. They care little for other people and are "without love." The opposition of the Chinese Christian to "worldly people" is used to contrast the value system and world view of the Chinese church with undesirable elements of the value system and world view of both Chinese and American culture. Speakers often criticize such traditional elements of Chinese behavior as "playing mah-jongg" or "eating lots of food." Undesirable elements of American culture include the perceived lack of concern for the unity of the family.

My son was telling me that the news has predicted that by 1990, the Women's Equal Rights Movement [ERA] will pass, that women shall be equal to men. But this is against what God had intended. Everything is twisted around in this world. . . . The world is of a rebellious kind. It is full of conflict. It is even worse in the European countries. The parents cease to discipline their children whenever the children threaten to leave their parents (pastor, new church).

Often, the worst of both Chinese and American culture are united in the representation of life in Hong Kong. Many church members have lived in Hong Kong at one point or another. The colony is often characterized as "without love" where the people are more concerned about appearances and keeping up with fads. Hong Kong is viewed as Chinese culture corrupted by Western in-fluence. The portrayal of Western culture in this light is typical for first-gen-eration Chinese immigrants. What makes this characterization different, however, is its context. It is not specifically American culture that is seen as bad; rather the conflict between the Chinese Christians and "worldly people" is couched in the context of the sacred-secular dichotomy. " 'Worldly people' base their faith upon feelings and emotions. They do not live by faith, but by their physical needs from the environment around them. They have no spiritual life" (deacon, old church). This crystallization of the cultural conflicts in the sacred-secular dichotomy is an essential element in the process of identity for-mation for the immigrant Chinese Christians.

   The resolution of psychological conflict involves discussion of personal problems by participants at the prayer meeting, followed by sermons and lectures in which church leaders provide guidance, both spiritual and practical, to the audience through explanation, reassurance, advice, and information. Church leaders attempt to explain personal problems by relating personal disorder to the Chinese Christian world view. In an environment characterized as chaotic and violent, "trials arrive often; there are trials around us constantly" (pastor, new church). The world view of the Chinese church provides the members with an explanation for this environment and the trials it creates for the immigrant.

   Church leaders then reassure the congregation that there is hope for the resolution of their problems. As one Sunday School teacher stated: "See brothers and sisters, the Lord's resurrection shall bring to us glorious hope or else all of us shall be without hope. So, brothers and sisters, real love and joy will not grow unless through pain." Second, reassurance is provided in noting the permanence and stability of God: "Human beings are so undependable for we tend to change; the environment also changes and things around us change also. But our Father shall never change. I am always pleased to know that my Lord is permanent; He will not change. We often change our minds or find it hard to make up our minds" (deacon, old church). Third, reassurance is provided by arguing that all men are viewed as equals before God. Such equality can allow members to participate in church activities without harsh social pressures or cultural expectations: "I thank God that even one such as I, who does not have much talent or intelligence or social position, can serve Him. Thank the Lord that He did not eliminate His servants to be only those who hold a Ph.D. He did not say that only those who are extremely intelligent can serve him" (pastor, new church).

   The advice given in a Chinese church may be either spiritual or practical. Spiritual advice includes exhortations to pray and work for an uplifted church. Audiences are also encouraged to "depend on God." Prayer is encouraged because it supposedly gives one a certain amount of "power." According to one Sunday School teacher, "The more we pray, the more ability we will obtain, and vice versa. If we don't pray, we won't have any power." Audiences are encouraged to pray because they will obtain guidance as well as power.

   Although the bulk of discourse involves the dispensing of spiritual advice, practical advice is given as well. Audiences are advised, for example, to employ common sense when making decisions, to exercise self-control, not to succumb to fads and spend money foolishly, to practice filial piety and respect church elders, and to concentrate on their business endeavors.

   Advice, whether practical or spiritual, however, is not enough to persuade the audience to change their behavior. The strategies of rhetoric employed by church speakers must also "demonstrate" to the audience that such advice is both feasible and effective in solving the problems at hand. This demonstration usually occurs in the form of the personal testimony. In one such testimony, the pastor of the old church, who also is an acupuncturist by profession, demonstrates how prayer and faith can deliver one from personal misfortune:

I remember once I was treating a patient. So the patient said: "Your needle has pierced close to my heart. I was in the hospital for two days." I thought she would take me to court. I had just started my practice and I was afraid. And I used to be very careful. And even though I did not think I had done anything wrong, I was afraid that the court action would have my name in the newspapers and I would have a bad reputation. At that time it was suppertime. So I asked my wife to wait awhile. I would go pray. So I went into the bedroom and prayed. I had an overwhelming sensation of peace. I do not know if any of you have had this great flood of joy and peace. So I came out and told my wife. I said: "Don't worry about it. Everything is going to be all right. Because Jesus told me so." This overwhelming sensation of peace did not come from me. After two days, this woman who was a patient called. "I really should not blame you for your needle because I have heart trouble. Actually I had a weakness in my heart. That is why I was in the hospital." Can you imagine? My needle is only a half an inch and she said it had almost pierced her heart!

For those who have experienced or are afraid of experiencing similar misfortunes, such testimony has a profound impact.

Finally, and perhaps most important of all, Christianity is transformed to aid in the formation of a Chinese Christian identity as a means of resolving the crisis of identity associated with immigration. In the church, the Christian minister seeks identification with a Chinese audience through his sermons, lectures, and speeches. His strategy for persuasion in turn becomes a part of the audience's identity formation as Chinese Christians. It does so by demonstrating to the audience the utility of that combined identity in adjusting to the new environment. Thus the congregations are informed by speakers that by adopting a religious identity as Christians and retaining their ethnic identity as Chinese, they can not only adjust successfully to life in the United States but also shield themselves from a chaotic, immoral environment. The discourse helps members to articulate their individual anxieties in ethnoreligious terms (Palinkas 1982). This not only contributes to the maintenance of their ethnic identity but encourages their continued membership in an ethnic church as a means of resolving these individual problems.

CONCLUSION

San Diego's Chinese Christian churches have indeed profoundly influenced the course of social change for immigrants. Historically the original Congregational Mission helped to acculturate Chinese immigrants and facilitate their dispersal throughout the city and county. Today Chinese churches help their members cope with the social, cultural, and psychological conflicts associated with immigration. In both instances the churches have enabled immigrants to retain much of their traditional culture and society while aiding them in the acculturation process.

From this analysis we can reach two major conclusions. First, the experience of Chinese immigrants in San Diego appears to conform to Francis L. K. Hsu's hypothesis that "as the human relationships supplied by the family and the wider kinship net weaken and dissipate, church affiliation or other differences will certainly hold the possibility of becoming more relevant to the Chinese" (1971:64). Where there existed strong networks of traditional voluntary associations to serve as substitutes for the patterns of kinship, the Chinese church was never very popular nor well attended. In San Diego, however, where such associations have never been strong or pervasive, the church has played a central role in the social organization of the community. This role is evident in the churches today.

Second, Christianity in general and the Chinese Christian church in particular appear to mediate the opposition between the Chinese and Western cultural systems through two distinct processes. One is the integration of what is perceived by both church leaders and the general audience to be the best elements of both cultural systems. This is usually defined in terms of successful adjustment to life in the United States, which in turn is further defined in terms of a reduction of anxiety and uncertainty. The second process is the separation of the desirable elements of either cultural system, both in terms of existing values and sentiments and adjustment to or accommodation of new ones, from the undesirable. Both processes are aimed at resolving the social, cultural, and psychological conflicts present in this arena. In this sense, the Chinese Christian church is unlike the ethnic churches of the European immigrants: it serves as both a force for stability in a new and chaotic environment and a force for change enabling the immigrant to adapt to that environment.

8

The Culture of Spontaneity and the Politics of Enthusiasm: Catholic Pentecostalism in a California Parish

MICHAEL D. MURPHY

All variation is abhorrent to Catholic thought (Durkheim 1951:158).

INTRODUCTION

Emile Durkheim notwithstanding, an organization of the immense scale and longevity of the Roman Catholic church has not thrived by adopting a posture of unrelenting rigidity in all matters at all times. To pursue its manifest goals of extending and maintaining its influence over all the peoples of the earth, church officials have often found it appropriate both to tolerate a measure of local variation in religious expression and to undertake periodic ecclesiastical reforms intended to transform the religion worldwide. On occasion reforms initiated by the hierarchy have even stimulated local interpretations of Catholic religiosity. The emergence and dramatic success of Catholic Pentecostalism in the United States during the late 1960s and early 1970s is an excellent example of the sort of cultural adjustments made possible by the willingness of the leaders of the church to react to the requirements of a changing world.

Catholic Pentecostalism—arguably the most important lay movement to emerge within the twentieth-century American church—was made possible by the reforms of the Second Vatican Council and is, in part at least, a reaction to the demystification of religion embodied in those reforms (see McGuire 1975). The ecumenicalism advocated by the Council and its call for a renewal of personal religious commitment moved some Catholic laymen to seek inspiration from an unanticipated source—the burgeoning Neo-Pentecostal movement in American Protestantism.

The development of Catholic Pentecostalism has been thoroughly documented both by early participants in the movement and by social scientists (Ranaghan and Ranaghan 1969; O'Connor 1972; Keifer 1973; Harrison 1974a, 1974b; McGuire 1974, 1975; Bord and Faulkner 1983). Briefly, in the fall of

1966 several lay members of the Catholic theology department at Duquesne University formed a prayer and discussion group. Among other concerns these lay theologians sought an appropriate response to the call for revitalization issued by the Second Vatican Council. In the ecumenical spirit of Vatican II, these laymen befriended Protestants who were involved in the growing Neo-Pentecostal movement. In January of 1967 these Catholics were introduced to an Episcopalian who invited them to attend a Pentecostal prayer meeting led by a Presbyterian. By the third or fourth of these multidenominational meetings, all of the Catholic participants had experienced "baptism in the Spirit" and were "speaking in tongues." In February they organized a weekend retreat during which a number of their students were initiated into what became the first Catholic Pentecostal prayer community in the world. Soon afterward important prayer communities were established at the Universities of Notre Dame and Michigan. From these three university centers the movement spread quickly throughout Catholic North America. Michael I. Harrison conservatively estimates that by mid–1973 over 75,000 Catholics were active members of approximately 1,250 Catholic Pentecostal groups called "prayer communities" (Harrison 1974a:50–51). The year 1973 is the culmination of what Richard J. Bord and Joseph E. Faulkner (1983:117–120) have called the "Building Phase" of the Charismatic Renewal Movement. Growth continued for a time in subsequent years, but not at the same dramatic pace. This chapter will focus on one local expression of the movement during the exuberant period of its greatest expansion. The "ethnographic present" of this chapter, then, is 1973; those readers interested in subsequent developments in Catholic Pentecostalism, including its eventual waning, are advised to consult Bord and Faulkner (1983) and Meredith McGuire (1982).

Attempts to understand the phenomenal early success of this movement within the American church have included examinations of the strategies of its national leadership (Bord and Faulkner 1983), of the attractions of the Pentecostal movement for Catholics (McGuire 1975), of the recruitment process itself (Harrison 1974b), and of the methods by which enthusiasm is maintained after initial commitment (Harrison 1975). Efforts have also been made to explain why Catholic Pentecostalism has succeeded while other post–Vatican II Catholic movements have not (McGuire 1974) and why Catholic Pentecostalism has thrived while a similar movement in a Protestant denomination has failed (Harrison and Maniha 1978). These and other studies suggest that the mutual accommodation of an ecclesiastical hierarchy tolerant of change and a movement leadership determined to remain acceptable to church authorities have clearly been crucial to the rapid expension of this controversial innovation in American Catholicism.

One source of complications in this process of accommodation is that the response of the ecclesiastical hierarchy occurs on at least three different organizational levels: the Vatican, the diocese, and the parish. It is unlikely that the movement would have thrived if the Vatican had not allowed bishops to make their own decisions about its acceptability and desirability. On the diocesan level the responses of bishops range from outright prohibition to active promotion of Pentecostal activities. Similarly, on the parish level, the local priests may facilitate—even participate in—Catholic Pentecostal activities, or they may discourage them from taking place on church property and impede them in other ways. In short, some local variation has developed because each prayer community must adjust to the particular attitudes of its local bishop and parish priest.

Equally important in understanding the success of the movement—and the local variation that characterizes it—is the position taken by its lay leaders towards the hierarchy. Many observers have noted the strong desire of Catholic Pentecostal leaders to avoid the appearance of challenging either the doctrines of the church or its priestly authorities (Harrison 1974b; McGuire 1974; Lane 1976; Harrison and Maniha 1978). Although some leaders are much more concerned about offending the hierarchy than others (see Fichter 1975:115ff.; Bord and Faulkner 1983:125–46), in general there has been a remarkable effort to stay in the good graces of priest, bishop, and pope.

In keeping with their desire to develop new forms of religious expression while remaining firmly within the embrace of Mother Church, the leaders of the movement have endeavored to minimize and control the influence of Protestant Pentecostalism in their activities (Lane 1976:175–76). Indeed this attempt to distance the movement from Protestant influences is best evidenced by an alternative name preferred by some participants, namely, "Charismatic Renewal" (Lane 1976:167). Not only does this label avoid the term "Pentecostal" with its obvious Protestant connotations, it also neatly underscores the view that participants in the movement seek to invigorate, not replace, traditional Catholic beliefs and rituals.

Many national and local leaders of Charismatic Renewal (e.g. Gelpi 1971) believe that if their Pentecostal activities are to receive the blessings of the church then they must avoid three potential pitfalls: excessive emotionalism, heresy, and spiritual elitism. People writhing on the floor in ecstatic trance states, speaking in tongues, shouting and screaming, and delivering wild apocalyptic prophecies are all part of the Pentecostal stereotype harbored by many Catholic clergy and laymen. The leadership of the movement recognizes the need to combat the negative association of Pentecostalism with unseemly, even psychopathological, emotionalism by teaching Catholic Pentecostals to conform to a brand of enthusiasm considerably less frenetic than that of many of its Protestant counterparts.

Another serious problem for the leaders of the Charismatic Renewal movement is the potential for Pentecostal activities, particularly prayer meetings, to become occasions for the espousal of heresy. The simple fact that Catholic Pentecostalism developed out of contact with Protestant Neo-Pentecostalism makes it doctrinally suspect in the eyes of some of the clergy. Moreover, Pentecostalism emphasizes direct unmediated communication between the believer and the supernatural in the form of prophecies and other revelations. Ecstatic communications always have the potential for contradicting official doctrine. The movement leadership disavows heresy by frequently stressing that nothing that Catholic Pentecostals believe or do supplants or denies the dogma and ritual of the church.

Finally, there is danger that those who become flushed with Charismatic excitement might come to consider themselves morally or spiritually superior to non-Pentecostal Catholics who are not "filled with the Spirit." The leadership of the movement attempts to prevent the emergence of elitist sentiments among Charismatic Catholics, while they seek to convince mainstream Catholics and clergy that such notions are not secretly subscribed to by those who have been "baptized in the Spirit."

The impressive ability of the leaders of Charismatic Renewal to guide participants in the movement away from the three outlined pitfalls testifies to the subtlety of their political skills. Although many political scientists and some anthropologists would limit political analysis to issues concerning governance and political structures, politics may also be considered as "a focus of study rather than . . . a type of subject matter" (Swartz 1978:2). This perspective holds that much of social life, not just that part concerned with governance, may be profitably analyzed from the perspective of actors drawing upon culturally defined resources in order to influence one another in the pursuit of goals (Swartz 1968:1). If F. G. Bailey is correct in asserting that "the same principles serve for political competition and political alliance alike in great issues and small" (1971:3), then a wide variety of goal processes must be investigated, not just those that involve weighty matters of state or take place in smoke-filled caucus rooms. If the principles, strategies, and tactics governing the manipulations of statesmen and politicians are different in kind or degree from those of goal seekers in other social arenas then this can only be determined by subjecting the latter to the same sort of analysis applied to the former.

In the case at hand, the leaders of the movement are acutely aware that to accomplish their goal of being *Catholic* Pentecostals, they must represent no threat to the church hierarchy. Their delicate task is to foster the religious enthusiasm of Pentecostalism among Catholics while ensuring that they neither contradict the teachings of the church nor run afoul of its officials. Their most important resource in implementing this goal of accommodation is the uniform body of beliefs, values, and ritual procedures that constitute the culture of Catholic Pentecostalism. This system of understandings has been carefully crafted to complement rather than challenge traditional Catholic beliefs and rituals. But to be effective as a political resource this cultural code must be transmitted to neophytes, and standards for proper behavior in ritual contexts must be enforced. In other words, the attainment of the goal depends upon the success of religious socialization.

Attempts to explain the rapid expansion of Catholic Pentecostalism during the early 1970s have stressed the importance of this process of religious socialization. Some scholars have described the development of a national level of organization that has sought to standardize and disseminate the culture of Charismatic Renewal through general publications, newsletters, lecture tours, and handbooks for local-level leaders (e.g., Lane 1976; McGuire 1982: 62–63; Bord and Faulkner 1983). Other work has centered on how established prayer communities recruit and socialize new members through the use of programmed "Life in the Spirit" seminars and other techniques (e.g. Harrison 1974b; 1978). Somewhat neglected, however, is the analysis of the social and, I would argue, political processes by which new prayer communities are founded and through which the first generation of members is socialized.

This chapter concerns the politics of the establishment in 1973 of a Charismatic prayer community in a conservative southern Californian parish, referred to here as "St. Anne's." By examining this prayer community during its formation and early development, much can be learned about (1) the cultural code of Catholic Pentecostalism, and its articulation specifically to avoid clashes with ecclesiastical authorities; (2) the transmission of this code to neophytes when they outnumber the virtuosi; (3) the social process by which new prayer communities are established; and (4) the political sources of local variation within the movement.

What follows is divided into three parts. First, I will outline the culture of Catholic Pentecostalism as it was conceptualized by the leaders and fully socialized members of St. Anne's prayer community approximately three months after its formation in 1973. Particular attention will be given to those Catholic Pentecostal beliefs and rituals that deviate from mainstream American Catholicism and that represent potential for heresy, excessive emotionalism, and spiritual elitism. In each case I will demonstrate that Catholic Pentecostal beliefs and practices are fashioned to avoid the appearance of challenging official church doctrine and authority. Second, I will describe the process by which a Pentecostal prayer community developed in St. Anne's parish. The conservative nature of this parish will be shown to have shaped the unique social organization and practice of Catholic Pentecostalism there. That St. Anne's is the only "clergy-led" prayer community in its diocese can be understood as an appropriate political response to the local situation. Third, I will describe the techniques by which the leadership of St. Anne's Charismatics routinized and controlled the expression of Pentecostal enthusiasm during the important ritual of the prayer meeting. Successful routinization not only diminishes the likelihood of conflict between movement participants and church authorities, it also promotes the spread of Catholic Pentecostalism by motivating some participants to establish new communities.

CATHOLIC PENTECOSTALISM AT ST. ANNE'S

The Catholic Pentecostals of St. Anne's explicitly seek an intense personal relationship with their God that goes far beyond the simple satisfaction of the obligations imposed on all Catholics by the church. They favor active, daily involvement in their religion and direct, unmediated communion with their God. Many Catholic Pentecostals have developed a theocentric world view in which the distinction between the sacred and the mundane is so blurred that even rather ordinary events, like finding an open parking space, are interpreted as evidence of divine intervention in their lives.

Catholic Pentecostals, then, desire both to amplify their experience of the supernatural and to expand its scope to include all aspects of their everyday lives. They believe they need only turn to the New Testament accounts of the early Christians to learn how to intensify and extend their experience of the sacred. Finding guidance in biblical accounts, St. Anne's Catholic Pentecostals believe that there are four principal means—in addition to those prescribed by the church—by which their goal of "getting closer to God" may be attained: (1) becoming baptized in the Spirit; (2) receiving the charisms, or gifts, of the Holy Spirit; (3) participating in prayer meetings; and (4) developing a prayer community.

Baptism in the Spirit

Catholic Pentecostals believe that a most important step in the renewal and intensification of their spirituality comes when they are "baptized in the Spirit," just as once they were sacramentally baptized with water. The significance of baptism in the Spirit is seen in the dramatic biblical account of Pentecost Sunday:

When the day of Pentecost arrived, all the believers were gathered together in one place. Suddenly there was a noise from the sky which sounded like a strong wind blowing, and it filled the whole house where they were sitting. Then they saw what looked like tongues of fire spreading out: and each person there was touched by a tongue. They were all filled with the Holy Spirit and began to talk in other languages, as the Spirit enabled them to speak (The Acts of the Apostles 2:1–4).

It is from this event as reported in the Acts of the Apostles that Pentecostalism has drawn its name and its theological orientation. Just as the original disciples were emboldened by the Spirit, so modern-day Pentecostals believe that a second baptism in the Spirit can renew and inflame their commitment to God.

Although a wide range of experiences is reported as accompanying baptism in the Spirit, most Charismatic Catholics believe that its bests indicator is the initial experience of "speaking in tongues," or glossolalia. This coupling of baptism in the Spirit and glossolalia is problematic, however, because not everyone is capable of entering easily into the mildly altered state of consciousness required for glossolalia (see Bord and Faulkner 1975:259). Since baptism in the Spirit is considered to be an initiation into Catholic Pentecostalism, there is danger both that nonecstatic Catholics be discouraged from participation and that ecstatic Catholics develop notions of spiritual superiority.

To avoid the emergence of a glossolalic elite and to expand the basis for recruitment, the leadership of St. Anne's prayer community plays down the significance of glossolalia, stressing that being able to speak in tongues is neither a necessary nor a sufficient condition for baptism in the Spirit. Unlike many Protestant forms of Pentecostalism, Charismatic Renewal does not encourage people to step forth to receive the Spirit unless they have benefited from some sort of preparation for the experience. This preparation has been institutionalized throughout the movement in the form of relatively standardized "Life in the Spirit" seminars (Harrison 1974b; Bord and Faulkner 1983).

The Charisms

An important feature of Catholic Pentecostalism at St. Anne's is its emphasis on the charisms or gifts of the Holy Spirit (McGuire 1982:42–48). St. Paul, in I Corinthians 12:1–11, enumerates the various charisms that were manifested in early Christian communities. They include the gifts of wisdom, knowledge, healing, power to work miracles, prophecy, discernment, tongues, and the interpretation of tongues. Charisms are special means provided by God to assist those who wish to attain a greater degree of spirituality. Leaders of the Charismatic movement at St. Anne's exhort would-be Catholic Pentecostals to be receptive to these gifts of the Holy Spirit, stressing the spiritual and emotional benefits to be gained from them. While Catholic Pentecostals believe that the charisms are intended for all, not everyone has the more dramatic gifts of tongues, interpretation of tongues, and prophecy. There is, in fact, an unequal distribution of the charisms within the prayer community; some members appear to have many of the gifts and others none at all.

In addition to those charisms mentioned in the New Testament, others have been identified by my informants. Particularly important are the gifts of "tears" and "memory." Tears refers to "holy weeping" and occurs when one is filled with happy emotion while contemplating the work and presence of God. The gift of memory helps people overcome psychological obstacles (called "blocks") to spiritual goals by recollecting their origins in early traumatic experiences. Both of these gifts are enthusiastically recommended to those Charismatics who feel that their baptism in the Spirit is in doubt because they have not spoken in tongues.

Space does not permit an adequate discussion of each charism so only those revelational gifts that are both highly valued by participants and considered potentially dangerous politically will be described in detail. They are valued because Charismatics believe them to be important means of direct contact with the supernatural; they are dangerous because they can be occasions for heresy or the expression of elitist sentiments.

A "prophecy" is a message from God to the Christian community (see McGuire 1977; Bord and Faulkner 1983). It is believed that if God chooses to speak to a group of worshippers he often will do so through an individual who has the gift of prophecy. Consequently, the gift is important not only to the individual recipient but to the entire community of believers. Occasionally a person who delivers a prophecy during the prayer meeting will preface it by saying something akin to "I have a prophecy" or "This is what just came to me." The use of the first person singular, the "King James" biblical vocabulary employed, and the content of the message indicate clearly that God is speaking through the individual (see McGuire 1977).

Most prophecies are by no means precise forebodings of things to come, as the common-sense notion of a prophecy might imply. Rather they are broad normative statements in which God, speaking through his human mouthpiece, professes his love for the people, enjoins them to love him in return and to pray to him, warns them of the spiritual dangers of the modern, secular world, or communicates some similar statement reflecting Charismatic theology. Whenever prophecies make specific predictions or stray from the standard Catholic Pentecostal beliefs, they become cause for concern among the leaders. The theological and the political problem with prophecy is that it is represented not as the potentially fallible opinion of an individual but as a revelation from God. Therefore, all sorts of statements contrary to church teachings could conceivably be given considerable support if presented as "prophecy."

St. Anne's Charismatics believe that the "gift of tongues" is another excellent means of communication with the supernatural, but this gift is rather more complex than prophecy. Speaking in tongues, or glossolalia, is a vocalization that conveys denotative meaning neither to the speaker nor to the listener (Hutch 1980; Goodman 1972; Hine 1969). It is considered to be a divine rather than a human language, and although it has no semantic component in the usual sense, Catholic Pentecostals believe it to be a very important form of prayer and revelation. Speaking in tongues may take the form of a personal prayer in which an individual communicates directly to God his or her innermost feelings. One informant lauded the gift of tongues because it enabled her "to pray quietly to God when I can't find the words to express the feelings I am experiencing." In describing their state of mind after speaking in tongues in private, Charismatics report feeling "relieved," "satisfied" or "euphoric." Private glossolalia is encouraged by the Charismatic leadership of St. Anne's because it is believed to be an excellent means of enhancing spirituality by "yielding" to the work of the Holy Spirit.

When speaking in tongues takes place in a public context its social significance changes entirely because public glossolalic utterances are viewed as messages to the community from God. In this case rather than expressing private feelings and sentiments the glossolalic serves as a mouthpiece for the Spirit. Glossolalia performed in inappropriate public settings is strongly discouraged; when it occurs in a proper setting, such as the prayer meeting, it is expected that an interpretation of the utterance be forthcoming by someone other than the glossolalic. "Interpretation of tongues" is also a charism, and if a public episode of glossolalia is not followed by such an interpretation then it is considered to be without relevance to the community and is discouraged. Since the speaker may not interpret his own ecstatic productions, each of St. Anne's glossolalics has a partner who usually interprets his or her utterances. Although a "good" interpretation should approximate in length the glossolalic episode, the interpretation is not thought of as a literal translation of divine words, phrases, or sentences. The gift of interpretation does not give its recipient the ability to break up the glossolalic utterance into meaningful units; rather a person receives an interpretation all of a piece through a direct revelation from God. The interpretations are rendered very much like the prophecies described earlier so that the clear impression is given that it is God speaking to the assembled through the individual.

The leaders of St. Anne's prayer community stress the necessity for treating the charisms with respect, reverence, and a certain amount of delicacy. As in the case of baptism in the Spirit, the dual problem of the leadership is to generate the expression of the charisms among the least ecstatic members of the community, while they control the enthusiasm of those most given to religious ecstasy. An important example of the former is the attempt to teach people how to speak in tongues (see Bord and Faulkner 1983:81; McGuire 1982:61). The neophyte is told to pray privately in a quiet setting, to relax and "let the Lord be the driver because he will steer the sounds in the manner that he chooses." The would-be tongue speaker is advised that he must make the sounds and that he may learn his "heavenly language" in a manner similar to his earthly one. As he prays a sound might come to him, and, like a baby, he must repeat this sound over and over until it becomes "spontaneous." As other sounds come, he is told, they too should be cultivated in the same manner. By employing this method several community members who at first found it impossible to speak in tongues gradually acquired a glossolalic "vocabulary." After much practice on their part, it became impossible to distinguish their utterances from those produced by people who received the gift spontaneously.

One of the most important means of controlling the expression of the charisms is itself a "gift of the Holy Spirit": the gift of discernment. This gift determines whether an utterance, thought, or act is "moved by the Spirit," a product of egotism, or a connivance of Satan. The Charismatics of St. Anne's believe that God provides them with this gift so that they can evaluate purported charismatic manifestations. In the course of the prayer meeting there are occasions when someone gives a teaching or "witnesses" to the assembled. If another individual feels that the content of the offering is either wrong or merely inappropriate in that setting, he is said to "discern" that it is not Spirit-filled. Discernment, therefore, provides the basis for denying claims to the heavenly origin of some propositions or actions. All charismatic manifestations are subject to discernment.

The Prayer Meeting

The principal ritual of Catholic Pentecostalism is the prayer meeting. Just as the Catholic mass is modeled after the Last Supper, the prayer meeting commemorates the original gathering of disciples on Pentecost Sunday. This weekly gathering at St. Anne's Parish Hall is considered the ideal setting for the proper manifestation of the charisms. Catholic Pentecostals believe that during the course of the prayer meeting the Holy Spirit descends among the faithful in order to facilitate their spiritual development, just as the Spirit appeared in the midst of the disciples on Pentecost Sunday. Charismatics maintain that the Holy Spirit is not merely present but that he actively guides the meeting. Catholic Pentecostals believe that each prayer meeting is unique, reflecting not only the particular needs of those assembled but also the aims of the Holy Spirit for that occasion. Consequently, the prayer meeting is conceptualized as a highly variable ritual process that should not be characterized by overt human orchestration.

The prayer meeting is composed of a sequence of discrete components, called "offerings" by some informants. Among the most important of these offerings are "testimonies," "sharings," and "witnessings" in which participants speak of how their personal experiences reflect the reality or desirability of divine intervention in everyday life; "teachings" in which a participant reads from the Bible (usually selections from the Psalms or the New Testament) or presents a short discourse on some religious topic; "prayers of praise" in which God is exalted and thanked for his bounty and assistance; "prayers of petition" in which a request for a specific intervention is made of God; "songs" in which one of a variety of hymns is sung by the assembled; "announcements" in which the leaders or others tell of upcoming events; the various charisms such as "speaking in tongues," "interpretation of tongues," "prophecies," "discernment," and "singing in tongues"; and, finally, periods of prayerful "silence" considered not as meaningless transitions between offerings, but as important meditative offerings in their own right.

Aside from understandings about how to enact the various offerings, rules have emerged concerning their proper frequency and sequencing. Some of these rules and the means by which they came to be shared at St. Anne's will be discussed below. Suffice it here to note that an important source of organization for this ritual is the "theme." It is believed that the Holy Spirit usually intends that some specific message will emerge during the course of the prayer meeting. Importantly, the theme becomes clear only slowly as a pattern is perceived in the various offerings and participants shape their participation accordingly.

The prayer meeting is politically problematic because it is an occasion during which the statements and actions of Catholic Pentecostals are under great public scrutiny and are likely to diverge dramatically from mainstream Catholic conceptions of proper religious comportment. Again, the problem is that extreme emotionalism and heretical statements may create difficulties for the prayer community with members of the church hierarchy and with noncharismatic parishioners. This political dilemma is exacerbated by understandings about the proper construction of a prayer meeting. Because the credibility of the prayer meeting rests upon the belief that it is divinely inspired, conspicuous supervision by the leaders is undesirable. It is a clear admission of collective failure "to move with the Spirit" if the leaders of the prayer meeting must frequently and openly contradict or disavow the performances of any of the participants. The leadership must employ great subtlety in its efforts to control the ritual, and the success of the prayer meeting depends upon participants' quickly learning and observing the limits of spontaneous religious enthusiasm.

The Prayer Community

St. Anne's Catholic Pentecostals speak often of the great feeling of mutual concern that develops among the members of a prayer community. The usual rationale given for strengthening the bonds of community, however, is not the creation of a satisfying sense of camaraderie, but rather the development of a collective basis from which each person may better attain the goal of "getting closer to God." The "Christian community" of the prayer group is offered as an alternative to an "American society" that diverts the individual from a Spirit-filled life. For St. Anne's Charismatics the prayer community is a valuable source of support and inspiration for the individual who must struggle against the imperfections of his own personality, the social pressures of a wanton society, and the powerful meddling of Satan.

Although the prayer meeting is the principal setting in which members of St. Anne's prayer community interact, it is only one of many activities available to the membership. For example, a community picnic is held each Sunday afternoon. Members of the community frequently invite each other to dinners, "coffees," and other informal gatherings. Charismatic Catholics are also much more given to participating in religious events outside their own parish than are mainstream Catholics; some members of St. Anne's prayer community averaged as many as five nights a week attending Charismatic events, both in their own and in other communities.

The strong sense of community characterizing St. Anne's Charismatics is also evident in the very obvious concern of members for each other's spiritual, emotional, and physical well-being. If any member of the community is taken ill he is regularly visited and administered to by others. If anyone experiences an emotional crisis the prayer community mobilizes immediately to help him weather it successfully.

Charismatic Catholics believe that their prayer communities evolve differently and that some groups are more successful than others in advancing the spiritual goals of their members. Similarly, it is recognized that, because of the special nature of their personalities or spiritual needs, some individuals are better served by membership in one community rather than another. Some prayer communities are so successful at engendering sentiments of moral community among some members that they give rise to smaller "convenant communities" in which Catholic Pentecostal families and individuals pool their financial resources and attempt to create a communal domestic setting that optimizes the collective pursuit of spirituality (see Connor 1972; Bord and Faulkner 1983:132–39).

Many of St. Anne's Charismatics are so committed to the prayer community that other social and religious activities are curtailed as their devotion to the prayer group increases. This has been one source of criticism from non-Pentecostal members of the parish who claim that such lay groups as the parish council and the Altar Society have suffered because both lay manpower and pastoral attention have been diverted to the prayer community. Since recruits to Charismatic Renewal tend to be active and devout Catholics prior to their association with the movement (e.g. McGuire 1974), this can cause a problem for clergy who "lose" the help of some of their most involved laymen.

While Catholic Pentecostals proclaim the desirability of each Catholic layman attaining a personal, ecstatic, and unmediated relationship with the supernatural, they also believe that this is best accomplished in the context of a group that is, in crucial respects, hierarchical. All prayer communities in St. Anne's diocese are presided over by a male leader who appoints an advisory group (called the "core") whose function is to assist him in guiding the prayer community. Within this general organizational format, however, one finds a great deal of variation in the nature and extent of the control exerted by the leadership over the other members of the prayer community. Charismatics explain this variation as being inspired by the Holy Spirit who fosters the development of an organizational structure appropriate to each community's needs; some communities require firmer direction than others. This organizational flexibility allows Catholic Pentecostal groups to respond effectively to variations in the local receptivity to their movement and its aims, and it makes just as important a contribution to the success of the movement as does the reworking of Pentecostal beliefs to conform more closely to Catholic doctrine.

THE DEVELOPMENT OF A PRAYER COMMUNITY

To anyone unfamiliar with the surprisingly widespread appeal of Charismatic Renewal in the early 1970s, St. Anne's parish would seem a most unlikely place for Pentecostalism to take hold. Located in a wealthy suburb of a southern California city, St. Anne's counts among its parishioners a large number of well-to-do middle-aged and elderly people. Both the suburb and the parish itself are noted for their political and social conservatism. Although the parish does include Catholics who are students or faculty members at a nearby university, many parishioners are retired professionals, business people, military officers, and their families who have adapted only with some difficulty to the liberal reforms of Vatican II.

Despite the generally conservative reputation of the parish as a whole, by early 1973 a number of devout parishioners were attending prayer meetings at St. Joseph's, a nearby parish. St. Joseph's is located in a neighborhood composed of a mixture of middle- and working-class families, as well as a large number of students and other single people. A sizable and thriving Catholic Pentecostal prayer community had developed in the parish, and although it enjoyed the support of the priests, it was run entirely by laymen.

Because of the size of St. Joseph's community, special care had been taken to develop an appropriate organizational structure to maximize its goals. The community was guided by a leader who relied heavily on a ten-member advisory "core" that did much of the organizational work necessary to maintain and expand the community. Members of the core had been assigned to lead a variety of "ministries" for the prayer community: a "book ministry" was in charge of disseminating written material concerning the Charismatic Renewal movement; a "healing ministry" helped people overcome their physical, emotional, and spiritual problems; and a "teaching ministry" organized instructional seminars for those who were new to Charismatic Renewal and sought baptism in the Spirit. In short, the St. Joseph's prayer community was large, well organized, and well integrated into parish life.

Half a dozen parishioners from St. Anne's were participating regularly in the Charismatic activities at St. Joseph's and had become baptized in the Spirit when some members of the core began to encourage them to establish a new prayer community in their own parish. At first the Charismatics from St. Anne's were skeptical of the likelihood of such controversial activities being accepted at their conservative parish. Eventually, however, one of them prevailed upon the wife of the parish deacon to visit a prayer meeting at St. Joseph's and to see firsthand what Charismatic Renewal was all about. Although initially leery, the deacon's wife was very impressed with the religious fervor displayed at the prayer meeting. After attending several prayer meetings she convinced her husband that he also should look into Charismatic Renewal.

The deacon is a vigorous man who approaches his religious duties with seriousness and thoroughness. His exemplary performance of the duties of his office and his steadfast support of the ecclesiastical hierarchy had earned him the respect and friendship of Father Richards, St. Anne's parish priest. Even more suspicious of Catholic Pentecostalism than his wife, the deacon's initial skepticism was based on his belief that it was likely to promote dissension within the church by undermining ecclesiastical authority. Ultimately, his wife persisted and he reluctantly attended a prayer meeting. Yet he, too, was very impressed with the level of devotion expressed in such an orderly fashion. On only his third visit to St. Joseph's the deacon was asked to assist the community's "healing ministry" in praying for a member's recovery from a serious illness. He was taken to a small "prayer room" where he joined the others in deep prayer for the sick man. Afterward the healing ministry asked the deacon if he would like them to pray for his spiritual development. He could only accede, so the members of the ministry laid hands upon the deacon and began to pray ardently for him. Within several minutes some of the Charismatics began to speak softly in tongues. To his considerable surprise the deacon spontaneously broke out into tongues himself. This experience, which he later described as the most intensely religious moment of his life, was discerned by the healing ministry as indicating baptism in the Spirit.

From the moment of his baptism in the Spirit, the deacon focused his great energies upon understanding this exciting new dimension in his spiritual life. After a short period of intense study and discussion with experienced Catholic Pentecostals, he was persuaded that his original doubts about the movement were unfounded and that the spiritual benefits to be gained from it were great. Both the deacon and his wife received a great deal of attention from the leader (and his wife) of St. Joseph's community and from other members of the core of that group. Within one month after baptism in the Spirit the deacon and his wife were attending four or five Pentecostal activities per week.

The deacon did not hesitate to discuss his new religious insights with his confessor and friend, Father Richards. Eventually the deacon and his wife convinced their priest to go with them to a prayer meeting. Father Richards was duly impressed but cautious. At the urging of his Charismatic friends, Father Richards invited a priest, Father Royce, to come to St. Anne's for one month of "renewal." Father Royce, a dedicated Catholic Pentecostal possessed of charisma in the commonsense as well as the theological meaning of that term, is a "facilitator" for the movement who often travels in promotion of its aims.

Father Royce accepted the invitation to preside over a period of renewal with the explicit understanding that this would coincide with the establishment of a prayer community. On the first Sunday of the renewal Father Royce delivered guest sermons for a number of masses. A fiery speaker who forcefully challenges Catholics to become more involved in their religion, Father Royce explained in detail why he thinks participation in Charismatic Renewal is an excellent means of doing this. Many of the more conservative members of the parish were upset by his flamboyant manner and by the content of some of his statements; a few complained to Father Richards about allowing such "radical" goings-on. Only eleven people, including all of the parish's experienced Charismatics, attended the first prayer meeting called by Father Royce. The following Sunday Father Royce again delivered a number of stirring sermons, and his call for people to attend the Wednesday prayer meeting was better heeded; over thirty people were present for the second meeting. Despite some opposition in the parish, approximately fifty people were attending by the time Father Royce left.

At the beginning of the month of renewal the Charismatics who had been attending St. Joseph's prayer meetings were assembled separately by the deacon, Father Royce, and Father Richards. Designated as the "working core," they were asked to pray to God to make clear who should emerge as the leader of the nascent St. Anne's prayer community. A few days before Father Royce's final prayer meeting, he and Father Richards decided that the deacon should be the leader of the community. Although not consulted in this decision the members of the working core approved unanimously of this choice.

Before leaving, Father Royce explained that the leader of the community should have ultimate authority on important matters. If his decisions or manner consistently created discord then he should be replaced, but in the normal course of events the best sort of community is not necessarily a democratic one. The decision-making process in St. Anne's reflected this position from the very start.

Once installed as the leader, the deacon immediately began to shape the community as he felt appropriate. For example, he scheduled the weekly meeting of St. Anne's core for the same evening and time as the general prayer meeting at St. Joseph's. Although some members of the core openly regretted this because it cut them off from contact with their "mother" community, all accepted the decision and the deacon's explanation for it: the core had to devote all of its efforts to ensuring the success of the fledgling community. In another early decision, the deacon invited several married couples to join the core and indicated his desire to add other couples to the group as time went on. He did not seek the advice or consent of the members of the core concerning who would join their ranks. Although no member of the core made an issue of the decision, several did note that the core group at St. Joseph's was much more regularly a part of the decision-making process. But even those who made this comparison felt that the situation at St. Anne's required firm control by the leader.

Decision making at St. Anne's is just one feature of this particular group that led Charismatics throughout the diocese to characterize it as a "clergy-led" prayer community. Many Charismatics feel that the full backing of the clergy and their active participation are essential to the success of a Pentecostal prayer community in a conservative parish. Most Charismatics agreed that the notoriously conservative parishioners of St. Anne's, although reassured by the leadership role of the deacon, would not be likely to tolerate any "scandal." The deacon and the members of the core were most concerned that the prayer meetings be properly conducted. Let us now consider how that concern was acted upon.

THE ROUTINIZATION OF RITUAL

Beginning with the fourth prayer meeting after Father Royce's departure, I attended twelve consecutive weekly meetings. The transformation of both the prayer community and its principal ritual was remarkable in that short period of time. Not only did the community grow from fewer than 50 to more than 150 members, but the prayer meeting changed from a relatively awkward affair to a smoothly performed and doctrinally sound ritual.

Most of the participants in the earlier meetings were familiar neither with the politically crucial nuances of the beliefs characterizing the movement nor with the procedural understandings concerning the proper realization of the "offerings" of a prayer meeting. As a consequence, these first meetings were plagued with performances deemed unacceptable by the leadership because of their content, their length, or the style in which they were delivered. From the perspective of the deacon and the members of the core, some participants were not "moving with the Spirit" but rather expressing "egotism," some were monopolizing the meetings by making too many offerings, and still others were reluctant to contribute offerings at all.

By the end of the period of observation most of the problems had been eliminated and the prayer meetings were models of controlled "spontaneity" (McGuire 1982:75–106): heretical statements were rare, the ratio of active to passive participants had increased, no single participant contributed more than two or three offerings per meeting, and, finally, the expression of emotion had taken on the decidedly muted quality typical of the more mature prayer communities in the diocese.

How was this transition from awkward to flawless performance effected? This question is particularly interesting given a cultural restriction placed on the leadership: overt management of the ritual directly undermines any claim to its divine inspiration and direction. Given the necessity for circumspection, how was the leadership able to convey to its neophytes the basic understandings and values underlying the movement? Undeniably important in this socialization process were the straightforward pedagogical efforts of the leadership both inside and outside the immediate context of the prayer meeting.

Many of the "teachings" delivered by the deacon and members of the core were fashioned to clarify beliefs and explain proper participation in the prayer meetings. With very few exceptions these teachings were of a very general nature rather than specific references to inappropriately performed offerings. Efforts were also made to communicate the culture of the movement at the end of each prayer meeting when participants were encouraged to ask questions about what had occurred. Indeed, the core members often approached newcomers, offering unsolicited explanations of Charismatic Renewal and interpretations of the more usual features of the prayer meetings. Newcomers also were invited to the weekly picnics where informal teaching took place in a convivial atmosphere.

Two months after he assumed leadership of the prayer community, the deacon began a series of "Life in the Spirit" seminars that introduce mainstream Catholics to Charismatic beliefs and practices. Without underestimating the significance of these direct attempts to impart the culture of Catholic Pentecostalism, we can now turn to the more indirect processes of cultural transmission that occurred during the meetings of the core and the prayer meetings themselves.

The core meetings were very important in the initial attempts of the deacon to gain unobtrusive control over the prayer meeting. Each week the core would gather to pray, to manifest the charisms, and to discuss matters of concern to the prayer community. At the outset these core meetings were tightly controlled by the deacon, who spent a great deal of time discussing just those issues of procedure that could not be made explicit during the regular prayer meeting. The deacon often illustrated his teaching by voicing concern for specific neophytes who he felt were experiencing difficulties in "opening themselves up to the Spirit" during the prayer meeting. The deacon explained how the content of an individual's offerings or the manner and frequency of his performance reflected a spiritual problem.

These teachings had two important consequences. First, by criticizing specific performances the deacon conveyed to the core a standard for behavior in the prayer meeting. In other words, the routinization process began by the development of shared understandings among the members of the core. Second, certain individuals were identified as requiring special attention if they were to advance spiritually. The following case illustrates just how effective the core could be in unobtrusively establishing standards for performance and bringing about desired changes in the behavior of some newcomers to the movement.

One ardent participant, "Sarah," used the prayer meeting to complain at length about her medical and marital problems. At the end of each of her many rambling "witnessings," this middle-aged lady would ask the assembled to pray to God on her behalf. After two prayer meetings in which she repeated this performance about six or seven times, the deacon decided to discuss her case during a meeting of the core. He noted that Sarah was contributing far too many offerings and that this discouraged others from participating. He also criticized the content of her offerings because of their undue emphasis on petition of, rather than praise for, God. Her unsatisfactory behavior was explained as stemming from her inability to cope with her various problems, and the deacon suggested that she might require special assistance in surmounting these "blocks" in order to attain a higher level of spirituality. Although the deacon said no more on the subject, the members of the core quickly acted on his teaching. The next day two female members of the core paid the first of many visits to Sarah. During these visits they encouraged her to talk about all of her difficulties and they prayed for the alleviation of her suffering. During the first visit, the two members of the core gently pointed out that the meeting should not be dominated by requests for assistance from God but rather should be devoted to glorifying him and his words.

At the following prayer meeting one of the core members talked to Sarah before the beginning of the meeting and then sat next to her after it started. Several times as Sarah seemed to be on the verge of offering a witnessing, her companion rose and spoke about the importance of prayers of praise. Several other members of the core gave similar teachings and eventually the deacon "discerned" that the Holy Spirit's theme for the meeting was the necessity to glorify God and not merely ask for his intercession. After this announcement several people, including Sarah, gave testimonies of gratitude for all that God had done for them. Over the course of the next few weeks the members of the core spent a great deal of time with Sarah and this seemed to influence the nature of her participation in the prayer meetings. Sarah reduced the number of her offerings and substantially changed their content: rather than asking for additional divine intervention in her life she gave thanks for all that was being done for her already. The case of Sarah illustrates how the core meetings, by identifying the problems of specific individuals, facilitate the development of shared understandings about the content and form of acceptable prayer meeting offerings.

Although the avowed purpose of the core meeting was to discuss issues of belief and procedure while identifying individuals who were in need of special help, it also had an important unavowed consequence: preparation for the upcoming prayer meeting. During the core meeting the deacon invited each member of the core to "share" any recent spiritual experiences or insights. After such a "sharing" the deacon would offer a commentary in which its appropriateness for the general prayer meeting was made obvious. If he was enthusiastic about a sharing, it was often used during the prayer meeting; if he expressed reservations, it would not be offered at the general meeting except in a suitably altered form. The core meeting, therefore, served as a testing ground for potential sharings and teachings, though even here every effort was made to sustain the impression that the Holy Spirit was providing inspiration and direction. One member of the core who agreed that the core meeting could be viewed as preparation for the prayer meeting explained it as the Holy Spirit's means of guiding the leaders of the community: "He doesn't just tell us things. He wants us to work on these problems ourselves."

Guided by these weekly preparations, the members of the core, through their unspoken coordination and without any apparent direction from their leader, provided a basic structure to the early prayer meetings. Their efforts were reinforced by the presence of a number of experienced Charismatics from St. Joseph's. The members of the core and their friends from the "mother" community dispersed themselves throughout the meeting room and took turns presenting exemplary offerings. Certainly at first these religious virtuosi dominated the meetings, albeit unobtrusively. These dozen well-socialized Catholic Pentecostals, in their expert renditions of the offerings, served as models for those neophytes making their own initial attempts at participation in the ritual.

Despite the constraint against too much explicit guidance, the leadership very effectively managed to communicate their approval or disapproval of the performances of Catholic and Protestant Pentecostals alike. That this discreet process of communication was effective as a means of social control is due at least in part to the desire of most neophytes to learn acceptable forms of religious behavior and to avoid embarrassment.

The display of affirmation takes a number of different forms. An acceptable offering often is followed by a chorus of concurrence, delivered with varying degrees of enthusiasm. Typical examples of approval are "Praise Jesus!" "Praise the Lord!" "Amen, brother [or sister]!" "Right on!" and so on. The exclamations are intended to confirm the content of the offering. An even greater affirmation is registered when a participant shapes the content of his own performance to that of a preceding offering. A participant may thank his predecessor for the insight of his contribution, or he may actually adjust his own performance to tie in with the preceding one.

A particularly well-done offering will sometimes be mentioned several times during the course of the meeting and ultimately be discerned as embodying the theme of the Holy Spirit's message for the assembled. Especially powerful or inspirational offerings will even be invoked in succeeding prayer meetings. For example, "Joan," a particularly devout Charismatic, delivered an articulate and passionate witnessing in which she described the great changes that had occurred in her life since she had become baptized in the Spirit. She placed special emphasis on how the sense of confusion and doubt that used to plague her spiritual life had been replaced with a peaceful clarity of mind that she had never before experienced. Her dramatic offering was warmly received with a round of affirming exclamations followed by a prayerful period of silence that gradually gave way to an episode of collective singing in tongues. In the very next offering another Charismatic explained how he, too, had experienced a wonderful calmness since he had become a Catholic Pentecostal. Several other people gave testimonies along the same lines and finally a member of the core discerned that this was the evening's theme. After the meeting was over a large number of people, including the deacon, congratulated Joan for her sterling offering. The following week the deacon again praised Joan's witnessing and delivered a long and obviously well-prepared teaching about it.

Like many other recipients of strong collective affirmation, Joan obviously enjoyed the attention that her successful offering garnered for her. In succeeding meetings most of Joan's offerings revolved around the peace of mind that she received from her Charismatic involvement. In some sense she specialized in the kind of testimony that brought her greatest approval. Indeed, it was not uncommon during the early meetings at St. Anne's for neophytes to repeat versions of a successful offering over and over. This can probably be explained by the fact that most neophytes very much want their performances to be approved of and legitimized.

Varying degrees of disapproval may also be communicated through a number of standardized, negative reactions to an offering. The mildest form of censure is simply to ignore an offering. Often an offering unacceptable in length, content, or delivery is followed by an embarrassing (rather than "prayerful") silence. Although the discomfiture experienced by the author of a defective offering is often painfully obvious, the embarrassment is usually brief because the silence soon gives way to another offering, and the meeting proceeds with no mention of the performance and its perceived defects.

A stronger form of rejection involves following an undesirable offering with a caution. Often no direct mention is made of the offending performance in these cautionary statements. Frequently after an unacceptable performance one of the leaders or the deacon himself would deliver a teaching that, while not making explicit reference to the offering, would directly contradict it. For example, one woman, freshly baptized in the Spirit, became so enthralled with the prayer meeting that she quickly came to dominate the ritual with her frequent contributions. Inevitably, before a period of silence could develop, she offered another "sharing" or "witnessing." Finally, the leader responded to one of her offerings by delivering a "teaching" on the importance and necessity of periods of prayerful silence. Embarrassed by this indirect criticism, the woman in question subsequently reduced the frequency of her offerings.

The most direct and confrontational form of negative response is invoking the gift of discernment to judge that an offering is *not* "Spirit-filled" or "moved by the Spirit." It might be discerned that the offering had been distorted by "egotism" (defined as the urge to assert self over God's will) and therefore is not a genuine expression of the Spirit. Even worse, an offering may be determined to be a false message sent by Satan to confuse the members of the community and impede their spiritual progress. The leadership used the gift of discernment in this way only sparingly, partly because it indicates the failure of the meeting to be open to the guidance of the Spirit, and partly because of the anger or anxiety it usually produces in the speaker, as the following incident illustrates.

During one of the prayer meetings a man who was attending only his second or third Charismatic ritual proclaimed that he had received a prophecy from God. He then delivered a vigorous attack against the doctrine of the infallibility of the pope, concluding with a general condemnation of the ecclesiastical authorities for being out of touch with the needs and concerns of modern Catholic laymen. His offering obviously alarmed many people, and after a tense moment of mutterings, the deacon responded with a teaching on the legitimacy of papal infallibility, the role of the pope in God's plan for salvation, and the absolute necessity of the ecclesiastical hierarchy. He finished by warning that although the Spirit moved among them during the prayer meeting, this did not preclude the possibility that Satan would send false messages, only apparently from God, to produce dissension and divisiveness among the faithful. Mortified, the man who made the antipapal remarks fled the meeting room. The deacon sent one of the core members after him and then spoke at length about the problem of attempted satanic disruptions of Charismatic activities. He stressed that being the victim of the Devil's evil work was no cause for shame; such interference was a clear indication that the Devil feared the success of Catholic Pentecostalism and was trying to undermine it. Although the deacon later tried to placate the man whose offering caused the furor, the man ceased to have anything to do with St. Anne's prayer community.

Most of the neophytes learned and responded very quickly to the cues provided them by the leader, the members of the core, and their guests from St. Joseph's. The effectiveness of this process of cultural transmission could be observed in the progressive routinization of the prayer meeting. Despite the fact that during this crucial period new recruits were joining the prayer community, the performances gradually came to approximate the standards set by the leadership. Two months after this study began one member of the core volunteered the observation that the prayer meeting was "more Catholic" at that point than it had been in earlier meetings. Asked to explain, she noted that the number of questionable offerings had decreased, that much of the initial awkwardness had disappeared, that many more members of the community were actively contributing to the meeting by their offerings, and finally, that the expression of the charisms, especially speaking in tongues and prophecy, managed to be "both enthusiastic and proper." My informant attributed all of these positive developments to the Holy Spirit working through the leadership.

A number of important structural developments accompanied the gradual routinization of the prayer meeting. The Protestant friends of the prayer community gradually stopped attending the meetings. The fact that the leadership often found it necessary to follow the offerings of a Protestant with a qualification or even a denial undoubtedly discouraged most of the non-Catholics from participation. The Charismatics from St. Joseph's also stopped attending the prayer meetings as the ritual came increasingly under the control of the deacon and the core. One of the former visitors explained that his presence was no longer necessary because St. Anne's community was "firmly established" and needed to develop in a manner appropriate to the needs of its membership.

If the prayer meeting became increasingly predictable, the core meetings became rather less so. Partly this was a consequence of the confidence that the leader had developed in the core. They had learned their lessons well and strict control over the core meetings was no longer necessary. These later core meetings were characterized by much more ecstatic expressions of the revelational charisms. Moreover, the meeting became an occasion for the lively discussion of the beliefs and practices comprising Catholic Pentecostalism. In short, as the prayer meeting became less cause for concern, the deacon relaxed his control over the core meeting.

Yet another factor may have contributed to the opening up of the core meeting. Some of the members of the original core, and a few other virtuosi, grew to regard the later prayer meetings as too controlled, too tame, for their own spiritual needs. They found in the core meeting an ideal setting for the unfettered expression of the charisms and for give-and-take in the discussion of the culture and the social organization of Charismatic Renewal. Because the core meeting is not as public as the prayer meeting, there is less danger of unusual offerings producing problems either with the ecclesiastical hierarchy or with conservative parishioners.

A number of these restive Charismatics explored other outlets for the more ecstatic manifestations of the Spirit. In one case two members of the core established a convenant community with several other couples. In another case, several people attended the weekly meeting of a prayer group that purposefully limited its membership to a small number of advanced and devout Catholic Pentecostals. Their intimate prayer meetings were characterized by the fervent and joyful expression of the charisms, by the animated exchange of ideas, and by the Pentecostal interpretation of the events of their everyday lives. Indeed a number of such groups, auxiliary to the larger prayer communities, were to be found scattered throughout the diocese.

Perhaps most fitting of all, several members of St. Anne's prayer community participated in the establishment of yet another Catholic Pentecostal prayer community. After merely three months St. Anne's Charismatics not only enjoyed great success within the parish, but also attracted people from neighboring parishes that lacked prayer communities of their own. In a repetition of the very process by which their own community had been established, but now with the roles reversed, some of the original members of the core urged several of their visitor friends to build a Charismatic Renewal prayer community in their own parish. These efforts met with success and some of St. Anne's core members plunged into the effort "to plant the seed of Charismatic Renewal" in yet another parish of the diocese.

CONCLUSION

Because of their traditional focus on non-Western societies, anthropologists have had a better opportunity than most to appreciate the cultural plasticity of the Roman Catholic church. Yet such flexibility is not limited to the church's efforts to establish itself among exotic peoples. What has been described here is an entirely Western case in which certain aspects of a rival vision of Christianity are incorporated—with modification—into the corpus of Catholic belief and ritual. The successful emergence and expansion of this pocket of enthusiastic variation within the American church invites analysis from many different perspectives, if for no other reason than to temper the Catholic church's reputation for resisting innovation at all costs.

I have adopted a political perspective in examining the process by which a new Charismatic prayer community was established and its members properly socialized during the movement's period of greatest expansion. A fundamental goal of most leaders and mature participants in the Charismatic Renewal movement has been to reach (and sustain) a compromise with local representatives of the ecclesiastical hierarchy. Such a compromise allows Charismatic Catholics to practice a modified form of Pentecostalism and still remain in good standing with the church.

The peaceful coexistence that the Charismatics of St. Anne's seek with their bishop, their priest, and the mainstream, conservative Catholics of their parish requires that Catholic limits be placed on Pentecostal enthusiasm. New members of the prayer community, accordingly, must be quickly socialized to avoid heretical statements, to moderate the expression of religious ecstasy, and to disavow sentiments of spiritual superiority over non-Pentecostal laymen and clergy. The principal resource drawn upon by the leaders of St. Anne's in socializing neophytes is that body of understandings that makes up the culture of Catholic Pentecostalism. Although it would be misleading to exaggerate the orthodoxy of all Catholic Pentecostal beliefs (see especially Fichter 1975:39–57 and Bord and Faulkner 1983), many of them clearly have been shaped to render Pentecostalism more palatable to ecclesiastical authorities and mainstream laymen. These careful modifications of the culture of Pentecostalism contribute to the success of the movement by diminishing the potential for conflict with ecclesiastical authorities, and by widening the base of recruitment among laymen to include people who will not defy the hierarchy.

Flexibility in the leadership style and social organization of the local prayer community also contributes to the spread of the movement by permitting Charismatic groups to range from the very democratic and innovative to the rather authoritarian and cautious (see McGuire 1975:96–97, 1982:75–76; Bord and Faulkner 1983). This organizational variability allows prayer communities to take hold in a wide variety of parish settings. An innovative, lay-run Pentecostal group very likely would have encountered a good deal more resistance from the conservative members of St. Anne's parish than did the group that was tightly controlled by the deacon and supported by the parish priest.

The task of avoiding conflict with non-Pentecostal Catholics is made all the harder because Pentecostal theology provides mechanisms by which new content may enter the cultural system in the form of prophecies and other purported messages from the supernatural. These avenues of revelation, if not carefully monitored and controlled, can lend an aura of legitimacy to statements that undermine rather than advance the goal of compromise. Consequently, an important contribution to the success of the movement as a whole has been the effectiveness of religious socialization in general and the routinization of the prayer meeting in particular.

As the case of St. Anne's reveals, the necessity to refrain from overt orchestration of the ritual places an important constraint on the leader's effort to prevent the prayer meeting from becoming a platform for heresy. If the socialization of recruits during the ritual is unpleasantly noticeable, then the illusion of divinely inspired spontaneity is difficult to sustain. Through the unobtrusive methods outlined earlier, the leaders of St. Anne's prayer community were able to instruct neophytes in the content and form appropriate for each of the offerings; by positively and negatively reinforcing the initial attempts of inexperienced Charismatics to participate actively in the ritual, standards for performance were effectively and quickly enforced.

But if too little control over Pentecostal enthusiasm undermines the goal of compromise, too much control vitiates Catholic Pentecostal activities, rendering them unsatisfactorily predictable and unexciting. The self-imposed limits on overt control of the ritual illustrate the importance movement leaders place on maintaining, as much as possible, the sense of the dramatic, the ecstatic, and the visionary. Enthusiasm too bridled is neither emotionally fulfilling for experienced participants nor sufficiently inspirational for potential recruits.

As St. Anne's prayer community increased in size and the socialization efforts of its leaders bore fruit, the content and form of the prayer meeting grew less objectionable but became too predictable. While this trend satisfied the political goal of restraint, it also changed the psychological impact of the ritual on some of its most experienced participants. Of the various means by which understimulated Charismatics sought exciting alternatives or complements to the routinized prayer meeting, perhaps the most interesting was the participation of some in the establishment of a new prayer community in the diocese. Attracted to the exciting and rather unpredictable early phase in the development of a prayer community, these devout Charismatics promoted the expansion of the movement in their capacities as instructors and exemplars.

Catholic Pentecostalism is the outcome of an attempt to weld a compromise, a mutual accommodation, between enthusiastic innovation and traditional orthodoxy. As such it represents an instructive example of the cultural subtlety and organizational flexibility of which the Catholic church is capable. Indeed, this periodic cultural and organizational elasticity is an important reason why the Roman Catholic church is—in terms of longevity, scale, and resources— the most successful corporate group in human history.

9

Political Religion and Religious Politics in an Alpine Italian Village

GEORGE R. SAUNDERS

Every religiously grounded unworldly love and indeed every ethical religion must, in similar measure and for similar reasons, experience tensions with the sphere of political behavior (Weber 1963:223).

The politicization of religion is a well-known phenomenon in the modern world, and almost always entails transformations in the religious system. Examples are readily available in the anthropological literature. Gananath Obeyesekere (1970), for instance, has described the ways in which traditional Buddhist beliefs, rituals, and priestly roles in Sri Lanka have changed through politicization in opposition to Western Christianity, and Clifford Geertz (1973b) has shown how in Java the peaceful coexistence of Islam and the Hindu-Indic tradition has been broken through their politicization. To some extent, this politicization is intrinsic to ideological struggle in complex societies, in which religion necessarily becomes self-conscious and willful rather than nonreflective and automatic (see for example Geertz 1971; Bellah 1970; and Sartre 1972). It is still religion, in most places in the world, that provides the deepest sense of "meaning" for most people, that orients them in general ways to action, and that defines for them sources of power, morality, and comfort in times of distress. But it rarely does so any longer without a complicating reflectiveness. As one of Geertz's Javanese informants remarked of the conflict generated at a funeral, "You can't even die any more but what it becomes a political problem" (1973:156).

In this respect, Italy is particularly interesting. In many ways, it led the Western world in the conceptual separation of church and state that now characterizes many highly modernized societies. The Italian Renaissance is certainly one logical historical home for such secularizing and rationalizing processes. In Italy, though, as in most other Western nations, the full secularization of the

Valbella, Italy

state has not occurred, and politics and religion have continued to be mutually relevant domains of both public and private life. Italy is certainly "modern" in the sense suggested above: there is a high degree of self-consciousness and very little consensus about the proper relationship between religion and politics. This may be surprising to those who are accustomed to thinking of Italy as a homogenous Catholic country, the home of the pope and the international center of the Roman Catholic church. The uninformed outsider might reasonably have expected that at least in Italy the nature of Catholicism would be unproblematic, the issue of church and state would have been resolved (in one way or another), "folk" and official versions of the religion would be reasonably congruent, and so forth. In fact, however, the place of religion in public life may be even more problematic and ambiguous in Italy than in much of the rest of the world.

The purpose of this chapter is to examine a particular transformative effect of this ambiguity. In contemporary Italy, the problem centers especially on the ways in which Catholicism, ostensibly an apolitical religion, and "communism," ostensibly an areligious political movement, are conceptualized as opposing ideologies, each of which may (or may not) be relevant in either political or religious spheres of action. I will begin with some background discussion of the modern history of church-state relations in Italy, and then move to a consideration of local-level processes in the alpine village of Valbella. I will examine both social and psychological factors that bear on the politicization of religion, focusing on three closely related issues. The first concerns two psychological variables, namely attitudes toward authority and dependency, important in understanding the transformation of Christianity. The second is the symbolic significance of the tension between social hierarchy and class solidarity, or, to put it differently, between individual patronage and collective action for economic and political purposes. The third is the importance of the idea of "separate spheres" for men and women in Italian village life.

HISTORICAL AND NATIONAL CONTEXT

Italy has been the homeland of Roman Catholicism more or less continuously since the accession of the emperor Constantine early in the fourth century. For much of that history, the church has also been the state, at least in the central part of the peninsula. Modern Italy was unified as a nation, however, in the 1860s, and the unification involved the seizure by the new Italian state of all but a tiny part of the papal territory. It was at the expense of the church, then, that Italy became an integrated nation, and this fact has played a major role in modern church-state relations. In protest against the "illegal" seizure of church lands, Pope Pius IX in 1874 promulgated the policy of *non expedit*, which prohibited loyal Catholics from voting, holding office, or otherwise giving even indirect support to the Italian government (Zariski 1972:21). This policy was continued and elaborated by his successor, Pope Leo XIII, who also internationalized the conflict by prohibiting sovereigns of other Catholic countries from coming to pay official visits to the Italian government (Salvemini 1973:144ff.). Over time, the position of the church softened, partially in response to the need to protect remaining church property and the rights of individual Catholics in Italy, and partly simply in recognition of the enduring reality of the situation. In 1913 the Gentiloni Pact made it possible for Catholics to participate in the Italian government (Kertzer 1980a:103). In 1919 the Italian Popular Party (*Partito Popolare Italiano*, PPI) was formed under the leadership of a Sicilian priest and Catholic Action leader, and its goal was explicitly to unite Catholics for political action.

Church and state were officially reconciled in the Concordat of 1929, which the Vatican and Mussolini found to their mutual advantage. Since this time, the Catholic church has officially held a privileged position in Italy, although the formal recognition of this relationship has not diminished the national ambivalence about it. The Concordat and the Lateran Pacts were also incorporated into the controversial Article 7 of the postwar constitution, which recognizes Roman Catholicism as the "sole religion of the state" (Di Renzo 1967:76). Significantly, the Italian Communist party (PCI), in an attempt to demonstrate the compatibility of communism and Catholicism, supported this clause in the constitution. It was the only party other than the PPI's successor, the Christian Democratic party (*Democrazia cristiana*, or the DC), to support continuation of the privileged status of the Catholic church.

In the immediate postwar period the DC emerged as the representative of Catholic interests. By building from the organizational strength of the church, it also established itself as the most powerful party in the new state. At the national level it has retained this position from 1948 until the present, although in recent years the Italian Communist party has not been far behind in votes and has held control of many municipal, provincial, and regional governments.

The DC has no formal ties to the Vatican, and the relationship is theoretically an informal one based on ideological similarities between the church and the party. Nevertheless, the DC has in practice generally proposed legislation that directly reflects official church policies. Sometimes it has done so even when it was apparent that such policies were at odds with the ideas of many DC voters. In 1974, for example, the party initiated a referendum designed to force the repeal of a law that allowed divorce (although even under this law the conditions and procedures for getting a divorce were among the most prohibitive in Europe). This referendum was soundly defeated at the polls. Again, in 1981, the party attempted to repeal a liberal abortion law, but the vote was almost two to one to retain it. In these cases, the party leadership has shown its allegiance to the policies of the church in opposition even to the will of a large proportion of its own constituents.

Even the DC leadership has shown ambivalence about the relationships between the church and the party. Alcide DeGasperi, the party's major figure in the early postwar period, once made this ambiguous statement:

We know that the state is completely independent in its relationship with the Church. We want, as the Church itself wants, to maintain this independence. But we know that we have first of all the moral duty, and since the Concordat, the juridical duty as well, to surround the Holy See with the most absolute respect. And we must above all remember that in the last hundred years of Italy's history the activity of the clergy has been directed to the moral reconstruction of Italy and that of healthy and free democratic institutions (quoted in Di Renzo 1967:59–60; see also Carrillo 1965:131–51).

In recent years, as the church has appeared to take a more conservative stand on social issues, many within the DC—especially in its leftist factions—have urged the party to exercise greater independence from the church and its dogma, with attention focused instead on social issues in a broadly interpreted "spirit of Christianity." There are paradoxical problems in such an orientation, however, since, as David I. Kertzer has pointed out, the DC "recognizes that its mass appeal is dependent on its identification with the Church" (1980a:81). This is especially true at the local level. Gaetano Salvemini has noted that "there are two churches in Italy: the local popular church, which is to be found in the parishes; and the Vatican, which is an international institution having its seat in Rome" (1973:159). This distinction is crucial: official policy and its realization at the local level are altogether different matters. Though many DC politicians today are somewhat embarrassed by the open partisanship of priests in their Sunday sermons (see, for example, C. White 1980:152–53), they nonetheless understand that many Italians vote DC precisely because they believe that it is their obligation as Catholics to do so. "False consciousness" this may be, but if the DC were effectively to differentiate itself from the church, it would undercut a major source of its own electoral strength.

It is not only the Christian Democratic party that is ambivalent about the relationship between church and state, however. In practice, if not in theory, similar ambiguities are found in the positions of the leftist parties, particularly the Communist party. At first glance, its policies seem clear: despite its earlier support of Article 7 of the Constitution, the PCI now fully endorses the separation of church and state. As former party Secretary Enrico Berlinguer said following the defeat of the abortion referendum, "Italians—non-believers and believers—have demonstrated their will to safeguard the lay character of the state against any kind of religiosity" (*Post-Crescent*, Appleton, Wisconsin, 5/19/81:A–6). PCI leaders (as well as leaders of the other lay parties) would like, at this point in history, to complete the conceptual differentiation of church and state that the DC must, for the reasons noted earlier, be careful to resist. The continuing significance of the problem is also emphasized in the remarks of Giovanni Spadolini, the first non-DC prime minister of the postwar era, who on taking office in 1981 said that his premiership was "a historic event because it established for the first time the practice of rotation of the Prime Ministership between the secular and the Catholic forces in the country" (*New York Times* 6/29/81:1).

The Italian Communist party's situation is the reverse of that of the Christian Democratic party. Though the PCI supports the differentiation of politics and religion, it must struggle to avoid being characterized as "antireligious." In order to build a broadly based, popular party in a country in which less than 1 percent of the population is officially non-Catholic, the PCI has tried not to make party membership and church membership totally incompatible. It has promoted an image of itself as the party of religious freedom, rather than one that might put severe restrictions on the church (which is the way the church and the DC in turn have tried to portray the PCI). Following Antonio Gramsci, the PCI has competed politically more at the social than the ideological level (Kertzer 1980b:327), but has allowed for the compatibility of Catholic belief and Communist political action. In short, again, it has worked for the conceptual differentiation of religion and politics, such that an individual's actions in one sphere are irrelevant with respect to the other.

For example, a significant symbolic expression of this position was that the wife of former PCI Secretary Berlinguer was a practicing Catholic, and he sometimes dropped her at the church as he left for some party function. In the Italian context, this was a vivid statement both of the potential compatibility of religion and politics and of the appropriate male and female domains of interest and responsibility. I will return to this latter point later in the chapter.

At the local level, nonetheless, the policy of differentiation often leads to competition between the PCI and the church for the social loyalty of individuals. Many Communist party organizations, especially in Italy's "Red Belt" in the regions of Umbria, Tuscany, and Emilia-Romagna, put considerable pressure on their members not to participate in church activities. Political allegiance has a strong social foundation, and for a PCI member to attend church on a regular basis (or for an active Catholic to attend PCI meetings) would be disruptive to the separate social networks of the two groups. In fact, this is one of the situations in which the ambiguity sometimes leads to social conflict or psychological tension. As Kertzer has shown (1975, 1980a), the Communist party has to a great extent been successful in supplanting parish churches as the sponsor of secular and political "rites of community" (in Bologna, at any rate), but a large percentage of Communists continue to turn to the church for "rites of passage"—baptisms, weddings, and funerals. Such rites have to do with fundamental processes of "making meaning" in important life situations and events, and here the Christian world view retains its hegemony in Italian culture. Indeed, the problem here is precisely the conflict between psychoculturally based "meaning" and socially based party allegiance, and this conflict often forces people into floundering justifications and apologies for their actions. When a PCI member chooses to baptize his or her children, he creates potential for social conflict; surely he does so because baptism symbolizes for him something beyond those social ties, something significant enough that he may buck his friends and his own ideological commitments in order to retain that sense of connection (however minimal) to a meaningful other world. It is clear that in many ways the

Christian consciousness of such a person has been transformed, but that "core" meanings are still encapsulated in the symbols of Christianity.

On the whole, then, there appears to be an advantage for the church and the DC in the promotion of "integralism," the attempt to provide a totally integrated institutional and ideological framework for life, in which politics and religion are inextricably linked. The church depends on the DC to defend its interests in the Italian state, and the party recognizes that it draws much of its electoral strength from its linkage to the church. The secular parties, on the other hand, find it advantageous to convince the Italian people that religion and politics are two distinct, mutually irrelevant domains of life. Both sides, however, demonstrate ambivalence about the proper general relationship between politics and religion, and the matter remains highly problematic.

What I am getting at here is that it is precisely because of this ambiguity and ambivalence that the relationship between specific political and religious ideologies is polemicized. The mutual relevance of politics and religion in specific contexts is negotiable and manipulable. The outcome of disputes, conflicts, and competitive trials depends on the ability of the actors to convince others that a particular situation is or is not one in which either politics, or religion, or both, are relevant features of the contest (cf. Bailey 1969). I do not mean to imply that people always have conscious control over their political and religious attitudes, but the general ambiguity makes conscious manipulations particularly possible. It is not automatically acceptable to discuss religious views at a political rally, but it may be so; and a sermon is not automatically an occasion for the pronouncement of political opinions, but it may be so. And furthermore, an ordinary man's decision to join the Communist party does not automatically entail a family fight about religion, but it may. Furthermore, because of the problematic nature of the relationship, Christianity itself is transformed and modified in order to maintain or improve its competitive position. With this in mind, let us examine some aspects of the relationship between politics and religion at the local level.

POLITICS AND RELIGION IN VALBELLA

Valbella is a mountain village, located in the province of Cuneo in the Maritime Alps of northwestern Italy. In the 1970s the village had a population of about 2,400, with about half residing in the central section on the floor of the valley and the remainder in some forty hamlets distributed around the valley walls and alpine terraces. Mountainous and undeveloped for tourism, Cuneo has long been one of the poorest provinces of industrial northern Italy. Until the 1950s the majority of Valbella's population was engaged in mixed farming on small, labor-intensive, family operations. There were few occupational alternatives locally, and it was common for young people to migrate for work to southern France, America, or the large industrial cities of northern Italy (see Saunders 1979). In the 1970s the exodus from the farms accelerated, although since some industrial jobs became available in the province itself, the depopulation of the village slowed somewhat. The opening of industrial concerns in the surrounding areas made it possible for many young people to find work close to home, so that they often maintained local residence and stayed in daily contact with their parents and adult siblings. Still, a large number of young families eventually left the village in order to be closer to schools, hospitals, movie theaters, and other amenities of modern life. On the whole, the community changed dramatically in the quarter century following World War II, from a relatively homogeneous farming village to a mixed community of factory workers, farmers, bureaucrats, pensioners, and students.

The extent of these changes can be illustrated with a few statistics. In 1951 the population was over 3,200, and 73 percent of the labor force was engaged in agriculture. By 1981 the population had declined by more than a quarter, to less than 2,300, and only 27 percent of the labor force was engaged in agriculture. Perhaps more significant is the fact that of the 156 men between the ages of fourteen and twenty-nine in the 1981 labor force, only 22 (14 percent) were farming. Finally, the age cohorts of the village have shifted: in 1951, 20 percent of the population was under the age of fifteen and 13 percent over the age of sixty-five. By 1981 only 15 percent was younger than fifteen, and 20 percent was older than sixty-five.

The general political and religious orientations of the community have been moderately conservative, though there has also been some diversity. For most of the postwar period, the dominant political party has been the Catholic DC. In the 1980 administrative elections, for example, the DC received slightly over 40 percent of the votes, and the second strongest party was the PCI, with about 14 percent. The PCI vote has tended to be very stable since the war, and the party activists have been the now largely middle-aged to elderly men who participated in the armed resistance movement against the Germans and the Italian fascists at the end of the war. In the 1980 election, the Socialist party (PSI) polled about 10 percent. Its composition differed from that of the PCI, and it drew primarily young men, especially factory workers but also bureaucrats and teachers. It was a much more visible party than the 10 percent vote would indicate, with frequent open meetings and agitation on local issues. Its members were more likely than those of other parties to declare their party loyalty in bar or *piazza* discussions. The PSI would probably have had much more local strength had it not been for an unpopular action taken in 1979 by the regional council, then dominated by the PSI and the PCI. Some years earlier, the previous regional council had decided to develop a large hospital complex in Valbella, and many people had seen this as the first ray of hope for the survival of the village as a viable community. The hospital would have provided close to one hundred jobs directly, and would also have attracted more commerce to the village. However, when the structure was half completed, the new regional council decided that it was economically extravagant and shut down the construction. Many Valbellans regarded this as "typical" partisan political warfare (they took it as a punishment for the village's continued support of the DC), and many of those who had favored the PSI became disaffected.

In the 1980 election, perhaps the most interesting block of votes consisted of those that were blank or void. A full 12 percent, or the third largest block of votes, were invalid, and it is probable that a fair number of the votes for other minor parties were also "throw-aways." This fact reflects the profound alienation of many voters from the political process, an alienation not unlike the alienation from the church. We will return to this issue in the course of the analysis.

PRAYER AND ANTIPRAYER IN THE JUNE ELECTIONS

In the week before the 1980 elections, the parish bulletin of the Church of San Donato in Valbella included the following:

Prayer for the June Elections

Our father who art in heaven and governs the universe, grant us the favor of having truly Christian representatives [in government] so that, through them, Your name may be glorified and Your kingdom of faith and love extended to all of the people. May Your will be done by those who govern us, as it is done by the Angels and Saints in heaven. Oh Lord, give us material welfare, but above all the bread of truth, of justice, of liberty; pardon the many public offenses that have insulted and continue to insult your divine majesty; free us, Oh Lord, from the danger that the Catholics, in the coming elections, may forget the gravity of their duty and give their vote to candidates or parties that do not offer the moral certainty of respecting and defending fully the doctrine of Your Gospel, the rights of religion and of the Church in private and public life. Grant us that all united and in concord we may press together around the standard of Your cross, to win the holy battle, for the triumph of Your name and for the salvation of our souls. Amen.

By chance, immediately under the prayer was printed the short notice, "The page of the offerings and other notices will be printed next month." (Usually, donations to the church—other than the small offerings in the Sunday collection basket—are announced in the parish bulletin.)

A couple of days later, a photocopied "Antiprayer for the Elections of June" was distributed anonymously on doorsteps around town. It was considerably longer than the original prayer, and since many of the references were to particular events and people not individually relevant to the discussion here, I will not reproduce it all. I have excerpted enough to render the tone and some of the content of the antiprayer.

Antiprayer for the Elections of June

Dear baby Jesus, who art so good, come down from heaven just once and descend upon the earth. Come to take away all the men of good will: Tanassi, Rumor, Leone, and Gui. . . . Valbella is a little town and the newspapers don't make it here, but our good priest Don Martino illuminates us from evening to morning with the Divine message—to vote for the Catholics [the DC]. Oh Lord, pardon the Italians, who don't know how to vote; don't continue to punish them with torrential rains. Have faith and hope because your cross is only the symbol of "Libertas." We, unfortunately, as good Catholics, do not identify with it, much less participate in your rich Sunday banquets. . . . Be quick if you want to save us from our fate; don't send the Winged Angel to mark "the crossed shield" on the ballot. . . . We bless you and glorify you, because your "dear friends" hold power tightly in their hands. Nevertheless, may your will be done. Amen.

Separated from the prayer itself, in response to the notice in the parish bulletin, was the following brief note: "The offerings will not be published in this nor in future issues, because nobody ever offers us anything."

The prayer and the antiprayer for the June elections encapsulate some of the most important political and religious attitudes of Valbellans. Before elaborating on them further, let me clarify a few of the references in the "Antiprayer." The "men of good will" named were national politicians of the DC and the PSDI (the Italian Social Democratic party) implicated in a serious scandal involving payoffs from the Lockheed Corporation. Giovanni Leone was the president of Italy, and he resigned under a cloud during this episode of corruption. Don Martino is the local priest, and presumably the author of the prayer in the parish bulletin. "Libertas" and the "crossed shield" are symbols of the Christian Democratic party, and they appear on the ballot itself. Though my translation may not do justice to the irony, the references here are highly sarcastic. "Dear friends" (*cari amici*), for example, is a common Italian way of describing corrupt patrons, people of power and influence who are willing to use their resources (illegally, if necessary) to help their friends and clients. The appended "nobody ever offers us anything" is clearly class-conscious, a statement that ordinary people suffer at the hands of the religious and political authorities. On the whole, the "Antiprayer" is a bitterly sarcastic parody of church and DC corruption, clientelism, and the complacent "ignorance" of Italian voters. On the other hand, though vehemently anticlerical, it is, in the end, not intended to be disrespectful to God and Jesus. The authors claim for themselves the genuine status of "good Catholics" (that is, *not* the kind who frequent the church and vote for the DC). And the final "may your will be done" seems genuine enough, though perhaps reflecting the attitude (also found in other passages in the antiprayer) that the system is unchangeable. Let us examine some of these characteristics in more detail.

HIERARCHY, PATRONAGE, AND CLASS SOLIDARITY: CLERICS AND ANTICLERICS

Though political parties were not mentioned by name in the "Prayer for the Elections of June," there was no ambiguity about the message. Catholics were reminded directly that they had a grave duty to vote for parties that would guarantee fully the rights of the church, and only one party makes such guarantees. Furthermore, the faithful were put on notice that this was not a mundane affair, but rather a "holy battle," and the coup de grâce was the final suggestion that an individual's vote had direct relevance for the "salvation of our souls." I do not know whether this prayer was composed personally by Valbella's priest or made available from diocesan sources, but it was certainly in keeping with Don Martino's past actions. Don Martino, the priest, was not a fiery politico, but a humble, retiring, almost painfully shy man whose parishioners sometimes complained that he hid from them. But his abhorrence of communism and his commitment to the DC were well known, and stories abounded of his work in campaigning, both privately and publicly, for the party. He appeared to find it quite appropriate to suggest to parishioners that good Catholics had only one political choice.

Don Martino was not unusual, in this respect, for an elderly Italian priest. The use of the pulpit for partisan political messages was common. Parishioners varied, however, in their reactions to such political propaganda. The message meant different things to different people, and though the matter is complex, we can at least sort out some of the variables that help distinguish the attitudes of different kinds of people in Valbella.

In the first place, the priest, the church, and the Christian Democratic party all symbolized for most Valbellans a common type of social relations: the system of patron-client relationships so well known in Italy (cf. Galt 1974; Silverman 1965; C. White 1980), in which hierarchy and vertical solidarity are the normative patterns of social alliance. That is, they promoted and depended on the personal loyalty and submission of individual, ordinary people to those of greater status, authority, and power. Though Christianity can certainly be interpreted as an ideology of revolutionary class solidarity, for Valbellans the church symbolized rather patronage and vertical alliance. The priest could refer to Christians as "all united and in concord," but implied that such unity is attained only when "pressing around the standard of the cross"—that is, when subjugating themselves in obedience to a higher authority. The idiom of Christianity in Valbella, then, was the idiom of patronage, and it depended on individual ties to those superiors—human and supernatural—who could help one through life. The help people hoped for, however, did not come cheaply; it had to be paid for with devotion, attentiveness, loyalty, and perhaps votes.

In practical, material terms, the priest of Valbella was a distinctly unimpressive patron. There was precious little that he could offer to parishioners, in the modern context, outside of religion itself. He did control a small charity fund, and he could write letters of recommendation, but on the whole his material influence was minimal. In fact, even the Christian Democratic party had few favors to dispense in Valbella, since the regional and provincial governments, which controlled a good portion of locally spendable funds, were dominated by other parties. Still, the idea that such favors were possible, and that it was important to stay on the right side, was very prevalent. The DC mayor of

Valbella, for example, though a local by birth, actually resided in Rome and returned frequently for holidays, council meetings, and public events. Part of his electoral appeal was precisely that he lived in Rome, and so was thought to have important connections that could benefit the community. In addition, though Valbellans may not have expected positive favors from the *signori* (see Bailey 1971) of the church and the party, many were afraid of offending these elites, fearing that such people could harm them or at least make their lives more difficult. Ordinary people were often reminded, in subtle or not-so-subtle ways, that their well-being was in the hands of other, superior people. The municipal doctor (*medico condotto*) who served the village until 1977 was said by villagers to dispense birth control information only if the person could produce a note of permission signed by the priest (which would almost surely have been impossible). While such information is readily available from other sources, this kind of statement—that people must work through the proper higher authorities in order to take care of their own personal needs—is common in the idiom of patronage.

Certainly at the symbolic level, the attraction of an alliance with a superior was considerable. Supernatural patrons were regarded as important for health and well-being, and it was still common to request favors from patron saints or the Virgin. The local tradition is rich with examples: In the sixteenth century, for instance, after a plague had passed through Valbella, surviving villagers built four small churches on four mountain peaks surrounding the village. These are all dedicated to the Virgin and have remained places of sacred and festive importance. In one, the walls are lined with *ex voto* paintings—some quite recent—depicting the favors requested of the Virgin. And in the 1970s, trips to Lourdes, organized by the parish priest or by the diocese, were made annually by those in poor health.

What kinds of people in Valbella were attracted by patronage and the imagery of vertical solidarity—the idiom of both the church and the DC? Middle-class men, particularly professionals and moderately well-to-do merchants, were among the most visible supporters of the church and were the activists of the Christian Democratic party. They had enough wealth and prestige to be concerned about protecting it, had small favors to dispense, and, because they were themselves in the minority and hoped to stay there, feared the development of class consciousness. To suggest that their ideological commitment to Catholicism and the DC was self-serving is not to imply that it was insincere. It is merely to recognize that, as interpreted by these people and the priest, Catholicism was conservative and favored the interests of bourgeois males. And it is to acknowledge, with Marx, that these people have traditionally been the ideological leaders in village culture (Marx 1978:172). The symbolization and propagation of elite ideas are nicely illustrated in Stanley H. Brandes' analysis of the *cofradía* of *el Señor del Consuelo* (a manifestation of Christ in a large painting) in a southern Spanish town. As he remarks, "the Señor, in his own way, has come to represent law, order, stability and historical continuity, all of which are highly valued by the Monteros elite" (1980:195). Much of the religious symbolism salient in Valbella worked in precisely this fashion.

Others who found such ideas attractive were in fact socially and economically dependent, people with little or no "clout" of their own, who were in need of help and protection. Socialized to the ideals of the church, they expected their rewards in another world and knew that if they happened to be rewarded in this life it would be through "miracles," that is, through the personal intervention of a patron. They often had low aspirations and expectations, and took pride, when they could take it at all, in their humble morality. This group included particularly women of all socioeconomic positions (though not all women, by any means), children, and some "traditional," relatively unsophisticated farmers.

Other people, however, rejected the idiom of patronage and were skeptical that vertical solidarity is ever binding on the superior partner. There are strong characterological reasons for such rejection in some cases, but for the moment let us consider social aspects. One of the well-known contradictions of southern European society is the coexistence of Catholicism and anticlericalism (see especially Kertzer 1980a:120–124). The anticlerics in Valbella, such as the authors of the "Antiprayer," felt that the church and the DC worked to protect the rights of a few at the expense of the many, and particularly to the detriment of the poor and otherwise powerless citizens. Symbolically, the opposition to the church was often expressed in terms of class solidarity—the horizontal solidarity of those who are alike; and in this symbolism, the priests and the politicians and all those who attempted to act as patrons were seen as the villains. An excellent example of this sentiment is found in a "testimony" taken in Valbella by researcher Nuto Revelli. An eighty-two-year-old peasant reminisced to Revelli in this fashion:

> The priest used to say from the pulpit: "But you socialists, do you or do you not believe that God exists?" We couldn't answer him because we respected the Church. But we understood that the priest was using an arrogant manner for political propaganda. We were Christians, but we said, "Politics is one thing and religion is another. . . . " We weren't against religion; we said of the priests, "Do you believe in God? Or do you pretend to believe in order to dominate the little people (*il basso popolo*)?" (Revelli 1977:37).

Here the speaker shows clear disdain for the priests, whom he regards as hypocrites who pretend to believe for political ends. He also shows class consciousness, identifying with the "*basso popolo*" and arguing that religion is serving the interests of others. He believes in God (and even in the abstract church), but he demands the differentiation of politics and religion. (For a similar view from another part of Italy, see Pitkin 1985:219–22).

The sentiment expressed in this peasant's speech, like that in the antiprayer, is a rejection of the ideology of dependency, patronage, and hierarchy. These sentiments were most commonly expressed by young men, particularly students and factory workers. Many of these young men had had to work through the psychological and social problems of resisting their fathers' authoritative attempts to control their careers and their mothers' attempts to control their marriages. They were financially independent, but not well-off, and had had to struggle to establish their autonomy. This is not to suggest that such factors in personal history are the sole determinants of ideology and political allegiance, but they do help in forming "angry young men," and these were the Valbellans who most often rejected the church and the DC. They were the activists of the local section of the Socialist party, while the activists of the Communist party were mainly middle-aged to elderly men whose political formation had been more directly influenced by the experiences of World War II.

Other farmers did not show quite the political sophistication of the speaker quoted earlier. Indeed, the following excerpt from my field notes shows another orientation entirely:

Antonio and I were discussing the recent political election. He was not really sure how it came out, but thought that "nothing had changed." I asked him about his political preferences (which, though we knew each other well, had never been discussed), and he told me that he had always, for thirty-five years, voted for the same party, the Social Democrats [PSDI]. He said that he liked them because they were "halfway between the Democrats [DC] and the Socialists [PSI]." I asked him what he thought of the leader of the Social Democratic party, and he appeared troubled, and it became apparent that he didn't know who it was. After a minute he asked his fourteen-year-old daughter if it were Craxi [then Secretary of the Socialist party], and then, getting no answer, said "Yes, I think that is who it is." I asked him what he thought of the relationship between politics and religion. He did not understand my vague (and rather stupid) question, and said that he was "more for religion than for politics, because the politicians have nothing of substance, but religion is always there." He then continued, "After all, it must be true, because there is hardly any place in the world that is not Christian." On the subject of Communism, he said that he didn't think that the Communists would really take away everything that everybody owns, but that "Still, Communism is more or less like Mussolini—a dictatorship. Communism is lack of freedom. Italy may have its problems, but at least we are free to go anywhere we want. If we want to go to Sicily, we go. Instead, in Russia, people can't go where they want. There are some places in Russia, in the real Russia, that foreigners never get to see." He asked his daughter the name of the "real Russia," and when she again did not answer, he said, "You know, like Stalingrad, I think it's called that" (Field notes 6/11/80).

This man generally accepted the ideology of the church, though rather halfheartedly, and he was somewhat skeptical about the word of "authorities." There is no term in the literature, to my knowledge, to describe the political attitude analogous to "anticlericalism" in religion. I suppose that it is most often referred to under the rubric of "alienation," which it certainly is, in part. As I will indicate later on, I think that in Valbella there was a fundamental characterological similarity underlying the distrust of priests and of politicians. When this man said that "politicians have nothing of substance," he meant that their words were only words, and he, like many others, assumed that they were primarily in politics for their own gain.

These attitudes were very common among farmers, who tended to regard all political parties and the clergy as either irrelevant or antithetical to their lives (an attitude often justified by experience). They managed to make a barely passable living through their own hard effort, and they asked of the priests and politicians only that they be left alone. They distrusted all sources of local authority, but were generally more indifferent than passionate in these attitudes. They did not make much effort to inform themselves about events in the world and presumed that people everywhere were pretty much the same—working and struggling to survive. Many of the farmers regularly voted for the Christian Democratic party, but in an unreflective fashion. Several stated explicitly to me that the DC had done next to nothing to help small farmers, but that in the end they always voted DC anyway. Often such statements were followed by a comment such as "We are Christians, after all, so how could we vote otherwise?" This is precisely the attitude that the priest sought to reinforce with reminders like the election prayer.

Anticlericalism was also sometimes found without the class consciousness of the first testimony. A merchant expressed these feelings about the church and the priests during a conversation about her recent illness.

She started by saying how much she disliked the church, because it deceives people and is always "picking at them." It makes them "believe in illusions." She described how when she had been in the hospital, gravely ill and near the point of death, the doctor used to come in three times a day, and each time would ask her if he could send the priest to give her communion. She told the doctor that she knew that this meant that he thought she was going to die, but it didn't matter to her—it was against her principles to go to communion. Her father felt the same way, she told me, and he is in the hospital right now, but he has let them give him communion twice, because he doesn't feel quite strong enough "to fight them off." She thinks that this is disgusting behavior by the priests and the "Catholics." They should respect her principles and leave her alone, rather than hounding her about it. Her husband basically agrees with her, she said, although when it came down to it, he had the children baptized and sent them to first communion. She was opposed even to baptizing them, because she didn't believe in it. I asked if she was not at all a believer, and she replied, "Oh, I suppose I believe in something, but certainly not in what they believe in. If there is a heaven up there, though, I deserve it for what I've done, not for anything that has to do with the church" (Field notes 6/7/80).

Here, in the last sentence, this woman explicitly rejected the notion that the church could or should mediate or intercede for her. Though she did not express class solidarity, she rejected the morality (and perhaps the efficacy) of patronage, and emphasized her individual accomplishments.

These individualistic attitudes can also be related to characteristic features of social life in southern European villages. It has often been noted that such communities seem riddled with jealousies, that gossip is rampant, and that there is a general distrust of those who try to put themselves above others. Thus politicians and the priest, who hold formal offices, and more generally those who act the part of "*signori*," are frequently considered hypocrites. It is assumed that their real intentions are strikingly at odds with their public "faces," and that they have hidden motives and goals. In Valbella, proverbs such as "*Mangia ostia e caga diau*" ("he or she eats the communion wafer and shits the devil") captured this feeling that those who appeared most religious were in fact the most devilish. Thus anticlericalism without class consciousness may be related to the "atomistic" social relations of such communities, in which the priest and politicians, like everybody else, are thought to be trying to capture an unfair portion of the "limited good" (Foster 1965). To people like the woman just quoted, priests and politicians were particularly despicable, however, because they used the "normative cover" of the church and their offices to take advantage of other people.

On the other hand, to the extent that such attitudes were grounded in features of social organization, they could as easily be applied to "Communists" as to the priests. That is, the politicization (in the general sense) of morality means that anybody can be accused of hypocrisy, double-dealing, and hidden motives. This is illustrated in one informant's account of a baptism in which he had been the godfather. The godmother was known to be a Communist, and so this man (a farmer who only occasionally attended church but who considered himself a good Catholic, and who was certainly anti-Communist) watched her closely during the baptismal ceremony. At several points during the baptism (according to his account), she mumbled the ritual words rather incoherently instead of speaking them out loudly and clearly. The man became very anxious and was concerned that the child had not been properly baptized. After several weeks of worrying about it, he finally went back to the priest to discuss the matter, and was satisfied only when the priest assured him that the ceremony had properly "taken." This case illustrates the ambiguity about the relationship between politics and religion. If the situation had not been ambiguous, the anxiety and tension would never have occurred: either the Catholic parents would not have invited a Communist to be godmother, or as a good Communist she would have refused, or, finally, her position in the ceremony would have caused no one any difficulty. As it was, she was probably ambivalent herself, which is why the words were mumbled instead of spoken out clearly. In any case, the ceremony became an occasion for conflict, since the godfather later "told her off" for her behavior during the baptism.

In fact, the ambiguity surrounding the differentiation of religion and politics frequently fueled the fears of hypocrisy in the village. To many Catholics, there was no question about communism being an atheistic ideology incompatible with religious belief and practice. When they then saw local leftists acting as godparents, sending their children to first communion, and so forth, they assumed that they had ulterior motives. PCI members themselves often felt guilty—either because of their participation in religious activities ("Communist guilt"), or because of their lack of full participation ("Catholic guilt"), and they were likely to behave defensively.

DEPENDENCY, AUTHORITY, AND THE FAMILY

Conflicts over dependency and authority relations have both social and psychological components. We have concentrated on the social aspects earlier, and I have written extensively about the psychological aspects in other places (1979; 1981), so I will not review the entire issue here. It is important to note, however, that both dependency and authority were issues of considerable significance for people in Valbella. Socialization of young children was generally oriented toward fostering dependent, centripetal relations between parents and children. As a result, early dependency needs were highly gratified, but they became problematic later, when children experienced anxiety and frustration in their attempts to move away from the control of their parents. Similarly, relationships between parents and children were often quite authoritarian.

It is partly because people have strong reactions to dependency and authority that particular idioms in politics and religion become psychologically engaging. In Valbella, people resolved these issues in a variety of different ways, of course. On the whole, women seemed to be more comfortable with symbolic dependency, which was compatible with certain aspects of their normal social roles (though for comparison see Cornelisen 1977; Brandes 1975:116–117; Parsons 1969; Revelli 1985; and Saunders 1981). Many women seemed to form a genuine identification with the Madonna, taking her submissive, asexual, maternal character as their ego ideal, and symbolically manifesting their dependency in unquestioning loyalty to the church (and by extension to the DC). Through the interweaving of religion and family life, symbolized in the maternal role of the Madonna, a mother might become the representative of the church in her own family.

It has often been pointed out (e.g. Dubisch 1986; Reiter 1975; Saunders 1981) that men and women in southern Europe have had distinct and separate life-worlds, that they have occupied different spaces and been assigned different domains of responsibility and competence. Carl N. Degler, in a recent book on women and the family in America, refers to this physical and conceptual separation as "the doctrine of separate spheres" (1980). In general, in Valbella as in much of the Latin Mediterranean (cf. Wolf 1969:288), politics has been considered a male domain, and religion a female domain. The family has likewise been a female domain, and the external world a male domain. These are cognitive distinctions and they do not necessarily hold behaviorally, of course. And in claiming that politics has been a male domain, I do not mean to imply that women have not interested themselves in politics, but simply that they have not ordinarily done so publicly. In nearly two years of research in the village,

I attended many political meetings, and only once saw a woman at a formal (nonrecreational) party gathering, and she came as a silent companion to a man. Even at the meetings of the Communist and Socialist parties, where women's rights were sometimes discussed, there was a conspicuous absence of women themselves. One woman said explicitly to me, "Men are made for politics, women for the family."

The corollary assertion—that religion has been a female domain—requires some qualifications, since I have pointed out that bourgeois men played prominent roles in church activities. Nevertheless, attendance at mass was predominantly female. For example, it was informative to watch the course of a funeral in Valbella. The ceremony usually began with people assembling at the hospital chapel, several blocks from the church. Men and women walked behind the hearse from the chapel to the door of the church. There the women followed it inside, while most of the men peeled off and stayed outside to smoke; some went to a nearby bar. When the women emerged from the church, the men assembled again behind the casket to accompany it out of town toward the cemetery.

The rank and file of the active churchgoers, then, were women. Those men who did take active roles in the church were often in positions of authority. They were called upon by the priest to organize festivals and fund-raising projects, and they performed the readings at mass. Such positions of authority and responsibility were obviously limited, however, and the male activists were accordingly few. Most men had difficulty accepting the dependent and submissive roles that ordinary churchgoers assumed. Indeed, many men, especially young adults, found it excruciatingly embarrassing when they were prevailed upon to do such jobs as helping to carry the statue through the streets during a patron saint's festival. There is a sense in which the church was conceived of as having a feminine personality in general, and thus men who were not in positions of leadership felt that they were submitting to feminine authority, and this was anxiety-producing and threatening to their male identities.

Given such psychocultural attitudes toward religion, the ambiguity about the relationship between politics and religion can foster psychological as well as social tension. The "separate spheres" can at times overlap, and this creates difficulties. For example, women sometimes saw a DC vote as an essential statement of Christian commitment. Even women who would not contradict their husbands on other matters felt justified in asserting themselves in this area, because religion was, for them, within their domain—the domain of home and family. Women might become politicized and assertive when they thought that their husbands' or sons' politics were incompatible with their family religious commitments. The women's assertiveness, once manifest, made men angry and frustrated, but they were often reluctant to engage in direct conflict over the matter. Accordingly, at a Communist party meeting in Valbella, a party leader lamented the fact that many men were "fiery revolutionaries" at the factory, but came home at night to be traditional, complacent, religious sons and husbands, so as not to disturb the peace of their homes. I once observed a middle-aged man joking to his eighty-year-old mother that he was going to vote for the PCI. She knew he was joking, but in a serious voice told me that if she thought it were true there would be real problems in the house. From behind her back, he grimaced his affirmation of this statement. Another man told me in private that he had voted against the repeal of the divorce law, but that I should not tell his wife, since she thought he had voted with the church.

The differentiation of religion and politics was thus problematic in Valbella. Men who did not share the opinions of their wives and mothers had two basic options: to keep quiet, or to attempt to convince them that politics and religion ought to be differentiated, and that their political activity had no relevance for the family's religious life. In such a small village, however, political commitments usually became common knowledge eventually, and such issues often created conflict in the family. In the process of working through these conflicts, religious and political ideas were transformed, if not in content, at least in the degree of consciousness and in their emotive impact. Such ideas could no longer be automatic and unreflective; rather, they had to be argued, justified, and consciously accepted or rejected. This in itself may be the most important transformation of Christianity, at the personal level.

Attitudes toward authority and dependency often shaped these transformations and can be expected to continue to do so. As women come more and more to reject dependent roles in society, they may be expected more often to take positions like that of the merchant described earlier. And to the extent that the leftist parties are able to maintain their images as parties of antipaternalistic collective action, they provide support for the antiauthoritarian motives of men, who are able to feel united and powerful against management, government, and perhaps against their own fathers. On the other hand, to the extent that people find it psychologically comfortable to submit to authority, and to the extent that they continue to feel the need to ally themselves individually with powerful people, the church and the DC will remain strong. This is not to suggest that dependency and authority are the only salient issues in the "making of meaning through symbols," but they are certainly significant. The symbolism of authority and dependency has traditionally favored the church and the DC, but the changing social and political context of life in modern Italy now allows for new transformations of such symbolism. I have suggested that there has been a general shift away from hierarchy and vertical solidarity and toward horizontal solidarity, individual autonomy, and rejection of authority. Such a shift implies transformations in the political and religious symbol systems, as well as a new manner of behaving in consonance with enduring psychological motivations.

A final matter has already been hinted at in several places. The shape of the symbolism of religion and politics is intricately related to the shape of relationships within the family, and these relationships have been changing in recent years. In Valbella there has been a strong movement from three-generation, stem family residence to nuclear family households (Saunders 1979). Along with this shift, there has been considerable democratization of intrafamily relationships (Saunders 1979, 1981). These changes have also resulted in diminishing emphasis on sex-differentiated socialization and will certainly mean, in the long run, diminishing likelihood of women identifying with the Madonna and the ideals of the church (cf. Collier 1986). As this occurs, either the church will experience further changes, adapting its ideology and symbol system accordingly, or there will be an increasing secularization of Italian society. Both processes are undoubtedly already under way.

Throughout this analysis I have emphasized the problematic nature of the relationship between politics, religion, and family experience, perhaps eventuating in a rather inconclusive and even contradictory set of propositions. Despite the "messiness" of such an approach, it is appropriate to one aspect of the theoretical perspective I am using here. All cultural and social systems are replete with contradictions, and all cultures encompass considerable internal inconsistency, ambiguity, and diversity. This diversity engenders conflict at the local level, as individuals and groups attempt to manipulate culture itself in order to gain power and control of important resources. Such internal contradiction is also the source of potential social and cultural change, and—in this particular case—of an important transformation of Christianity.

10

Transformations of Christianity: Some General Observations

GEORGE R. SAUNDERS

Christianity clearly provides a flexible symbolic system that can assume various forms and functions as it is adapted to local cultural, social, economic, and political exigencies. The studies in this book, along with other recent work on culture and Christianity, illustrate this flexibility, but also suggest some core issues around which the polemics of transformation generally develop—some of the salient problems with which Christians typically concern themselves in adapting the religion to local contexts.

It is worth noting that decisions about religious life are often intrinsically political. In the simplest sense, this means that they involve people pursuing public goals, developing strategies, and marshaling resources for the attainment of those goals (see Bailey 1969). The politicization of Christianity at the "macro" level presents some interesting problems. The relationships between Christianity, colonialism, and capitalism, for example, are particularly complex. Christianity has often been an instrument used by Westerners in the pacification of colonial areas, to control and subdue potentially rebellious native populations (Bultmann 1985). A consequence—and often even a direct goal—of Christianization has been the destruction of indigenous culture. Nevertheless, it should be remembered that Christianity developed in a stratified society and since its inception some sects have adapted its ideology specifically for opposition to domination, in some cases as the ideological arm of revolution (Garrett 1986). L. M. Lombardi-Satriani, for example, describes a popular Sicilian folksong in which a serf approaches the Crucifix praying that Christ destroy "the evil race of landowners." Christ responds with a rhetorical "And are your own arms paralyzed, or are they nailed up like mine? Those who want justice make it themselves; don't wait for others to do it for you" (Lombardi-Satriani 1974:144–45).

Many of the "nativistic" movements of colonial areas, though explicitly anti-European, have incorporated essential elements of Christian belief and ritual into their programs. The Christian influence is clear in the Handsome Lake Religion of the Seneca (Wallace 1972), "Kimbanguism" in Zaire (MacGaffey 1983), and in the Paliau movement of Manus (Schwartz 1962). William Wedenoja's description of the role of Christianity in the transformation of Jamaican society clearly shows how the religion may be adapted, both psychologically and socially, to marshal anti-European sentiment and so transform itself into a revolutionary force (see also Henry 1986; D. Brown 1986:48–49; MacGaffey 1986:208–11). It is therefore clear that Christianity's symbolic system can be employed to legitimate either radical or conservative causes.

When Christianity first arrives in an area, of course, it is directly associated with those who import it—the European missionaries and their home societies. Thus it is difficult, at the outset, for it to be used for anti-European purposes. Nevertheless, within a short time, transformations may take place that make it the effective property of the indigenous population. In Jamaica, Rastafarians say that the Bible was originally a black man's document, but that King James rewrote it to suit whites (Wedenoja 1978). Part of the Rastafarians' purpose in smoking ganja is to enable them to read between the lines of the King James Bible and find the original meanings. For Rastafarians (as for Melanesians), Christianity thus becomes a kind of puzzle, and part of the religious experience is the quest for these secrets that will grant access to material success and political power.

Politicization of religion may also take place through shifting alignments within a single society, as is demonstrated by the recent dramatic events in Iran, Afghanistan, and the Middle East (cf. Esposito 1986, Saiedi 1986). As I indicate in Chapter 9, church and state have never been effectively separated in Italy, and attitudes toward the church are important indicators of political values and of party affiliation. This articulation of religion and politics is in fact an extremely important component of social life in most places in the world, despite the suggestion by modernization theorists that "differentiation" and compartmentalization are integral aspects of life in industrialized societies. The symbolic system of Christianity, then, is dynamic and can be shaped, modified, and selectively emphasized in order to make it a more effective instrument of political action in a particular setting.

THE "HOLY FAMILY": KINSHIP AND CHRISTIANITY

Some of the most significant transformative sequences in Christianity have to do with family and kinship. The "Holy Family" is probably the most salient symbolic complex in the religion, but even here the flexibility of Christianity is evident. In its standard southern European versions, Christianity describes a minimal nuclear family—a father, a mother, and a child. From a cross-cultural point of view, this family is unique: Jesus seems to have neither siblings nor biological descendants, and he is peculiarly disconnected from lineage or wider kin ties. On the other hand, family and kinship are the images he uses to express his relationship to his followers.

It seems likely that the early Christian symbolization of the family was related to a developing universalistic, achievement-based ethic and a revolutionary ideology. That is, early Christianity—a religion of artisans in an agricultural society (Weber 1963:19)—played down the importance of inherited status and appealed to a mobile population without family ties, one willing and able to demonstrate total commitment to the religion rather than to relatives. In this case, Christianity was a vehicle for a fundamental modernization of social relations, the evolution from kinship- to contract-based social organization. This modernizing tendency is still operational, as when Jamaican Pentecostal preachers stress in their evangelistic sermons that converts may face opposition from kin, but that Jesus must come first. Similarly, in the Korean village of Ye-an, the few people who converted to Christianity were somehow marginal, without powerful lineages or important ancestors, and one attraction of Christianity was simply that it provided opportunities that did not depend on kin ties. In fact, given the pervasive significance of kinship in most societies, this may be a common motive for conversion, since Christianity provides the ideological justification for rejection of kin ties.

When Christianity is taken out of the European cultural tradition, then, the nature of kinship, lineage connections, and the role of ancestors often become problematic. In the indigenous religions of Melanesia, for example, there is a kind of lineage-based ancestor cult in which living and deceased members continue to interact. In particular, the recently deceased supervise the morality of the living, acting for the welfare of the lineage. In return, the living show continuing respect for the dead. When Christian missionaries arrived in Manus, many people converted, but this did not necessarily mean that they stopped believing in ancestral spirits (Schwartz 1962, 1976). It is important to note that for most people in the world the acceptance of a new religion does not necessarily imply the rejection of the old. The adoption of Christianity may be an additive process, with Christianity and the indigenous religion seen as alternative or complementary but equally "real," rather than as mutually exclusive realities. The conversion may depend not on the "truth" of one as opposed to another religion, but on other factors, such as the relative power of the Christian God and the ancestral spirits. Similarly, a person may reject the way of life associated with previous beliefs, but not necessarily reject the beliefs themselves.

It should also be pointed out that the antikinship bias of early Christianity is often modified in the transformative process. There are numerous examples from Africa, Melanesia, and other places where Christianity has fought a losing battle against the continued social relevance of kinship ties. Henry Warner Bowden notes that the Jesuits specifically used the Huron attachment to kinspeople to expand the number of converts: "After someone became a Christian, the Jesuits warned his relatives that death would separate them unless they too adopted the new faith" (1981:87). And in this book, both Michael French

Smith and Geoffrey M. White indicate that in Melanesia people sometimes interpret the concept of God as a Christian metaphor for "ancestor," and that churches have become the functional equivalents of ancestral shrines.

The nuclear family complex of Christianity provides rich material for symbolic elaboration. In different cultures, the distinctive figures in the symbolic family—Jesus, Mary, Joseph, and God the Father—are variably emphasized and differently conceptualized. In the popular Christianity of southern Europe, for example, Mary is unquestionably the most significant religious figure. As Anne Parsons (1964, 1969) points out, she is most often presented as an idealized mother—devoted and attentive to her child, submissive and long-suffering, and basically desexualized. In certain contexts even within southern Europe, however, she may be portrayed differently. In Seville in southern Spain, the gothic, maternal Madonna is much less popular than the Baroque, virginal, almost adolescent representation. The urban proletariat of Seville relates especially to one particular Madonna—the famous Macarena—in a fashion distinct from their manner of relating (at least overtly and consciously) to their own mothers. At the feast of the Macarena, men of the barrio carry her image in procession, addressing her with *piropos* (the witty words of the hustler) and treating her much as they would a beautiful young woman passing on the street. This is a transformation that probably would not "resonate" in Anglo-Saxon cultures (cf. Warner 1961:301–14).

It is also notable that in multiethnic areas, ethnic alternatives are available in representations of the Virgin. In Mexico, for example, Our Lady of Guadalupe has been taken to be an Indian version, but there are also Hispanic-Caucasian images. Each image seems to represent a separate supernatural figure, and each is a special patron with specific attributes and its own dedicated clientele (Wolf 1958). (For a different view of the historical development of Indian devotion to the Virgin of Guadalupe, see Taylor 1987).

The selective emphasis on different persons of the Trinity is also a key aspect of transformation. In southern Europe, where an important cultural complex focuses on the mother-son relationship, Jesus (as the Son) is usually the most clearly conceptualized and salient of the three persons. There are few representations of God the Father in popular art, and he inspires little devotional attention. In the Solomon Islands, on the other hand, the father-child relationship is much more affect-laden, and God the Father is the salient figure of the Trinity. In Jamaica it appears that God the Father replaces a distant African high God, and Jesus becomes a maternal figure reflecting the social center of the matrifocal family. Though such generalizations about these correspondences obviously oversimplify a very complex phenomenon, there can be little doubt that the social and psychological salience of family relationships is reflected in an appropriate transformation of the Christian symbol system.

THE MORAL BURDEN OF CHRISTIANITY

Even when people are primarily concerned with religion's material benefits (rather than ideological content), Christianity always imposes some moral burdens on the individual and the social group. The severity of this burden, the domains of life in which it is applied, the manner of its imposition, and the types of outlets provided in different cultural settings are all relevant to the analysis of the transformative process.

"Moral burden" here refers both to the behavioral prescriptions and proscriptions of the religion and to the consequences of "sin." In some denominations, a single sin can be fatal to the soul, while in others the cycle of sin, repentance, confession, and absolution is an ongoing part of life. In some cases, all that is demanded of the Christian is a profession of belief, faith, and surrender to the will of God, while others require constant regulation of behavior. The consequences of sin may be strictly personal and other-worldly, or may be social and this-worldly. Where one's sins can bring illness and death to one's children, for example, the moral burden is serious and immediate. Theodore Schwartz reports that at one point during the Paliau movement, the idea that "God is everywhere" and omniscient was developed by the people of Manus into the doctrine of the "think-think." The basic idea—that God can understand all of people's thoughts—is common in Christianity, but here it was taken to its extreme logical conclusion, in which all thoughts, however inconsequential or fantastic, had to be carried through, or else one would have "lied" to God. For example, if a man thought to himself that it would be nice to go eat some mangoes, but en route to doing so got sidetracked and did something else, then he was thought to have attempted to deceive God. He had "told" God in his silent thoughts that he was going to do one thing, and then had done another. During this period, people walked around purposefully, without letting others interrupt or distract them. The moral burden was such that they were obsessed and driven by their own thoughts. This obsessiveness is remarkably similar to the Iroquois attitude toward dreams, as detailed by Anthony F. C. Wallace (1958).

The Christian notion of "sin," of course, is a cultural concept with a very important psychological foundation. As Robert I. Levy (1973:326) notes, early missionaries to Polynesia saw the natives' lack of "sorrow for sin" as a problem. A word signifying a sense of guilt was absent from the Tahitian language, and the culture emphasized only outer behavior as morally significant. To the Jamaican Pentecostal, sin is likewise socially controlled, and means violation of taboos prohibiting the drinking of alcohol, public dancing, cursing, selfish behavior, fraternizing with sinners, cheating, boasting, fornication, and ill temper. These taboos are enforced by gossip and by church courts that, while highly effective in small communities, are inadequate in urban areas where people may remain relatively anonymous. This conception of sin as behavioral deviance reflects the "shame-oriented" nature of the Jamaican conscience, which may have its origins partly in the social order of plantation slavery. Socialization in Jamaica—unlike the West—does not regularly employ parental withdrawal of love as punishment of children, and consequently an extrapunitive rather than intrapunitive conscience predominates (cf. Spiro 1965:406–9). In addition, many of the Pentecostal taboos are not learned in childhood, but rather adopted only upon conversion. They serve partly to distinguish Pentecostals from other Christians and "sinners" and to promote group solidarity and identity. They are conformed to for the sake of conspicuous identification and maintenance of membership, and their violation does not result in the Calvinistic, guilt-ridden anguish that Western Christianity often expects.

Clifford Geertz's useful distinction between the "scope" and the "force" of a religion suggests some of the possible ways in which different cultures deal with the moral burden of Christianity, and some of the ways in which transformation may occur. "Scope" refers to the range of situations in which religion is thought to be relevant; "force" refers to its intensity and significance (Geertz 1971). If we consider the two variables, "force" and "scope," and assign each one of two values, "maximal" or "minimal," we have a set of four possibilities to describe the significance of religion for a group of people. In the case where both force and scope are minimal, the moral burden of Christianity must be considered minimal; we might describe this as a relatively "secular" society. Though guilt may still be salient psychologically, behavior is little constrained by "religious" considerations, and the foundations of guilt may be diffuse and vague. In the second case, where force is maximal but scope is minimal, we can speak of the compartmentalization of religion, the "bracketing" of the religious from other areas of life. Here the moral burden of Christianity may be extreme, but people have to confront it only in a limited number of contexts. For example, religion may focus on certain taboos that evoke considerable anxiety, and yet as long as these particular sins are avoided, little else is required of the individual. In this case, a potentially heavy moral burden may be combined with little or only periodic practical discomfort.

In the third case, where scope is maximal but force is minimal, religion permeates life, and yet its moral impact is moderate. Religion is ever-present, and yet of little psychological depth; the moral burden is constant but light. Here, though ritual may be associated with all sorts of everyday activities (for example, making the sign of the cross when passing a church, saying "God bless you" to babies), it may be only minimally attended to and evoke little emotion.

Finally, in some cases both the force and the scope of religion are great; it touches all aspects of life and demands constant vigilance. The classic case, perhaps, is Max Weber's Calvinism, which demanded single-minded dedication and a thorough, religiously oriented organization of activity. In this case, people must cope with the pressures of a substantial moral burden. Usually where both the scope and the force of religion are maximal, culture provides some opportunities for periodic release from this pressure, some opportunities to turn the system on its head, to fight back, and to express the ambivalence such systems generally inspire. (This ambivalence may also be the source of later transformations.) Peter Burke's (1978) analysis of Carnival in early modern Europe indicates that the approved collective gluttony, violence, and sexual license during this period contrasted with the moral burden of Christianity in the rest of the year. A classic example of the principle—though not from a Christian context—is provided in Max Gluckman's (1960) analysis of rites of rebellion in southeast Africa. Gluckman suggests that the temporary reversal of an established social order contributes to its continuing stability, by allowing for the release of otherwise proscribed emotions in a controlled setting. The reversal reaffirms the original values supporting the system, since there is a sense of the ridiculous in the reversal itself, in that it expresses a state of affairs that simply cannot obtain in ordinary life.

Apocalyptic sects, however, may have little need for such episodic release from moral burdens. To the extent that they predict a dramatic change in conditions in the near future, they may be able to defer such release. In fact, ritual may amplify rather than alleviate the moral burden, as indicated by the collective flagellations of some plague-period millenarian sects in the mid–1300s in Europe (Ziegler 1975). Similarly, American revivalist services often feature sermons that convince the listeners of their sinfulness and imminent damnation, and then offer to save them from it. In this case, the ritual amplifies the moral burden in order to convert people or to increase commitment.

Again, in cases of political, social, or military crisis, both force and scope may be amplified. History is replete with such cases, as in the puritanical theocracy headed by the monk Savonarola in fifteenth-century Florence (Weinstein 1970). Florence, the city of the Medici, of humanism and the revival of antiquity, a leader in the modernizing trend of "secularization," temporarily embraced an all-encompassing millenarian movement, in which much of the art and "pagan" culture of the preceding decades was summarily consigned to the bonfire.

During missionization, some of the most pronounced problems of "translation" of Christianity into native idioms have concerned the force and scope of the moral burden. Christian missionaries from western Europe have frequently been concerned with the sexual behavior of the indigenous people, an area in many respects outside the scope of traditional religion in Polynesia and Melanesia. In the Solomon Islands, people regard themselves as good Christians, and yet, to the missionaries' chagrin, they have effectively compartmentalized their sexual behavior; the moral burden of Christianity was simply untranslatable. Different missionaries have approached this problem differently, of course. In the Trobriands, Catholics appear to have been more rigid about it, and this may account for some of their difficulty in making converts. A Trobriand Methodist minister, on the other hand, has downplayed the significance of sexual behavior, and in his sermons speaks simply of the importance of love, implicitly allowing for the possibility of premarital sex (Hutchins 1976). Thus the moral burden in the field of sexual behavior may be transformed from its European intent, through adjustments in the force and scope of the religion.

TRANSFORMATIONS IN THE SERVICE OF GROUP IDENTITY

Two contradictory (and yet complementary) processes are evident in the transformation of Christianity. The first is the continual segmentation, schism, and differentiation of individual sects. The second is the "ecumenical" move-ment, in which sectarian and denominational differences are minimized to enhance religious solidarity. In general (but not always), the first trend is more salient at the local level, while the second is more evident at the level of national and international organization.

In local-level religious politics, schisms often develop around differing inter-pretations of issues in the "core reference system," the group's conceptualization of the definitive and essential features of Christianity. For example, two Jamaican Pentecostal sects are distinguished primarily by the fact that one baptizes in the name of Jesus alone, while the other baptizes in the name of the entire Trinity (Wedenoja 1976). This difference may appear trivial to outsiders, but is ex-tremely important to members of the two sects. The distinctions provide each group with important criteria for differentiating themselves, and encourage group solidarity and identity. The differences are symbolic, and the symbols selected for the definition of group boundaries may to some degree be arbitrary, as long as they serve to distinguish the two groups. (They may also, of course, be highly meaningful; in fact, they are probably most often selected because of salient psychological or cultural associations.) For example, Mary Douglas (1973) sug-gests that the significance of Friday abstinence from meat for the "Bog Irish" derives partly from its usefulness in differentiating them from other politicore-ligious groups in the environment. Schwartz (1975) uses the term "ethno-gnomic" to designate these traits that are selected as emblematic of the separate identity and community of distinct groups. He points out that groups in the same culture area may be hypersensitive to selected cultural, ethnic, and lin-guistic differences and correspondingly blind to similarities. Thus specific cultural traits become "diagnostic" of group membership, a process Schwartz refers to as "cultural totemism" (1975:116). Such totems may be particularly important in "nativistic" movements where conquered, colonized, or partially acculturated groups seek a new definition of themselves as distinct both from their precontact cultural identity and from the dominating cultural group (Wallace 1956). Given the effects of missionization, this process may thus be an integral part of many transformations of Christianity in third world areas.

The processes of schism and marginal differentiation also act to maintain the small scale of the realms of action and identity for individuals. Thus in some cases fragmentation may have as its primary purpose (recognized or not) simply the diminished size of the group. This partly explains the tendency to segmen-tation among modern Catholic charismatic groups, where much of the attraction of joining is the opportunity for active, individualized participation in a group religious experience. When the group gets too large, this opportunity is dimin-ished, as is the opportunity for participation in leadership roles. In short, schism amplifies the social space, defining separate realms in which leadership may be exercised and individual personalities developed.

On the other hand, in many cases of culture contact the subordinate group is less interested in differentiating itself from the dominant group than in assimilating to it. Just as religious disaffiliation establishes a boundary and a differentiated identity, religious affiliation may help establish an identification when desired. This is one of the most powerful bases for mass conversion of conquered or colonized peoples to Christianity: conversion is a statement of affiliation with wealthier and more powerful outsiders. And under the influence of missionaries, colonized peoples have often interpreted Christianity as the source of the power and wealth of Western societies.

The conditions of the sociocultural environment thus influence the definition of group boundaries, and the persistent strain between fragmentation and expansion is one of the most important dynamics in the transformation of Christianity. Expansion may take the form of ecumenism, which creates a larger but more heterogeneous group, but it probably more often occurs through proselytization, where the attempt is not to combine groups manifesting a wide range of differences but rather to expand the membership of a specific group at the expense of the others.

RECRUITMENT AND CONVERSION: WORLDLY AND OTHER-WORLDLY GOALS

The complexity of transformative processes is well illustrated in the conversion of new members to Christian sects or denominations. Conversion is necessarily a multifaceted experience, and it is obvious that not all conversions are of the same type. This banal observation deserves special emphasis when the cultural context is far removed from the familiar experience of Westerners. In the first place, individual conversions from one established religion to another within a society are likely to differ considerably—both psychologically and socially—from mass conversions effected through missionization, the rise of a new religion, or in the face of dramatic crises. In the latter cases, the content of the religion may be less important than the political context, economic factors, or even aesthetic considerations. Furthermore, the conversion may have little to do with "other-worldly" ideals, and may depend much more on a set of on-the-ground hopes and expectations.

These pragmatic factors are particularly evident in colonized third world areas, where Christianity was often just one suitcase in a whole load of baggage that the colonialists brought with them. In much of Melanesia, for example, the success of the missionaries depended a great deal on natives' perceptions of their wealth and power. Where missionaries arrived alone, in comparative poverty and often in bad health, with little back-up support from governmental or commercial agencies, they tended to make few converts. When the missionaries arrived on impressive ships with military support, however, and brought with them marvelous samples of Western technology, they met a pragmatic population already culturally disposed to believe that material well-being and power are dependent on a correct relation to the supernatural. The very technological and military superiority of the Westerners was an indictment of native religion.

Christianity was perceived as a part of a whole Western cultural complex, and the link between religion and power was unquestioned. Conversion was therefore frequently—if not inevitably—oriented less to points of doctrine than to a source of power.

This point is important. Potential converts in isolated areas have usually had no opportunity to observe firsthand the home societies of the missionaries, and often develop misconceptions about the importance of Christianity in the sociocultural systems of the colonial powers. In the village of Kragur, Papua New Guinea, the people initially saw Catholicism as comprehensive and definitive of European life. Whether or not the missionaries intended to convey such an impression, the people conceived of Christianity as a kind of "total institution" (cf. Goffman 1961). They hoped that conversion would bring them the whole cargo of European wealth, power, and technical knowledge. And certainly, in seeking conversions, many missionaries have deliberately used people's lack of familiarity with Western life to convince them of the power of Christianity. Karl G. Heider describes such a case in the missionization of the Dani: "One missionary told me that when he gave penicillin shots, he had the patient pray with him to Jesus. Then, when the yaws were cured, he would point out that the Dani owed the cure to Jesus" (1979:13).

Indigenous Melanesian religions are consistently "this-worldly" in orientation, and often only vaguely conceptualize life after death or "salvation." Thus the ostensible ends of the missionaries' Christianity have been difficult to translate and communicate in the Melanesian context. It should thus not be surprising that when the anticipated benefits of conversion have not materialized, people have become disillusioned and skeptical. Often they have continued to believe that Christianity is the source of Western power, but suspect that the missionaries have censored essential information needed to make the religion effective— that is, to bring them their deserved share of wealth and power. A common belief in Manus, according to Schwartz (1962), was that the missionaries had removed the key first page of the Bible before giving it to the natives (see also Worsley 1968:43).

The this-worldly, pragmatic considerations are not confined to Melanesia, however; nor do they concern only material goods. The shrines of southern Europe, such as St. Anthony's tomb in Padua, are filled with petitions for physical health, fertility, and success in love, as illustrated by the crutches, silver heart and kidney *ex votos*, wedding dresses, and photographs of babies deposited around them. Where the requests have not been honored, it is not uncommon to hear people cursing the saints or the Madonna for their inattention or deliberate stinginess.

Significantly, there are also cases where conversion has *not* taken place at least partly because Christianity did not provide the appropriate practical benefits. Griffin Dix's chapter points out that an essential requirement of religion for Korean villagers is that it provide effective cures for illness and injury, and Christianity is perceived as deficient in this respect. In Ye-an, Christianity has had to compete with an indigenous shamanistic tradition with much more impressive curing performances than the few corresponding Christian ceremonies. Accordingly (and for other reasons), there have been few converts in Yean. And in Jamaica and Haiti, Pentecostalism has succeeded where traditional denominations have not partly because its faith-healing practices are viewed as improved, modern equivalents of the African-based healing traditions.

Conversion may also be motivated by another kind of pragmatic consideration, where Christianity is perceived as an alternative to a dysfunctional indigenous system. For example, Christianity presented Solomon Islanders with a way out of the headhunting circle, which at the time of missionization had grown unusually troublesome and disruptive. As Christianity was perceived to place converts under the protection of a more powerful God, Christians were freed from the responsibilities (and dangers) of continuing to take heads to placate the ancestors. In Jamaica, Christianity has similarly provided the convert with a means of escaping anxiety-producing life situations. In the first place, Jamaican Christians are believed to be immune from sorcery, and so the convert receives a kind of protection—experienced as relief from anxiety—in exchange for commitment to the church. In addition, conversion can facilitate identity change, enabling people to give up self-destructive personal habits such as drunkenness and providing them with a concrete program (and a support group) for the effective management of their lives. Christians in Jamaica are also excused by their peers from participation in customary drinking obligations. As Melford E. Spiro (1965) has so cogently argued, individuals may use religious institutions as "culturally constituted defense mechanisms," in order to manage their personal conflicts and ambivalences.

The identity change accompanying conversion calls attention to the fact that it is both a personal and a public act. The interplay between psychological and political aspects of the conversion is illustrated in the frequent insistence of the convert that—before "seeing the light"—he or she had been skeptical about the new religion. Preconversion skepticism is a well-articulated tradition in Christianity: the most famous skeptic is probably Paul, the Christian tormenter turned tormented Christian. Schwartz (1962) has noted the phenomenon in the Paliau movement in Manus, where there appeared to be a subtle rule that the potential convert should first be a public skeptic, ridiculing the movement and vowing that he would never join. The process was so predictable that Schwartz refers to it as "ritualized skepticism." After such a display of public skepticism, the subsequent conversion seems more valid and significant to all involved.

More is involved than before-the-fact preparation, of course. Many of those who attend Jamaican Pentecostal meetings originally go out of curiosity and for entertainment, but find themselves caught up in the emotion of the service and have conversion experiences. Once this apparently involuntary and socially irrevocable act takes place in a public context, the individual usually becomes committed to Pentecostalism. In fact, the skeptic who is publicly converted may have an even greater motive for fanatical participation and proselytization than the willing convert, because he must reduce his cognitive dissonance (Wedenoja 1978; Festinger 1957, 1962; Festinger, Riecken, and Schacter 1956). He becomes a convert in order to explain the phenomenon to himself, and because he has already publicly committed himself. Takie Sugiyama Lebra has noted such a "bridge-burning" effect among Japanese *Tensho* converts in Hawaii after participating in a public dancing ritual (1970; see also Shupe 1981).

Similar phenomena also occur regularly among Catholic Pentecostals or "Charismatics" in the United States. When reminiscing about their conversion experiences, Charismatics often explicitly acknowledge that they—like other reasonable uninitiated people—had earlier doubted or even antagonistically rejected the reality of the charismatic experience. In this way, they retrospectively attempt to establish their own credentials as rational people. The ultimate implication is that the "real" (inspired) truth comes through a different channel than "mere" reason, and requires special insight or a special "gift" of enlightenment. The convert thus anticipates and subverts the outsiders' insinuations that believers are soft-headed and incapable of straight thinking. "I was once like you" is a largely incontestable statement.

This is not to imply that converts are consciously attempting to manipulate their own experience so as to make political statements. Indeed, the process is neither necessarily conscious nor primarily directed at others. Again, the reduction of cognitive dissonance is often a major factor. Having committed himself to the religion, an individual may then feel the need (perhaps unconsciously) to remove any lingering doubts. There is also considerable individual variation in the tolerance for dissonance, and perhaps those with the lowest tolerance make the most "noise" prior to conversion. Smith notes that in Kragur there is a psychosocial similarity between the strongest supporters of the local mission and its most vehement critics, and these people probably have less tolerance for dissonance than those with moderate attitudes. They have difficulty accepting vague, incomplete, or contradictory elements in their belief systems. Thus they fervently oppose Christianity, and then they equally strongly commit themselves to it when they convert.

The relation between dissonance and the transformation of the Christian symbol system is complex. Wallace's (1956) discussion of "revitalization movements" suggests that such movements often develop out of a creative attempt at cognitive resynthesis, and have the goal of reducing the dissonance resulting from the ineffectiveness of traditional culture in helping people through crises. Wallace calls the process "mazeway reformulation," in which the "mazeway" is an individual's view of his society and culture that, among other things, is expected to provide ways of coping with these difficulties. However, when the culturally prescribed behavior no longer effectively reduces anxiety, the situation is ripe for a cultural transformation—a prophetic revelation that results in culture change. Thus Wallace suggests that cultural and religious transformation may occur as an aspect of the dissonance-reducing process: people revise cognitive orientations, belief systems, ritual practices, and social organization in order to bring them into line with current perceptions of reality.

Such transformations, however, also produce their own dissonance. They shake people up, even if they are also satisfying. The "noise" created in the transformative process is itself invigorating and revitalizing. It creates new alternatives and demands new forms of commitment. Dissonance may also be useful in that it facilitates keeping the mind open to alternative possibilities, to the alternative realities that may sometimes emerge. There is thus often a kind of dual consciousness in religiosity: even in the moments of greatest commitment, people harbor lingering doubts that motivate them to "hedge their bets." For example, at the height of the Paliau movement in Manus, when commitment was at its peak, people threw into the ocean all of their money and possessions, including many important traditional ritual items. They later insisted that the jettison took place in the deep water beyond the reef; and yet, somehow, when the cargo ship failed to arrive and the fervor had subsided, they were able to recover much of the material. Though many argue that the recovery of these goods is itself a miracle, it is more likely that the dual consciousness was at work and protected people from more drastic losses. It is also Schwartz's impression that many of those who had not joined Paliau found the dissonance equally useful: they watched the movement closely, keeping in touch with the events as they progressed, so that if it became apparent that the cargo really was going to arrive, they could quickly jump on the welcoming bandwagon.

It is also apparent that many people live comfortably with contradictions in their belief systems, as long as there is no compelling reason for them to confront and resolve the paradoxes. In many places, the boundary between cult and orthodoxy, between indigenous religion and Christianity, is not firmly established, and people may cross from one to another with little difficulty. As Wedenoja points out, Jamaicans have for a hundred years attended both orthodox churches and syncretic cults, which they see as complementary. This kind of flexibility is especially evident where the ideology of the religion is less significant than its anticipated material benefits. In some settings, paradox may become apparent and dissonance occur only under special conditions. During normal times, contradictory beliefs may exist in the same environment without apparent difficulty. They become more salient during crises, and in fact the existence of these alternatives provides a variety of possible ways of responding to the crisis.

"Sudden" conversions are especially interesting, although most—despite their abrupt appearance—probably involve a rather thorough covert or unconscious preparation (Toch 1965:117). The sudden consciousness of transformation—the experience of "seeing the light"—provides the convert with a sense of conviction that some external power was involved. Like preconversion skepticism, this makes the experience seem more valid and interesting, and also provides a motivation and justification for dramatic personality change. Christian lore is replete with archetypical examples, such as the conversion of St.

Francis of Assisi, the wealthy, carefree, irresponsible youth who became the great advocate of poverty and the recipient of the Catholic world's first recorded case of stigmata. After sudden conversions, then, we often see profound transformations of personal identity: alcoholics stop drinking, aggressive people become quiet and humble, troubled people appear calm and contented, and so forth. Sometimes the personality change is evidenced in physical changes, in the person's posture, gait, facial expression, or clothing. Jamaicans told Wedenoja that Christians always have a special "aura" that is easily recognized by others. These changes are culturally conditioned, of course, since people know in advance how Christians are expected to act, though the behavioral adjustments may be considerable. In the Solomon Islands, for example, the character traits necessary for success and prestige prior to the arrival of Christianity were considerably devalued afterwards. The Christian in the Solomons must adopt a universalistic ethic, in which the entire Christian community (not just one's kinspeople) is dealt with in a moral fashion. Furthermore, the Christian ethic idealizes passive, cooperative behavior, in direct contrast to traditional leadership ideals of aggressive masculinity (G. White 1978, 1980).

Such changes may be more or less "deep" and enduring. In some societies, conversion itself seems to be a favored experience, and people go through a number of them in a lifetime. Each conversion may bring dramatic personal transformations, but within a short time the convert either slips back into old life patterns or moves on to other new ones. Robert Jay Lifton (1970) considers this a common sequence in modernized societies, and has identified a personality type—"protean man"—who converts to new ideologies in a serial fashion. On the other hand, at conversion the individual obtains rights and duties in a different social group and may engage in a general restructuring of social relations. If most of the convert's previous associates have also converted, this restructuring may be minimal. If not, it may be extensive. In some cases conversion may be motivated specifically by the desire to restructure social relations, again a political act. As indicated earlier, in Ye-an, Korea, only a minority of the population has converted to Christianity, and the converts are mostly "marginal" in some way or another. For these people, one attraction of Christianity is the possibility of social mobility, outside the standard system of prestige allocation, to be sure, but nonetheless a new social status (and a new support group). As Christians, converts have the opportunity to identify themselves through an alternative ideology, and they no longer need to accept judgements of their failure in the non-Christian social arena.

Finally, it should be recalled that many conversions occur as a result of proselytization. Sects attempting to win converts must assess the potential attractiveness of their message to particular audiences, and may thus (consciously or unconsciously) transform their own religion in attempting to appeal to the susceptibilities of the audience. Thus an understanding of transformations via recruitment and conversion requires consideration of the psychological and

cultural characteristics of both the existing congregation and the potential converts.

CONCLUDING REMARKS

The case studies in this book illustrate some of the transformative processes
at work in symbol systems of all kinds, as well as the reciprocal processes by
which symbol systems effect changes in social systems. There are distinct differences in the realized versions of Christianity in these individual ethnographic
examples. And yet there are also threads of unity—not universals, but elements
and processes that reoccur from time to time and place to place as focal issues
in the communication of the religion across cultural and temporal frontiers.

It is this communicative process that is of interest throughout the book, and
this is the theme that integrates the various chapters: Christianity is a dynamic
cultural system, transmittable and translatable according to regular principles
of culture change. The precise translation—the dynamic system of symbols that
emerges in a particular cultural context—depends on a variety of historical,
material, psychological, social, and cultural factors. Here we have begun to
enumerate some of those factors and some of the processes of culture change
that are particularly relevant in an anthropological perspective on Christianity.

References

Arbuckle, Gerald A.
  1978 The Impact of Vatican II on the Marists in Oceania. *In* Mission, Church and Sect in Oceania. ASAO Monograph No. 6. James A. Boutilier, Daniel T. Hughes, and Sharon W. Tiffany, eds. Pp. 275–99. Ann Arbor: University of Michigan Press.
Armstrong, E. S.
  1900 The History of the Melanesian Mission. London: Isbister and Co., Ltd.
Bailey, F. G.
  1969 Strategems and Spoils. New York: Schocken.
  1971 What Are *Signori? In* Gifts and Poison. Pp. 231–51. Oxford: Basil Blackwell.
Bailey, F. G., ed.
  1971 Gifts and Poison. Oxford: Basil Blackwell.
Barnett, Homer G.
  1957 Indian Shakers: A Messianic Cult of the Pacific Northwest. Carbondale: University of Southern Illinois Press.
Barrett, Leonard E.
  1974 Soul-Force: African Heritage in Afro-American Religion. Garden City, New York: Doubleday.
Barth, Gunther
  1964 Bitter Strength: A History of the Chinese in the United States, 1850–1870. Cambridge: Harvard University Press.
Beckwith, Martha Warren
  1929 Black Roadways: A Study of Jamaican Folk Life. Chapel Hill: University of North Carolina Press.
Beidelman, T. O.
  1982 Colonial Evangelism. Bloomington: Indiana University Press.
Beier, Ulli
  1975 The Cultural Dilemma of Papua New Guinea. Meanjin Quarterly 34:302–10.
Bellah, Robert N.
  1970 Father and Son in Christianity and Confucianism. *In* Beyond Belief. Pp. 76–99. New York: Harper and Row.

Berk, B. B., and L. C. Hirata
  1976   Mental Illness Among the Chinese: Myth or Reality? Journal of Social Issues
          29(2): 149–66.
Black, Peter Weston
  1978   The Teachings of Father Marino: Aspects of Tobian Catholicism. *In* Mission,
          Church and Sect in Oceania. ASAO Monograph No. 6. James A. Boutilier,
          Daniel T. Hughes, and Sharon W. Tiffany, eds. Pp. 307–54. Ann Arbor:
          University of Michigan Press.
  1982   The "In-charge" Complex and Tobian Political Culture. Pacific Studies 6:52–
          70.
  1983   Conflict, Morality and Power in a Western Caroline Society. Journal of the
          Polynesian Society 92:7–30.
  1985   Ghosts, Gossip and Suicide: Meaning and Action in Tobian Folk Psychology.
          In Person, Self and Experience: Exploring Pacific Ethnopsychologies. G. White
          and J. Kirkpatrick, eds. Pp. 245–300. Berkeley: University of California Press.
Bord, Richard J., and Joseph E. Faulkner
  1975   Religiosity and Secular Attitudes: The Case of Catholic Pentecostals. Journal
          for the Scientific Study of Religion 14:257–70.
  1983   The Catholic Charismatics: The Anatomy of a Modern Religious Movement.
          University Park: The Pennsylvania State University Press.
Bowden, Henry Warner
  1981   American Indians and Christian Missions. Chicago: University of Chicago
          Press.
Bowles, Gilbert
  1900   Jamaica and Friends' Missions. Oskaloosa, Iowa: The Western Word Publishing
          Company.
Brandes, Stanley H.
  1975   Migration, Kinship, and Community: Tradition and Transition in a Spanish
          Village. New York: Academic Press.
  1980   Metaphors of Masculinity: Sex and Status in Andalusian Folklore. Philadelphia:
          University of Pennsylvania Press.
Brathwaite, Edward
  1971   The Development of Creole Society in Jamaica 1770–1820. Oxford: Clarendon
          Press.
  1978   Kumina: The Spirit of African Survival. Jamaica Journal 42:44–63.
Brody, E. B.
  1969   Migration and Adaptation: The Nature of the Problem. *In* Behavior in New
          Environments: Adaptation of Migrant Populations. Pp. 13–22. Beverly Hills,
          California: Sage Publications.
Brown, Aggrey
  1979   Color, Class and Politics in Jamaica. New Brunswick, New Jersey: Transaction.
Brown, Beverly
  1975   George Lisle: Black Baptist and Pan-Africanist 1750–1826. Savacou 11/12:58–
          67.
Brown, Diana DeG.
  1986   Umbanda: Religion and Politics in Urban Brazil. Ann Arbor, Michigan: UMI
          Research Press.

Buchner, J. H.
  1854 The Moravians in Jamaica. Reprinted in 1971. Freeport, New York: Books for Libraries Press.
Bultmann, William A.
  1985 Christian Missions as the Handmaiden of Imperial Expansion: The Church of England Pacific Missions as a Case Study. *In* Religion in the Pacific Era. Frank K. Flinn and Tyler Hendricks, eds. Pp. 43–62. New York: Paragon House.
Burke, Peter
  1978 The World of Carnival. *In* Popular Culture in Early Modern Europe. Pp. 178–204. New York: Harper Torchbooks.
Burridge, Kenelm O. L.
  1978 Introduction: Missionary Occasions. *In* Mission, Church, and Sect in Oceania. ASAO Monograph No. 6. James A. Boutilier, Daniel T. Hughes, and Sharon W. Tiffany, eds. Pp. 1–30. Ann Arbor: University of Michigan Press.
Calley, Malcolm J. C.
  1965 God's People: West Indian Pentecostal Sects in England. London: Oxford University Press.
Carrillo, Elisa
  1965 Alcide deGasperi: The Long Apprenticeship. Notre Dame, Indiana: University of Notre Dame Press.
Cayton, Horace R., and Anne O. Lively
  1955 The Chinese in the United States and the Chinese Christian Church. New York: Bureau of Research and Survey, National Council of the Churches of Christ in the United States.
Chapman, M., and P. Pirie
  1974 Tasi Mauri: A Report on Population and Resources of the Guadalcanal Weather Coast. Honolulu: East-West Center Population Institute.
Chevannes, Barry
  1971 Revival and Black Struggle. Savacou 5:27–39.
Chinese Community Church of San Diego
  1953 Chinese Community Church Annual. Mimeo.
Chisholm, William
  1938 Vivid Experiences in Korea. Chicago: The Bible Institute.
Clark, C. A.
  1961 Religions of Old Korea. Seoul: The Christian Literature Society.
Collier, Jane F.
  1986 From Mary to Modern Woman: The Material Basis of Marianismo and its Transformation in a Spanish Village. American Ethnologist 13:100–107.
Comaroff, Jean, and John Comaroff
  1986 Christianity and Colonialism in South Africa. American Ethnologist 13:1–22.
Connor, John
  1972 Covenant Communities: A New Sign of Hope. New Covenant, April, 2–9.
Cornelisen, Ann
  1977 Women of the Shadows. New York: Vintage.
Counts, Dorothy Ayers
  1978 Christianity in Kaliai: Response to Missionization in Northwest New Britain. *In* Mission, Church, and Sect in Oceania. ASAO Monograph No. 6. James A. Boutilier, Daniel T. Hughes, and Sharon W. Tiffany, eds. Pp. 355–94. Ann Arbor: University of Michigan Press.

Crissman, Lawrence
   1967   The Segmentary Nature of Urban Overseas Chinese Communities. Man 2:185–204.
Curtin, Philip D.
   1970   Two Jamaicas: The Role of Ideas in a Tropical Colony 1830–1865. New York: Atheneum.
David, H. P.
   1969   Involuntary International Migration: Adaptation of Refugees. *In* Behavior in New Environments: Adaptation of Migrant Populations. E. B. Brody, ed. Pp. 73–95. Beverly Hills, California: Sage Publications.
Degler, Carl N.
   1980   At Odds: Women and the Family in America from the Revolution to the Present. New York: Oxford University Press.
DiRenzo, G. J.
   1967   Personality, Power and Politics. Notre Dame, Indiana: University of Notre Dame Press.
Dix, Griffin
   1977   The East Asian Country of Propriety: Confucianism in a Korean Village. Ph.D. dissertation, Department of Anthropology, University of California, San Diego.
   1979   How to Do Things with Ritual: The Logic of Ancestor Worship in a Korean Village. *In* Korea in Transition. D. McCann et al., eds. Pp. 57–88. Honolulu: Center for Korean Studies, University of Hawaii.
   1980   The Place of the Almanac in Korean Folk Religion. The Journal of Korean Studies 2:47–70.
Dolan, J. P.
   1975   The Immigrant Church: New York's Irish and German Catholics, 1815–1865. Baltimore, Maryland: Johns Hopkins University Press.
Douglas, Mary
   1973   Natural Symbols. New York: Vintage.
Dubisch, Jill
   1986   Introduction. *In* Gender and Power in Rural Greece. Pp. 3–41. Princeton, New Jersey: Princeton University Press.
Durkheim, Emile
   1951   Suicide. First published in 1897. New York: The Free Press.
Eilers, Annaliese
   1936   Westkarolinen: Tobi und Ngulu. Ergebnisse der OpSudsee-Expedition 1908–1910 (II B9, part 1). G. Thilenius, ed. Hamburg: Friedrichsen, De Gruyter Co.
Eisner, Gisela
   1974   Jamaica, 1830–1930, A Study in Economic Growth. Westport, Connecticut: Greenwood Press.
Elkins, W. F.
   1977   Street Preachers, Faith Healers and Herb Doctors in Jamaica 1890–1925. New York: Revisionist Press.
Esposito, John L.
   1986   Modern Islamic Sociopolitical Thought. *In* Prophetic Religions and Politics. Jeffrey K. Hadden and Anson Shupe, eds. Pp. 153–72. New York: Paragon House.

Fallowes, R.
  1929–34 Letters to His Sister. Canberra: National Library of Australia, ms. 2478.
Farwell, W. B.
  1885 The Chinese at Home and Abroad. San Francisco, California: A. L. Bancroft.
Festinger, Leon
  1957 The Theory of Cognitive Dissonance. Stanford, California: Stanford University Press.
  1962 Cognitive Dissonance. Scientific American 207 (4): 93–102.
Festinger, Leon, Henry W. Riecken, and Stanley Schacter
  1956 When Prophecy Fails. New York: Harper Torchbooks.
Fichter, Joseph
  1975 The Catholic Cult of the Paraclete. New York: Sheed and Ward.
Fingarette, Herbert
  1972 Confucius: The Secular as Sacred. New York: Harper and Row.
Firth, Stewart
  1975 The Missions: From Chalmers to Indigenization. Meanjin Quarterly 34:342–50.
Foster, George M.
  1965 Peasant Society and the Image of Limited Good. American Anthropologist 67:293–315.
Fried, Morton
  1987 Reflections on Christianity in China. American Ethnologist 14:94–106.
Furley, Oliver
  1965 Moravian Missionaries and Slaves in the West Indies. Caribbean Studies 5:3–16.
Gager, John G.
  1975 Kingdom and Community: the Social World of Early Christianity. Princeton, New Jersey: Prentice-Hall.
Galt, Anthony
  1974 Rethinking Patron-Client Relationships: The Real System and the Official System in Southern Italy. Anthropological Quarterly 47:182–202.
Gardner, William James
  1909 A History of Jamaica from its Discovery by Christopher Columbus to the Year 1872. . . . London: F. F. Unwin.
Garrett, William R.
  1986 Religion and the Legitimization of Violence. In Prophetic Religions and Politics. Jeffrey K. Hadden and Anson Shupe, eds. Pp. 103–22. New York: Paragon House.
Geertz, Clifford
  1971 Islam Observed: Religious Development in Morocco and Indonesia. First published in 1968. Chicago: University of Chicago Press.
  1973a Religion as a Cultural System. In The Interpretation of Cultures. Pp. 87–125. New York: Basic.
  1973b Ritual and Social Change: A Javanese Example. First published in 1959. In The Interpretation of Cultures. Pp. 142–69. New York: Basic.
Gelpi, Donald
  1971 Pentecostalism: A Theological Viewpoint. Paramus, New Jersey: Paulist Press.

Gluckman, Max
  1960 Rituals of Rebellion in South-East Africa. *In* Order and Rebellion in Tribal
        Africa. Pp. 110–36. Glencoe, Illinois: The Free Press.
Gaggin, J.
  1881 No. 32, Journal of the Jessie Kelly. Journals of Government Agents. 67 volumes.
        Suva, Fiji: Central Archives of Fiji.
Goffman, Erving
  1961 Asylums: Essays on the Social Situation of Mental Patients and Other Inmates.
        Garden City, New York: Anchor.
Goldie, J.
  1914 The Solomon Islands. *In* A Century of the Pacific. J. Colwell, ed. Sydney:
        n.p.
Goodman, Felicitas
  1972 Speaking in Tongues: A Cross-Cultural Study of Glossolalia. Chicago: Uni-
        versity of Chicago Press.
Granet, M.
  1975 The Religion of the Chinese People. M. Freedman, trans. New York: Harper
        & Row.
Grattan, Clinton H.
  1963 The Southwest Pacific Since 1900: A Modern History. Ann Arbor: University
        of Michigan Press.
Greenberg, Joseph
  1946 The Influence of Islam on a Sudanese Religion. American Ethnological Society,
        Monograph 10. Seattle: University of Washington Press.
Griego, Andrew
  1979 Rebuilding the California Southern Railroad: The Personal Account of a
        Chinese Labor Contractor, 1884. Journal of San Diego History 25:324–27.
Guiart, J.
  1970 Conversion to Christianity in the Pacific. *In* Millenial Dreams in Action. S.
        Thrupp, ed. Pp. 122–38. New York: Schocken Books.
Hallowell, A. I.
  1967 The Self and Its Behavioral Environment. First published in 1954. *In* Culture
        and Experience. Pp. 75–110. New York: Schocken Books.
Harrison, Michael I.
  1974a Sources of Recruitment to Catholic Pentecostalism: A Middle-Class Religious
        Movement. Journal for the Scientific Study of Religion 13:49–64.
  1974b Preparation for Life in the Spirit: The Process of Initial Commitment to a
        Religious Movement. Urban Life and Culture 2:387–414.
  1975 The Maintenance of Enthusiasm: Involvement in a New Religious Movement.
        Sociological Analysis 36:150–60.
  1978 Commitment Mechanisms and Routinization in a Social Movement. Journal
        for the Scientific Study of Religion 17:456–60.
Harrison, Michael I., and John Maniha
  1978 Dynamics of Dissenting Movements within Established Organizations: Two
        Cases and a Theoretical Interpretation. Journal for the Scientific Study of
        Religion 17:207–24.
Harvey, Kim
  1979 Six Korean Women: The Socialization of Shamans. The American Ethno-
        logical Society Monograph 65. St. Paul, Minnesota: West Publishing.

1987 The Korean Shaman and the Deaconess: Sisters in Different Guises. *In* Religion and Ritual in Korean Society. Laurel Kendall and Griffin Dix, eds. Pp. 149–70. Berkeley: Institute of East Asian Studies, University of California.

Harwood, F.
1978 Intercultural Communication in the Western Solomons: The Methodist Mission and the Emergence of the Christian Fellowship Church. *In* Mission, Church and Sect in Oceania. ASAO Monograph No. 6. James A. Boutilier, Daniel T. Hughes, and Sharon W. Tiffany, eds. Pp. 231–50. Ann Arbor: University of Michigan Press.

Hastings, S. U., and B. L. MacLeavy
1979 Seedtime and Harvest: A Brief History of the Moravian Church in Jamaica, 1754–1979. Kingston, Jamaica: The Moravian Church Corporation.

Heider, Karl G.
1979 Grand Valley Dani: Peaceful Warriors. New York: Holt, Rinehart and Winston.

Henderson, George E.
1931 Goodness and Mercy: A Tale of a Hundred Years. Kingston, Jamaica: Gleaner Company.

Henry, Paget
1986 Indigenous Religions and the Transformation of Peripheral Societies. *In* Prophetic Religions and Politics. Jeffrey K. Hadden and Anson Shupe, eds. Pp. 123–50. New York: Paragon House.

Hill, Robert
1983 Leonard P. Howell and Millenarian Visions in Early Rastafari. Jamaica Journal 16 (1): 24–39.

Hilliard, David
1978 God's Gentlemen: A History of the Melanesian Mission 1849–1942. St. Lucia: University of Queensland Press.

Hine, Virginia
1969 Pentecostal Glossolalia: Toward a Functional Analysis. Journal for the Scientific Study of Religion 8:211–26.

Hocart, A. M.
1922 Cult of the Dead on Eddystone. Journal of the Royal Anthropological Institute 61:301–24.

Hogbin, H. I.
1958 Social Change. London: Watts.
1970 Experiments in Civilization: The Effects of European Culture on a Native Community of the Solomon Islands. First published in 1939. New York: Schocken Books.

Hogg, Donald
1964 Jamaican Religions: A Study in Variations. Ph.D. dissertation. Ann Arbor, Michigan: University Microfilms.

Holden, Horace
1836 A Narrative of the Shipwreck, Captivity, and Sufferings of Horace Holden and Benjamin H. Nute. Boston: Russel, Shattuck, and Co.

Hsu, Francis L. K.
1971 The Challenge of the American Dream: The Chinese in the United States. Belmont, California: Wadsworth Publishing.

Huber, Mary Taylor
1987   Constituting the Church: Catholic Missionaries on the Sepik Frontier. American Ethnologist 14:107–25.
Hurwitz, Samuel J., and Edith F. Hurwitz
1977   Jamaica: A Historical Portrait. London: Pall Mall.
Hutch, Richard A.
1980   The Personal Ritual of Glossolalia. Journal for the Scientific Study of Religion 19:255–66.
Hutchins, Edwin
1976   The Christian Magician in the Trobriand Islands. Paper delivered at the annual meeting of the Southwestern Anthropological Association, San Diego.
Jackson, K. B.
1975   Head-hunting and the Christianization of Bugotu, 1861–1900. Journal of Pacific History 10:65–78.
Janelli, Dawnhee
1986   Ancestors, Women and the Korean Family. In The Psycho-Cultural Dynamics of the Confucian Family: Past and Present. Walter H. Slote, ed. Pp. 197–220. Seoul: International Cultural Society of Korea.
Janelli, Roger, and Dawnhee Janelli
1982   Ancestor Worship and Korean Society. Stanford, California: Stanford University Press.
Keifer, Ralph
1973   The Duquesne Weekend—1967. New Covenant, February, 1.
Kendall, Laurel
1985   Shamans, Housewives and Other Restless Spirits: Women in Korean Ritual Life. Honolulu: University of Hawaii Press.
Kertzer, David I.
1975   Participation of Italian Communists in Catholic Rituals: A Case Study. Journal for the Scientific Study of Religion 14:1–11.
1980a Comrades and Christians: Religion and Political Struggle in Communist Italy. Cambridge: Cambridge University Press.
1980b Ideological and Social Bases of Italian Church-Communist Struggle: A Critique of Gramsci's Concept of Hegemony. Dialectical Anthropology 4:321–28.
Knox, A.J.G.
1977   Opportunities and Opposition: the Rise of Jamaica's Black Peasantry and the Nature of the Planter Resistance. Canadian Review of Sociology and Anthropology 14:381–95.
Kwong, Julia
1984   Ethnic Organizations and Community Transformation: The Chinese in Winnipeg. Ethnic and Racial Studies 7:374–86.
Lane, Ralph
1976   Catholic Charismatic Renewal. In The New Religious Consciousness. Charles Y. Glock and Robert N. Bellah, eds. Pp. 162–79. Berkeley: University of California Press.
Lawrence, P., and Meggitt, M. J.
1965   Gods, Ghosts and Men in Melanesia: Some Religions of Australian New Guinea and the New Hebrides. Melbourne: Oxford University Press.

Lebra, Takie Sugiyama
  1970 Religious Conversion as a Breakthrough for Transculturation: A Japanese Sect in Hawaii. Journal for the Scientific Study of Religion 9:181–94.
Lee, Rose Hum
  1960 The Chinese in the United States of America. New York: Oxford University Press.
Levy, Robert I.
  1973 Tahitians: Mind and Experience in the Society Islands. Chicago: University of Chicago Press.
Lewis, Matthew Gregory
  1834 Journal of a West India Proprietor, Kept During a Residence in the Island of Jamaica. Reprinted in Westport, Connecticut: Greenwood Press.
Lifton, Robert Jay
  1970 Boundaries: Psychological Man in Revolution. New York: Random House.
Linyard, Fred
  1969 The Moravians in Jamaica from the Beginning to Emancipation 1754–1838. Jamaica Journal 3:7–11.
Lipphard, W. B., and F. A. Sharp
  1975 What is a Baptist? *In* Religions in America: Ferment and Faith in an Age of Crisis. Leo Rosten, ed. Pp. 25–38. New York: Simon and Schuster.
Liu, Judith
  1977 Celestials in the Golden Mountain: The Chinese in One California City, San Diego, 1870–1900. M.A. thesis, Department of Sociology, San Diego State University.
Lombardi-Satriani, L. M.
  1974 Antropologia culturale e analisi della cultura subalterna. Florence: Guaraldi.
Long, Edward
  1774 The History of Jamaica, Volume II. London: T. Lowndes.
Lyman, Stanford
  1970 The Asian in the West. Reno: Western Studies Center, Desert Research Institute, University of Nevada.
  1974 Chinese Americans. New York: Random House.
McEvoy, A. F.
  1977 In Places Men Reject: Chinese Fishermen at San Diego, 1870–1893. Journal of San Diego History 23:12–24.
MacGaffey, Wyatt
  1983 Modern Kongo Prophets: Religion in a Plural Society. Bloomington: Indiana University Press.
  1986 Religion and Society in Central Africa: The BaKongo of Lower Zaire. Chicago: University of Chicago Press.
McGuire, Meredith
  1974 An Interpretative Comparison of Elements of the Pentecostal and Underground Church Movements in American Catholicism. Sociological Analysis 35:57–65.
  1975 Toward a Sociological Interpretation of the Catholic Pentecostal Movement. Review of Religious Research 16:94–104.
  1977 The Social Context of Prophecy: "Word Gifts" of the Pentecostals. Review of Religious Research 18:134–47.

1982   Pentecostal Catholics: Power, Charisma, and Order in a Religious Movement. Philadelphia, Pennsylvania: Temple University Press.

McKinnon, J.
1975   Tomahawks, Turtles and Traders. Oceania 45:290–307.

MacPhail, E. C.
1977   San Diego's Chinese Mission. Journal of San Diego History 23:9–21.

Malzberg, Benjamin, and E. S. Lee
1956   Migration and Mental Disease: A Study of First Admissions to Hospitals for Mental Disease, New York, 1939–1941. New York: Social Science Research Council.

Marx, Karl
1978   The German Ideology: Part I. In The Marx-Engels Reader. Second edition. Robert C. Tucker, ed. Pp. 146–200. New York: W. W. Norton and Co.

Melanesian Mission
n.d.   The Southern Cross Log. Monthly Journal of the Melanesian Mission. Auckland.

Mohl, Raymond A., and Neil Betten
1981   The Immigrant Church in Gary, Indiana: Religious Adjustment and Cultural Defense. Ethnicity 8:1–17.

Morrell, W. P.
1960   Britain in the Pacific Islands. Oxford: Clarendon Press.

Nee, Victor, and Brett De Bary Nee
1974   Longtime Californ: A Documentary Study of an American-Chinatown. Boston: Houghton Mifflin.

North American Congress of Chinese Evangelicals (NACOCE)
1980   Chinese Church Growth Report. Pasadena, California: NACOCE.

Obeyesekere, Gananath
1970   Religious Symbolism and Political Change in Ceylon. Modern Ceylon Studies I:43–63.

O'Connor, Edward
1972   The Pentecostal Movement in the Catholic Church. Notre Dame, Indiana: Ave Maria Press.

Oliver, D. L.
1955   A Solomon Island Society: Kinship and Leadership among the Siuai of Bougainville. Boston: Beacon Press.

Palinkas, Lawrence A.
1981   The Force of Words: Rhetoric and Social Change in a Chinese Christian Community. Ph.D. dissertation, Department of Anthropology, University of California, San Diego.
1982   Ethnicity, Identity and Mental Health: The Use of Rhetoric in an Immigrant Chinese Church. Journal of Psychoanalytic Anthropology 5:235–58.
1984   Social Fission and Cultural Change in an Ethnic Chinese Church. Ethnic Groups 5:255–77.

Parrinder, Geoffrey
1961   West African Religion. London: Epworth.

Parsons, Anne
1964   Is the Oedipus Complex Universal? The Jones-Malinowski Debate Revisited. In The Psychoanalytic Study of Society, III. Warner Muensterberger and Sydney Axelrad, eds. Pp. 278–328. New York: International Universities Press.

1969   Paternal and Maternal Authority in the Neapolitan Family. *In* Belief, Magic, and Anomie. Pp. 67–97. New York: The Free Press.

Patterson, Orlando

1973   The Sociology of Slavery. Kingston, Jamaica: Sangster's.

Penny, A.

1876–1888   Diary. 11 Volumes. Sydney: Mitchell Library, B807–17.

1888   Ten Years in Melanesia. London: Wells Gardner, Darton and Co.

Phillippo, James M.

1843   Jamaica: Its Past and Present State. Reprinted in 1969. London: Pall Mall.

Pierson, Roscoe M.

1969   Alexander Bedward and the Jamaica Native Baptist Free Church. Lexington Theological Quarterly 4:65–76.

Pitkin, Donald

1985   The House that Giacomo Built: History of an Italian Family, 1898–1978. Cambridge: Cambridge University Press.

Ranaghan, Kevin, and Dorothy Ranaghan

1969   Catholic Pentecostals. Paramus, New Jersey: Paulist Press.

Ray, Benjamin C.

1976   African Religions: Symbol, Ritual, and Community. Englewood Cliffs, New Jersey: Prentice-Hall.

Reckord, Mary

1969   The Slave Rebellion of 1831. Jamaica Journal 3:25–31.

Reiter, Rayna R.

1975   Men and Women in the South of France: Public and Private Domains. *In* Toward an Anthropology of Women. Rayna R. Reiter, ed. Pp. 252–82. New York: Monthly Review Press.

Revelli, Nuto

1977   Il mondo dei vinti. Torino: Einaudi.

1985   L'anello forte. Torino: Einaudi.

Ross, H.

1973   Baegu: Social and Ecological Organization in Malaita, Solomon Islands. Urbana: University of Illinois Press.

Ryman, Cheryl

1984   Kumina: Stability and Change. ACIJ Research Review (African-Caribbean Institute of Jamaica) 1:81–128.

Saiedi, Nader

1986   What Is Islamic Fundamentalism? *In* Prophetic Religions and Politics. Jeffrey K. Hadden and Anson Shupe, eds. Pp. 173–95. New York: Paragon House.

Salamone, Frank A., ed.

1983   Missionaries and Anthropologists (Part II). Studies in Third World Societies, No. 26. Williamsburg, Virginia: College of William and Mary.

Salvemini, Gaetano

1973   The Origins of Fascism in Italy. Roberto Vivarelli, trans. New York: Harper and Row.

Sartre, Jean-Paul

1972   The Humanism of Existentialism. *In* Essays in Existentialism. Wade Baskin, ed. Pp. 31–62. Secaucus, New Jersey: The Citadel Press.

Saunders, George R.
    1979   Social Change and Psychocultural Continuity in Alpine Italian Families. Ethos
            7:206–31.
    1981   Men and Women in Southern Europe: A Review of Some Aspects of Cultural
            Complexity. The Journal of Psychoanalytic Anthropology 4:435–66.
Scheffler, H. W.
    1965   Choiseul Island Social Structure. Berkeley: University of California Press.
Schneider, Harold K.
    1981   The Africans: An Ethnological Account. Englewood Cliffs, New Jersey: Pren-
            tice-Hall.
Schneider, Jane, and Shirley Lindenbaum
    1987   Frontiers of Christian Evangelism: Essays in Honor of Joyce Riegelhaupt (In-
            troduction). American Ethnologist 14:1–8.
Schuler, Monica
    1979   Myalism and the African Religious Tradition in Jamaica. In Africa and the
            Caribbean: The Legacies of a Link. Margaret E. Crahan and Franklin W.
            Knight, eds. Pp. 6–79. Baltimore, Maryland: Johns Hopkins University Press.
    1980   "Alas, Alas, Kongo": A Social History of Indentured African Immigration into
            Jamaica, 1841–1865. Baltimore, Maryland: Johns Hopkins University Press.
Schwartz, Theodore
    1962   The Paliau Movement in the Admiralty Islands, 1946–1954. Anthropological
            Papers of the American Museum of Natural History 49:207–421.
    1963   Systems of Areal Integration: Some Considerations Based on the Admiralty
            Islands of Melanesia. Anthropological Forum 1:56–97.
    1968   Cargo Cult: A Melanesian Type-Response to Culture Contact. Paper written
            for De Vos Conference on Psychological Adjustment and Adaptation to Culture
            Change, Hakone, Japan.
    1975   Cultural Totemism: Ethnic Identity Primitive and Modern. In Ethnic Identity:
            Cultural Continuities and Change. George De Vos and Lola Romanucci-Ross,
            eds. Pp. 106–31. Palo Alto, California: Mayfield.
    1976   Personal Communication.
Seaga, Edward
    1969   Revival Cults in Jamaica: Notes Towards a Sociology of Religion. Jamaica
            Journal 3 (2): 3–15.
Sewell, William G.
    1862   The Ordeal of Free Labor in the British West Indies. Reprinted in 1968. New
            York: A. M. Kelley.
Shupe, Anson D., Jr.
    1981   Six Perspectives on New Religions: A Case Study Approach. New York: The
            Edwin Mellen Press.
Silverman, Sydel
    1965   Patronage and Community-Nation Relationships in Central Italy. Ethnology
            4:172–89.
Simpson, George E.
    1956   Jamaican Revivalist Cults. Social and Economic Studies 5:321–412.
    1978   Black Religions in the New World. New York: Columbia University Press.
Smith, Michael F.
    1978   Good Men Face Hard Times in Koragur [Kragur]: Ideology and Social Change
            in a New Guinea Village. Ann Arbor, Michigan: University Microfilms.

1982   The Catholic Ethic and the Spirit of Alcohol Use in an East Sepik Province Village. *In* Through a Glass Darkly: Beer and Modernization in Papua New Guinea. Institute of Applied Social and Economic Research Monograph 18. Mac Marshall, ed. Pp. 271–88. Boroko: Papua New Guinea Institute of Applied Social and Economic Research.

1984   "Wild" Villagers and Capitalist Virtues: Perceptions of Western Work Habits in a Preindustrial Community. Anthropological Quarterly 57:125–38.

In press. Business and the Romance of Community Cooperation on Kairiru Island. *In* Sepik Heritage: Tradition and Change in Papua New Guinea. Durham, North Carolina: Carolina Academic Press.

Smith, T. L.

1978   Religion and Ethnicity in America. American Historical Review 83:1155–85.

Spiro, Melford E.

1952   Ghosts, Ifaluk, and Teleological Functionalism. American Anthropologist 54:497–503.

1965   Religious Systems as Culturally Constituted Defense Mechanisms. *In* Context and Meaning in Cultural Anthropology. Pp. 100–113. Glencoe, Illinois: Free Press.

1966   Religion: Problems of Definition and Explanation. *In* Anthropological Approaches to the Study of Religion. Association of Social Anthropologists, Monograph No. 3. M. Banton, ed. Pp. 85–126. London: Tavistock.

Stonequist, E. V.

1937   The Marginal Man: A Study in Personality and Culture Conflict. New York: Russell and Russell.

Sue, S., and D. W. Sue

1973   Chinese-American Personality and Mental Health. *In* Asian Americans: Psychological Perspectives. S. Sue and N. Wagner, eds. Pp. 111–24. Palo Alto, California: Science and Behavior Books.

Swartz, Marc J.

1978   Politics as a Culturally Constituted Mechanism. Paper presented at the meetings of the International Society for Political Psychology, New York.

Swartz, Marc J., ed.

1968   Local-Level Politics. Chicago: Aldine.

Taylor, William B.

1987   The Virgin of Guadalupe in New Spain: An Inquiry into the Social History of Marian Devotion. American Ethnologist 14:9–33.

Thompson, Richard A.

1979   Ethnicity versus Class: An Analysis of Conflict in a North American Chinese Community. Ethnicity 6:306–26.

Thomson, A.

1914–1917   Diary. Manuscript in possession of Bishop Dudley Tuti, Jejevo, Santa Isabel.

Tippett, A. R.

1967   Solomon Islands Christianity. London: Lutteworth Press.

Toch, Hans

1965   The Social Psychology of Social Movements. Indianapolis and New York: The Bobbs-Merrill Company.

Vogt, Evon Z.
 1964   Ancient Maya Concepts in Contemporary Zincantan Religion. VIe Congres
        International des Sciences Anthropologiques et Ethnologiques 2:497–502.
Wallace, Anthony F. C.
 1956   Revitalization Movements. American Anthropologist 58:264–81.
 1958   Dreams and Wishes of the Soul: A Type of Psychoanalytic Theory among the
        Seventeenth Century Iroquois. American Anthropologist 60:234–48.
 1972   The Death and Rebirth of the Seneca. New York: Vintage.
Warner, W. Lloyd
 1961   The Family of God: A Symbolic Study of Christian Life in America. New
        Haven, Connecticut: Yale University Press.
Webb, Malcolm C.
 1986   Why Our Civilization Can Never Be "Moral": The Cultural Ecology of Chris-
        tian Origins. In The Burden of Being Civilized: An Anthropological Perspective
        on the Discontents of Civilization. Southern Anthropological Society Pro-
        ceedings, No. 18. Malcolm C. Webb and Miles Richardson, eds. Pp. 101–19.
        Athens: University of Georgia Press.
Weber, Max
 1951   The Religion of China. New York: Free Press.
 1963   The Sociology of Religion. First published in 1922. Ephraim Fischoff, trans.
        Boston: Beacon Press.
Wedenoja, William
 1976   Personal communication.
 1978   Religion and Adaptation in Rural Jamaica. Ph.D. dissertation, Department of
        Anthropology, University of California, San Diego.
 1980   Modernization and the Pentecostal Movement in Jamaica. In Perspectives on
        Pentecostalism: Case Studies from the Caribbean and Latin America. Stephen
        D. Glazier, ed. Pp. 27–48. Washington, D.C.: University Press of America.
Weinstein, Donald
 1970   Savonarola and Florence: Prophecy and Patriotism in the Renaissance. Prince-
        ton, New Jersey: Princeton University Press.
Weiss, M. S.
 1974   Valley City: A Chinese Community in America. Cambridge, Mass.: Schenk-
        man.
Welchman, H.
 1889–1908   Missionary Life in the Melanesian Islands. 12 volumes. Canberra: Na-
        tional Library of Australia.
White, Caroline
 1980   Patrons and Partisans: A Study of Politics in Two Southern Italian Comuni.
        Cambridge: Cambridge University Press.
White, Geoffrey M.
 1978   Personal communication.
 1979   War, Peace and Piety in Santa Isabel, Solomon Islands. In The Pacification
        of Melanesia. M. Rodman and M. Cooper, eds. Pp. 109–39. Ann Arbor:
        University of Michigan Press.
 1980   Social Images and Social Change in a Melanesian Society. American Ethnol-
        ogist 7 (2): 352–70.

1985a Premises and Purposes in a Solomon Islands Ethnopsychology. *In* Person, Self and Experience: Exploring Pacific Ethnopsychologies. G. White and J. Kirkpatrick, eds. Pp. 328–66. Berkeley: University of California Press.

1985b "Bad Ways" and "Bad Talk": Interpretations of Interpersonal Conflict in a Melanesian Society. *In* Directions in Cognitive Anthropology. J. Dougherty, ed. Pp. 345–70. Urbana: University of Illinois Press.

White, G. M., F. Kokhonigita, and H. Pulomana

1988 *Cheke Holo* Dictionary. Canberra: A.N.U. Pacific Linguistics Series C.

Whiteman, Darrell L.

1983a Melanesians and Missionaries: An Ethnohistorical Study of Social and Religious Change in the Southwest Pacific. Pasadena, California: William Carey Library.

Whiteman, Darrell L., ed.

1983b Missionaries, Anthropologists and Cultural Change. Studies in Third World Societies, No. 25. Williamsburg, Virginia: College of William and Mary.

Williams, Joseph J.

1932 Voodoos and Obeahs: Phases of West Indian Witchcraft. Reprinted in 1970. New York: AMS.

Wilson, E.

1935 Welchman of Bughotu. London: Society for Promoting Christian Knowledge.

Wolf, Eric R.

1958 The Virgin of Guadalupe: A Mexican National Symbol. Journal of American Folklore 71:34–39.

1969 Society and Symbols in Latin Europe and in the Islamic Near East. Anthropological Quarterly 42 (3): 287–301.

1982 Europe and the People without History. Berkeley: University of California Press.

Wong, Bernard

1982 Chinatown: Economic Adaptation and Ethnic Identity of the Chinese. New York: Holt, Rinehart and Winston.

Woodford, C. M.

1909 The Canoes of the British Solomon Islands Protectorate. Journal of the Royal Anthropological Institute 39:506–16.

Worsley, Peter

1968 The Trumpet Shall Sound. New York: Schocken.

WPHC

n.d. Western Pacific High Commission. Inward correspondence. Files located in the Western Pacific Archives, Suva, Fiji.

Yang, C. K.

1961 Religion in Chinese Society. Berkeley: University of California Press.

Zariski, Raphael

1972 Italy: The Politics of Uneven Development. Hinsdale, Illinois: The Dryden Press.

Zelenietz, M.

1979 The End of Headhunting in New Georgia. *In* The Pacification of Melanesia. M. Rodman and M. Cooper, eds. Pp. 91–108. Ann Arbor: University of Michigan Press.

Ziegler, Philip
  1975 Germany: The Flagellants and the Persecution of the Jews. *In* The Black Death: A Turning Point in History. William M. Bowsky, editor. Pp. 65–79. Huntington, New York: Robert E. Krieger Publishing Company.

Index

Contributors

PETER WESTON BLACK teaches anthropology at George Mason University in Fairfax, Virginia, where he is coordinator of the anthropology program. He earned his Ph.D. from the University of California, San Diego. He is interested in Micronesian ethnohistory, the cultural dimension of conflict resolution, and issues surrounding ethnopsychological framing of ethnicity and identity.

GRIFFIN DIX is Research Director, MacWeek, in San Francisco. He received his Ph.D. in anthropology from the University of California, San Diego, in 1977. He has been a research analyst at the San Francisco Newspaper Agency, Assistant Professor in Anthropology at the University of Santa Clara, and has conducted educational research at the American Institutes for Research in Palo Alto and marketing research at Bank of America. His publications include *The Computer Education Handbook* and a co-edited volume, *Religion and Ritual in Korean Society*.

MICHAEL D. MURPHY received his Ph.D. in anthropology from the University of California, San Diego, and is Associate Professor at the University of Alabama. He has pursued ethnographic work in California, Jamaica, Mexico, and Spain. Dr. Murphy's work has appeared in journals and magazines in Mexico, Spain, and the United States. His current project centers on folk Catholicism in southern Spain, where he has conducted fieldwork as a Research Fellow of the U.S.-Spanish Joint Committee for Educational and Cultural Affairs.

LAWRENCE A. PALINKAS, Ph.D., is Deputy Head, Occupational Medicine Department and Manager of the Social Epidemiology Program at the Naval Health Research Center in San Diego, California. He is also an Assistant Adjunct Professor in the Department of Community and Family Medicine, School of Medicine, University of California, San Diego. Dr. Palinkas is currently engaged in research for the U.S. Navy on health and performance of Antarctic winter-over personnel. He has also conducted studies on ethnic differences in illness and disease risk and the processes of adaptation to stress associated with sociocultural change.

GEORGE R. SAUNDERS is Associate Professor of Anthropology at Lawrence University in Appleton, Wisconsin, and received his Ph.D. from the University of California, San Diego, in 1977. He has conducted research in the Italian alpine village of Valbella (a pseudonym) on five occasions, including a year period in 1974–75, and during the summers of 1972, 1979, 1980, and 1985. He has also worked with Laotian Hmong refugees in Wisconsin. His current research interests focus on the history of Italian anthropology, particularly the work of Ernesto DeMartino, and on the recent popularity of Protestantism in Italy.

MICHAEL FRENCH SMITH has conducted field research in Papua New Guinea's Manus Province in 1973 and on Kairiru Island, East Sepik Province, in 1975–76 and 1981. In 1982 he did research on family farms in Appalachia. His publications deal primarily with time, work, and social change. He received his Ph.D. in anthropology from the University of California, San Diego, in 1978. Since then he has held teaching or research positions at U.C.S.D., the State University of New York College at Geneseo, George Mason University in Virginia, and Virginia Polytechnic Institute and State University. He is presently director of research for Public Sector Consultants, Inc., a public policy consulting firm in Lansing, Michigan. He is also working on a book about social change on Kairiru Island that focuses on grass-roots perceptions of progress and development.

WILLIAM WEDENOJA is an Associate Professor and Coordinator of Anthropology at Southwest Missouri State University, where he teaches courses on primitive religion, culture and personality, and human evolution. Dr. Wedenoja wrote his dissertation on the psychodynamics of Balm and Revival cultism in Jamaica, and received his Ph.D. in psychological anthropology from the University of California, San Diego, in 1978. He has been studying Jamaican religion, personality, and mental health, with a particular emphasis on ritual trance, for fifteen years, and has also done fieldwork in other Caribbean islands, the Ozark highlands, and British Columbia. His publications include "Jamaican Psychiatry" (*Transcultural Psychiatric Research Review* 20:233–58, 1983), and *The Heritage of the Ozarks* (Little Rock: August House, 1984), a book on multicultural education.

GEOFFREY M. WHITE is a Research Associate at the Institute of Culture and Communication of the East-West Center in Hawaii. He received his Ph.D. in anthropology from the University of California, San Diego, in 1978. He returned there as a Visiting Lecturer in 1985–86, and has also taught at the University of Hawaii. His field research in Santa Isabel, Solomon Islands, has dealt with social identity, cultural change, and problems of ethnographic method. His publications include a dictionary and three co-edited volumes: *The Pacific Theater: Island Representations of World War II* (University of Hawaii, 1988); *Person, Self and Experience: Exploring Pacific Ethnopsychologies* (University of California, 1985); and *Cultural Conceptions of Mental Health and Therapy* (Reidel, 1982).